THE VISIONARIES

ALSO BY WOLFRAM EILENBERGER

Time of the Magicians

The VISIONARIES

Arendt, Beauvoir, Rand, Weil, and the Power of Philosophy in Dark Times

Wolfram Eilenberger

Translated by Shaun Whiteside

PENGUIN PRESS NEW YORK 2023

PENGUIN PRESS
An imprint of Penguin Random House LLC
penguinrandomhouse.com

Originally published in German as *Feuer der Freiheit* by Klett-Cotta, Stuttgart

Pages 371 and 373–74 constitute an extension of the copyright page.

LIBRARY OF CONGRESS CATALOGING-IN-PUBLICATION DATA
Names: Eilenberger, Wolfram, 1972– author. | Whiteside, Shaun, translator.
Title: The visionaries : Arendt, Beauvoir, Rand, Weil,
and the power of philosophy in dark times /
Wolfram Eilenberger ; translated by Shaun Whiteside.
Other titles: Feuer der Freiheit. English
Description: First U.S. hardcover edition. | New York : Penguin Press, 2023. |
Originally published: Feuer der Freiheit. Stuttgart : Klett-Cotta, 2020. |
Includes bibliographical references and index.
Identifiers: LCCN 2022049207 (print) | LCCN 2022049208 (ebook) |
ISBN 9780593297452 (hardcover) | ISBN 9780593297469 (ebook)
Classification: LCC B105.W6 E3513 2023 (print) | LCC B105.W6 (ebook) |
DDC 190—dc23/eng/20230123
LC record available at https://lccn.loc.gov/2022049207
LC ebook record available at https://lccn.loc.gov/2022049208

Printed in the United States of America
1st Printing

Book design by Daniel Lagin

For Venla and Kaisa

Women on the way

Did you imagine
I would hate life,
And flee to the desert?

—Johann Wolfgang von Goethe,
"Prometheus" (1789)

Fool me once, fool me twice
Are you death or paradise?

—Billie Eilish,
"No Time to Die" (2020)

CONTENTS

I

SPARKS: 1943

Beauvoir is in the mood, Weil in a trance,
Rand in a fury, and Arendt in a nightmare.

THE PROJECT

"What's the use of starting if you must stop?"[1] Not a bad way to begin. That was precisely the essay's intended subject: the tension between one's own finite existence and the obvious infinity of the world. After all, it took only a moment's contemplation of this abyss for every plan, every design, every self-appointed goal—be it conquering the globe or mere gardening—to be abandoned to absurdity.[2] In the end, it all boiled down to the same thing. Even if no one else did, time itself would ensure that whatever work one had done came to nothing, consigning it to eternal oblivion. Exactly as if it had never existed. A fate as certain as one's own death.

Why then do something rather than nothing? Or, to put it better in the form of a classical trio of questions: "What, then, is the measure of a man? What goals can he set for himself, and what hopes are permitted him?"[3] Yes, that worked. That was it, the structure she was looking for!

From her corner table on the second floor of the Café de Flore, Simone de Beauvoir observed the passersby. There they walked. The others. Each one a private consciousness. All moving about with their own concerns and anxieties, their plans and hopes. Exactly as she did herself. Just one among billions. The thought sent shivers down her spine every time.

Beauvoir had not agreed to this assignment lightly, not least of all because the subject was one that her publisher, Jean Grenier, had commissioned her to write about. For an anthology on the prevailing intellectual discourse of the day, he wanted her to write something about "existentialism."[4] But neither she nor Jean-Paul Sartre had claimed this term for themselves. It had merely been coined by the arts pages of the newspaper, nothing more.

The irony of the assignment was thus hard to overstate, because if there had been a leitmotif defining her and Sartre's journey over the past ten years, it was refusing to be put into boxes preassigned to them by other people. That kind of revolt had been right at the heart of her project—and still was today.

THE PRIME OF LIFE

Let the others call it "existentialism." She would deliberately avoid the term. And instead, as an author, she would simply do what she loved most since the earliest diary entries of youth: devote herself with the greatest possible concentration to her life's most concerning questions—whose answers she did not yet know. Strangely, they were still the same. Above all was the question of the possible meaning of her own existence. As well as the question of the importance of other people for one's own life.

But Beauvoir had never felt as certain and as free in this reflection as she did now, in the spring of 1943. At the climax of another world war, in the middle of her occupied city. In spite of ration cards and food shortages, in spite of chronic withdrawals from coffee and tobacco (by now Sartre was so desperate that he crawled around every morning on the floor of the café collecting the previous evening's stubs), in spite of daily checks and curfews, in spite of the ubiquitous censorship and German soldiers swaggering about with ever greater shamelessness in the cafés, even here in Saint-Germain-des-Prés. As long as she could find enough time and peace to write, everything else was bearable. Her first novel was due to be published by Gallimard in the autumn.[5] A second one lay completed in the drawer.[6] There was also a play in the works.[7] Now the first philosophical essay would follow. Sartre's work *Being and Nothingness*—over a thousand pages in length—was also at the publisher. Within a month his drama *The Flies* would premiere at the Théâtre de la Cité. It was his most political play so far.

In fact, all of this was the intellectual harvest of a whole decade during which she and Sartre had created a new style of philosophizing. Just as—because the one was inseparable from the other—they had invented new ways of living their lives: private, professional, literary, erotic.

Even during her philosophy studies at the École Normale Supérieure, when Sartre had invited her to his house to have her explain Leibniz to him, they had concluded a love pact of an original kind: they had promised each other unconditional intellectual fidelity and honesty—with an openness to other attractions. They would be absolutely necessary to each other, but also at times to others. A dynamic dyad in which the whole wide world would be reflected according to their will. Since then this plan had led them to many new beginnings and adventures: from Paris to Berlin and Athens; from Husserl via Heidegger to Hegel; from treatises and novels to plays. From nicotine and mescaline to amphetamines. From the "little Russian girl" and "little Bost" to the "very little Russian girl." From Nizan via Merleau-Ponty to Camus. It still carried her, indeed it carried her more resolutely than ever ("To live a love is to throw oneself through that love towards new goals"[8]).

By now they were able to meet their weekly timetable (maximum sixteen hours) as philosophy teachers without any great commitment. Rather than sticking to the coursework, they had their students discuss freely with one another after a brief introduction—always a success. It paid the bills, or at least some of them. After all, they didn't have to pay only for themselves, but also for large parts of their "family." Even after five years in Paris, Olga was finding her feet in her career as an actress. Little Bost was also struggling to make a name for himself as a free-lance journalist, and Olga's younger sister, Wanda, was still trying desperately to find something that suited her completely. Only Natalie Sorokin, the youngest of the new generation, was making her own way: at the very beginning of the war she had specialized in bicycle theft, and since then she had operated a well-organized black-market trade—obviously tolerated by the Nazis—in an increasingly wide assortment of goods.

THE SITUATION

The experiences of war and occupation had brought them closer together once again. Over the past few months, their life together had really sorted itself out, it seemed to Beauvoir, who was in practice the head of the family. They each enjoyed their role, without being reduced to it. They each knew their claims and rights, without insisting on them too rigidly. They were each happy in their own way, but without being bored when they were together.

Beauvoir was not worried about the impending judgment for her own sake alone. For over a year, investigators of the Vichy authorities had been making inquiries. Entirely by accident, Sorokin's mother had found an intimate correspondence between her daughter and her former philosophy teacher in a drawer. She had started investigations of her own and had finally gone to the authorities with the material. The method, she charged, was obviously always the same: first Beauvoir privately befriended the students or former students who looked up to her, then she seduced them sexually, and after a time she even passed them on to her partner of many years, the philosopher and writer Jean-Paul Sartre. This put her at risk of being charged with the crime of "incitement to debauchery,"[9] which would have involved consequences for Beauvoir, the least serious of them the permanent withdrawal of her teaching permit. So far, the only thing certain was that Sorokin, Bost, and Sartre had held their tongues when summonsed. Apart from the aforementioned letters to Sorokin, which were not in themselves finally incriminating, there was no direct evidence. On the other hand, Pétain's regime would have no shortage of evidence as to which side of the political spectrum Beauvoir occupied—and what she stood for with the whole of her existence.

For years Beauvoir and Sartre had lived together, not in apartments, but in hotels on the Left Bank. It was there that they danced and laughed, cooked and drank, argued and slept together. Without any external compulsion, without any hard-and-fast rules, and above all—as far as possible—without making false promises and renunciations. Might a mere glance, a casual touch, a *nuit blanche* not be the spark to light the flame of a life renewed once more? They tried to believe as much. In fact, for Beauvoir and Sartre, human beings were really at one with themselves only as beginners.

> One never arrives anywhere. There are only points of departure. With each man humanity makes a fresh start. And that's why the

> young man who seeks his place in the world does not initially find it . . . and feels forsaken.[10]

That was also a way of explaining why she had brought Olga, Wanda, Little Bost, and Sorokin to Paris, taken them under her wing, and supported, sponsored, and financed them in the city. It was to guide these young people out of their obvious abandonment and into freedom; to encourage them to make their own place in the world rather than simply occupying one already prepared for them. This was done as an act of love, not of subjection, of living Eros, blind debauchery. An act in which humanity was preserved. Because: "Man is only by choosing himself; if he refuses to choose, he annihilates himself."[11]

DEADLY SINS

Insofar as there was anything in her new philosophy that could take the place of "sin," left free after the death of God, it was the voluntary refusal of that very freedom. That deliberate self-destruction was to be avoided at any price, both for oneself and for others, both privately and politically. And in the here and now, in the name of life itself, and as a celebration of it. And not as the supposed "existentialist" Martin Heidegger seemed to be teaching from the depths of the German provinces, in the name of a "being-for-death." "The human being exists in the form of projects that are not projects toward death, but toward singular ends. . . . Thus one is not *for* death."[12]

Accordingly, the only being that counted was the being of this world. The only guiding values were worldly values. Their only true origin was the will of a free subject to grasp his freedom. That was what it meant to exist as a human being.

Hitler and his kind had had precisely this form of existence in their sights; they sought its annihilation and extinction. That had been their exact goal when they had invaded Beauvoir's country three years before—so that, after their final victory over the whole world, they could dictate to the last people on earth how they were to write their essays, or even only to tend their front gardens, right down to the smallest detail. No, she really had better things to do than worry about the judgment of that petit-bourgeois fascist. Let them take her teaching permit away! She would reassemble herself, piece by piece! At this very moment so many doors seemed to be opening at the same time.

MORALITY

Beauvoir was excited about the debates. In the evening there was going to be a general rehearsal of Sartre's latest play. After that, as ever, they would be out on the town. Even Camus had said he was coming. If her thoughts so far had been correct, they opened the possibility of a new definition of man as an acting creature. And one that was neither empty of content, as in Sartre's latest work, nor bound to remain absurd, as in Camus's writings. With her essay she would reveal an alternative. A third way of her own.

As far as she could see, this meant that the measure of genuinely human action was limited from within by two extremes: on the one hand, the extreme of totalitarian intrusion by external forces, and, on the other hand, the extreme of total asocial self-determination. In concrete terms, then, it existed between the inevitably lonely goal of conquering the whole world and the equally lonely endeavor of cultivating one's own front garden. In the end, and one had only to look out of the window, there were other people apart from oneself. Therefore the goals of moral engagement also had to be kept between two extremes: a self-emptied and necessarily undirected sympathy with *all* other suffering human beings, on the one hand, and exclusive attention to purely private concerns, on the other. Like a scene from real life: "A young woman gets irritated because she has leaky shoes that take in water. . . . However, another woman may cry about the horror of the Chinese famine."[13]

Beauvoir had once even personally experienced this situation herself. She (or rather an earlier version of her) had been the young woman with the leaky shoes. But the other, weeping woman was her then fellow fighter Simone Weil. Never again since then had she met a person who could burst spontaneously into tears because somewhere far away a disaster was happening that seemingly had absolutely nothing to do with one's own life. That other Simone in her life was still a mystery to her.

Beauvoir paused and looked at her watch. It was time. Tomorrow morning, she would go back to the Café de Flore and think again about this mystery.

THE MISSION

Like Simone de Beauvoir, early in 1943, Simone Weil resolved to embark on radically new paths. The seriousness of the situation left her no choice. That spring, the thirty-four-year-old Frenchwoman was more certain than ever that she was facing an enemy who justified the greatest possible sacrifice. For a person like Weil, fully imbued as she was with religious belief, that sacrifice lay not in giving up her own life, but in taking another.

"If I am prepared to kill Germans in case of military necessity," she recorded in her diary that spring, "it is not because I have suffered from their acts. It is not because they hate God and Christ. But because they are the enemies of every country in the world, including my own, and because sadly, to my acute pain, it is impossible to prevent them from doing harm without killing a certain number of them."[14]

In October 1942, she left New York, where she had fled into exile with her parents, on a freighter bound for Liverpool, to join the forces of Free France led by General Charles de Gaulle.[15] Nothing caused Weil greater pain during those crucial weeks and months of the war than the thought of finding herself far from her home and far from her people. Immediately after her arrival at the organization's headquarters in London, she informed the leading members there of her burning desire to be given a mission on French soil and, if necessary, to die a martyr's death for the fatherland. She would be happy to go as a parachutist—she had studied the handbooks on the subject in detail. Or else act as a liaison with the comrades on the ground, some of whom she knew personally, having worked years before in Marseille for the Catholic Resistance group around the journal *Témoignage chrétien*. But ideally, she would be at the head of a special mission that she had dreamed up herself, and that she was firmly convinced would be crucial to the war. Weil's plan was to set up a special unit of French nurses at the front who would be deployed only in the most dangerous places, to provide first aid in the middle of battle. She had acquired the requisite medical knowledge through courses with the Red Cross in New York. At the front line, this special unit would be able to save many valuable lives, Weil explained, and in support of her proposal she presented the members of the executive committee with a list of selected surgical specialist publications.

But the actual value of the unit would lie in its symbolic power, its *spiritual* value. Like all wars, she continued animatedly, this one was primarily a war of mental attitudes—and hence one of propagandistic skill. Yet in this sphere the enemy had so far proved to be greatly superior, to evil ends. One need only think of Hitler's SS and the reputation that now sped ahead of it throughout the whole of Europe.

> The SS are a perfect expression of the Hitlerian inspiration. If one may believe neutral reports, they exhibit at the front the heroism of brutality, and carry it to the extreme possible limits of courage.... We can and ought to demonstrate that our courage is quantitively different, is courage of a more difficult and rare kind. Theirs is a debased and brutal courage, it springs from the will to power and destruction. Just as our aims are different from theirs, so our courage too springs from a wholly different inspiration. There could be no better symbol of our inspiration than the corps of women suggested here. The mere persistence of a few services in the very center of the battle, the climax of inhumanity, would be signal defiance of the inhumanity which the enemy has chosen for himself and which he compels us also to practice. The challenge would be all the more conspicuous because the services would be performed by women and with a maternal solicitude. These women would in fact be only a handful and the number of soldiers they could help would be proportionately small; but the effect of a moral symbol is independent of statistics. It would illustrate with supreme clarity the two roads between which humanity today is forced to choose.[16]

Once more in her country's history, Weil explained, the important thing was to counter the spirit of idolatry with a salutary and authentic form of faith. In short, what she had in mind was a kind of female anti-SS in the spirit of the Maid of Orléans: the plan had already been set out in writing. When Simone Weil delivered it to Maurice Schumann in person, he promised his former fellow combatant that he would present it to de Gaulle in person. And he personally accompanied her to her accommodation in the barracks.

As Schumann had predicted, it took de Gaulle less than three seconds to dismiss the "Nursing Unit"—"But she is mad!"[17]—which was why any other kind of deployment on French soil, they agreed, was out of the question in Weil's case. Far too dangerous. You only had to look at her. Emaciated and practically blind without her glasses. Purely physically, she wouldn't be able to cope with the demands required, let alone the mental ones.

For all the eccentricity of her appearance, Schumann pointed out, Weil was a person of the highest integrity, and above all of unique intellect: she had graduated in philosophy from the elite École Normale Supérieure in Paris, she was fluent in several languages, a gifted mathematician, with years of experience in journalism and work with trade unions. These abilities could be very useful.

Rather than sending her to the front to die for her ideals, Weil's superiors entrusted her with a different special mission: for the phase after the victory over Hitler, and the subsequent assumption of power by the government in exile, she was to draw up plans and scenarios for the political reconstruction of France.

Deeply disappointed, but without any open contradiction, she accepted the task, holed up in a hotel room at 19 Hill Street in Mayfair, repurposed as a study—and set about her intellectual work.

INSPIRED

In the history of humanity, there can have been few individuals more productive than was the philosophical Resistance fighter Simone

Weil during only four months in that London winter of 1943: she wrote treatises on constitutional and revolutionary theory and on a political new order for Europe, and one investigation of the epistemological roots of Marxism, and another of the function of political parties in a democracy. She translated parts of the Upanishads from Sanskrit into French, and wrote essays on the religious history of Greece and India, and on the theory of the sacraments and the sacredness of the individual in Christianity and, under the title *The Need for Roots*, a 300-page redesign of the cultural existence of humanity in the modern age.[18]

As her "plan for an association of front-line nurses" suggests, Weil represented the actual needs of the moment in the realm of ideals and inspiration. As the continent that gave rise to two world wars within only two decades, her analysis suggested, Europe had already been suffering from a devastating hollowing of its guiding values and ideals, both culturally and politically. In fact, she told the military chiefs of staff of the French Resistance in February, in an essay of the same name, this war was "A War of Religions."[19]

> Europe remains at the center of the drama. From the fire scattered over the world by Christ—the same fire, perhaps, that Prometheus brought—there were still a few live embers in England. It was enough to prevent the worst. But it was only a respite. We are still lost unless those embers and the flickering sparks on the Continent can be fanned into a flame to kindle the whole of Europe. If we are only saved by American money and machines we shall fall back, one way or another, into a new servitude like the one which we now suffer. It must be remembered that Europe was not subjugated by invading hordes from another continent, or from Mars, who have only to be driven out again. She is wasted by an internal

> malady. She needs to be cured. . . . The conquered peoples can only oppose the conqueror with a religion.[20]

To bring this healing process under way, first militarily, and then politically and culturally, the continent must therefore be filled with "a new inspiration"[21]—according to Weil notably from the writings of Plato as well as the New Testament. Because in the darkest of times anyone who wanted true healing should draw on sources that were not only from this world.

This applied most specifically to her homeland, France, which, as the source of *liberté* in 1789, had fallen further than any other among the warring nations. In the summer of 1940, subjugated almost without a fight by Hitler's troops in only a few weeks, it now relied on outside help for its liberation, and had as a nation lost any guiding faith in itself. In other words, it was deeply shaken in terms of the most profound and important of all human spiritual needs: that of "roots."

> To be rooted is perhaps the most important and least recognized need of the human soul. It is one of the hardest to define. A human being has roots by virtue of his real, active and natural participation in the life of a community which preserves in living shape certain particular treasures of the past and certain particular expectations for the future. This participation is a natural one, in the sense that it is automatically brought about by place, conditions of birth, profession and social surroundings. Every human being needs to have multiple roots. It is necessary for him to draw well-nigh the whole of his moral, intellectual and spiritual life by way of the environment of which he forms a natural part. . . . Uprootedness occurs whenever there is a military conquest. . . . But when

> the conqueror remains a stranger in the land of which he has taken possession, uprootedness becomes an almost mortal disease among the subdued population. It reaches its most acute stage when there are mass deportations, as in German-occupied Europe.[22]

This was Simone Weil's assessment of the situation, as philosophical mastermind appointed specially by the shadow cabinet of General de Gaulle in the spring of 1943. Weil was born Jewish, but for years she was deeply inspired by Christianity; this analysis of a spiritual deficit at the foundation of the murderous events of the time serves as a source of her almost superhuman-seeming philosophical production.

IN A TRANCE

As if in a trance, she allowed the whole range of her unique mind to flow onto the page. Hour after hour, day after day. Without getting enough sleep. And above all, as in previous years, without eating enough. In her London notebook she writes: "In view of the general and permanent condition of humanity it may be that to eat one's fill is always a kind of theft. (I have been guilty of many kinds.)"[23]

On April 25, 1943, this trance came abruptly to an end. Weil collapsed in her room and lost consciousness. She was discovered by a colleague several hours later. Having regained consciousness, Weil categorically forbade the colleague to call a doctor. She had still not entirely abandoned the idea of her combat unit. Instead she called Schumann directly, and he replied that no final decision had been made on the question of deployment in France—in principle, anything was possible, particularly if she received prompt treatment. Only then did Weil agree to be taken to the hospital.

MORONIC

If the New York author and philosopher Ayn Rand had wanted to find the epitome of all the values that, in her view, were responsible for the disaster of the World War, she could have found no more suitable candidate than the very real Simone Weil in London. In that spring of 1943, nothing seemed more devastating to Rand than the willingness to sacrifice her own life in the name of a nation. Nothing could be more morally fatal than the will to stand by others first and foremost. Philosophically, nothing could be more absurd than blind faith in God. Metaphysically, nothing more confused than the attempt to anchor one's guiding values in a realm of unworldly transcendence. Existentially, nothing more insane than personal asceticism for the salvation of the world.

This attitude and the ethics behind it are the actual enemy. They must be overcome and unconditionally opposed wherever they appear. This irrationalism must not be granted so much as an inch. Certainly not in terms of one's own survival.

As Rand had painfully learned in ten years as a freelance writer, in the United States these were ultimately business-related questions. Which was why, in a letter of May 6, 1943, to her editor Archibald Ogden, she had fumed more than ever before. Regarding his mention of faith, she writes, "I don't know what that word means. If you mean 'faith' in a religious sense—in the sense of blind acceptance—I don't have any faith in anything or anybody, I never have had and never will have. I go by facts and reason," thus setting out the actual foundations of her approach toward the world. And she even deploys them against Ogden in defense of her own interests: "What evidence has the firm of Bobbs-Merrill given me of its competence to handle the business side of a book's publication? Whom is it that I must have faith in, and on what grounds?"[24]

She had worked on *The Fountainhead* for seven years. Her energy and creativity, but above all her philosophy, had gone into this work. And now the novel was to be presented in the already thin publicity material as a love story among architects. The publicity department had so far not even seen fit to communicate the fact that the author of the book was a woman and not a man: "I suppose *faith*—the blind faith of a moron—is all one can feel for publicists who do this. . . . Is that the kind of faith you ask me to feel?"[25]

A rhetorical question, obviously. In her life, Rand had been seen as all kinds of things, but never as a moron. In fact, it was clear to everyone who talked to her for even a few minutes that they were dealing with an intellect of a unique clarity and, more important, an uncompromising nature. As far as she was concerned, the fundamental problem that needed to be solved concerned not her own existence, but everybody else's. The mysterious thing for Rand was not what her fellow humans thought and did, but *why* they did it: why could they not simply think and, moreover, act stringently? What exactly was preventing all these people from following their own purely fact-based judgment? She could do it, after all.

OUTRAGEOUS

Why did her editor, a day before the official publication date of the book, not state the obvious? The two or three advertisements promised in the contract were mere window dressing. In fact, the publishing company had just waved the book through. The marketing department had decided that, if at all, *The Fountainhead* would have to make its own way into the bookstores or the bestseller lists. After all, it could not have escaped anyone that this 700-page book, with its main character, the apparently superhuman architect Howard Roark, was really a philosophical manifesto masquerading as a novel. A weighty monument of ideas, full of page-long monologues, which also had the barely marketable quality of challenging all intuitions on which the moral sensibility of the mainstream American public was based.

Where Rand was concerned, this was precisely the unique promise of the work. That was also how it was to be presented and advertised: as a *transformative* literary reading experience that would open up a fundamentally different vision of the world to its readers, leading them from the cave into the light in order to see themselves and the world clearly for the first time. The author had assured her closest circles that 100,000 copies would be the minimum she could expect [26]—as well as a Hollywood adaptation of the novel featuring her favorite actor, Gary Cooper, in the role of Howard Roark.

What, *in purely rational terms*, suggested anything to the contrary? Certainly not the quality of her work. And certainly not the contemporary importance of its message! Was the current state of the world, and even America itself, not obvious enough? Did every single citizen of the country not sense that something had gone fundamentally askew? That it was more urgent than ever to save a whole culture from self-destruction? To heal it, with the power of free speech, with solid argument? To use, not least, the world-transforming power of storytelling, to cure it of the deep confusion that, in the spring of 1943, seemed poised to bring it crashing down in a global orgy of violence?

READY FOR BATTLE

The goal that Rand had set herself with her novel was above all to illuminate the "struggle between individualism and collectivism not in politics but in the human soul."[27] *That* was its actual theme; the struggle between autonomy and definition by others, between thinking and obeying, between courage and humility, between creation and copying, between integrity and corruption, between progress and decay, between Me and all the others—between freedom and oppression. Along the way to the true liberation of the individual from the yoke of altruistic slave morality, the works of Max Stirner and Friedrich Nietzsche had been a mere rhapsodic prelude. It was only with hers, Ayn Rand's philosophy, that enlightened egoism could be given an objectively explicable foundation! It was in exactly this spirit that the author also presented her hero Howard Roark—as the redeemer from all the evils of the present day—letting him take the stand as the defendant in the crucial trial at the end of her novel. As a pioneering embodiment of a freedom-loving existence of pure creative reason. Roark's credo was also Rand's own:

> The creator lives for his work. He needs no one else. His primary goal lies within himself. . . . Altruism is the doctrine which demands that man live for others and place others above himself. . . . The nearest approach to it in reality—the man who lives to serve others—is the slave. If physical slavery is repulsive, how much more repulsive is the servility of the spirit. The conquered slave has a vestige of honor. He has the merit of having resisted and of considering his condition evil. But the man who enslaves him in the name of love is the basest of creatures. He degrades the dig-

> nity of man, and he degrades the conception of love. But this is the essence of altruism.[28]

Rand knew the warning her hero was talking about. She had experienced firsthand what it felt like to live in a society of state-produced slaves. Like so many formerly affluent Jewish families, the Rosenbaums of Saint Petersburg had been expropriated in the October Revolution. After the looting and destruction of the pharmacy run by their father (Lenin: "Loot the looters!"), Ayn, still called Alisa at the time, had fled with her parents and two sisters to Crimea in late 1918. Thousands of kilometers, first by train, then later on foot. Admittedly, in 1921, the family was able to move back to Saint Petersburg (Petrograd; Leningrad from 1924). But their now largely penniless father, as a former representative of the "bourgeoisie," was no longer able to continue his profession as a pharmacist.[29]

In the autumn of 1921, Rand enrolled at the university, studying history and philosophy, and after graduating in 1924, she switched to the State Institute for Cinematography. But her true goal at this time was a different one: the nineteen-year-old highflier wanted nothing more than to leave the Soviet Union, she wanted to have nothing more to do with its utopia of the "new man," but instead to make herself, through her own efforts, the person she was: a creator of her own worlds. She wanted to reach freedom, the country of her favorite film stars and directors—America!

Early in 1926, her parents managed to send her to relatives in Chicago on a tourist visa. Six adventurous weeks later (Riga, Berlin, Le Havre, New York), she was on the bus to Hollywood, to make her living as an author and screenwriter. Alisa Rosenbaum was just twenty-one at the time, she spoke barely a word of English, and she wanted from now on to be known only as "Ayn Rand." If the old world could not be saved,

Alisa could become someone else in the new one. She swore that she would rather die than ever return to her homeland.

ONLY LOGICAL

Since then she had fought every day for her American dream. While Rand felt she was closer than ever to the goal of her life with the publication of *The Fountainhead,* her parents and her two younger sisters had been threatened with death by starvation in Leningrad, besieged for over two years by Hitler's Wehrmacht. That was if they were alive at all. Rand did not have the slightest possibility of finding out. The few reports of the naked struggle for survival that flew as rumors across the Atlantic were beyond any kind of humanity. About a million people were supposed to have died by the spring of 1943 in Leningrad. All the dogs and cats had been killed for food long since. There was even talk of systematic cannibalism.[30] No, nobody needed to tell her anything. She had experienced it all herself. The hunger. The typhus. The deaths. Since then her eyes had been opened, and her philosophical vision sharpened.

In Rand's view of things, Hitler's and Stalin's lust for blood followed a single logic, which was that of a violent state subjugation of each individual human being in the name of an ideally exalted collective. Whether that collective was called "class" or "*Volk*," "nation" or "race," there was a difference only at first sight. Because in their inspirations, their methods, and above all their inhuman effects, these "totalitarianisms"[31] (the common term with which Rand summed up the political threats that had existed from the early 1940s onward) were identical. Totalitarianism had first succeeded in Russia, then in Italy, and finally in Germany. No country was safe from it. Not even the United States. But the actual secret behind the success of totalitarian forces in the systematic subjugation of the broad masses lay not in their actual support, but in a general dull indifference.

With America's successful entry into the war under the New Deal president Franklin Roosevelt, for Rand the whole world risked being destroyed by a single false idea, a fundamental philosophical misunderstanding: the ennoblement of self-sacrifice for others in favor of a collective sanctified by propaganda. That altruistic intellectual blockade was precisely what needed to be broken down. This war was a war of ideas!

> These horrors are made possible only by men who have lost all respect for single, individual human beings, who accept the idea that classes, races and nations matter, but single persons do not, that a majority is sacred, but a minority is dirt, that herds count, but Man is nothing. Where do you stand on this? There is no middle ground.[32]

Rand had set down these words for a political manifesto as early as 1941. Given the geopolitical situation she now thought of developing that text as quickly as possible into a nonfiction book. By the spring of 1943, she felt more firmly resolved than ever to throw herself with her full intellectual might into that war of ideas. Out of pure self-interest, for her *own* threatened freedom and integrity. For everything that was dear to *her* in this world and no other. Who else would she have done it for?

THE FOREIGNER

Not far from Ayn Rand's apartment in Manhattan, Hannah Arendt also saw that the time for a fundamental redefinition of things had come. But in a much less combative spirit. “Very few individuals,” the thirty-six-year-old philosopher wrote in an article in January 1943, “have the strength to conserve their own integrity if their social, political and legal status is completely confused.”[33] Exactly ten years after being driven out of Hitler’s Germany, Arendt wasn’t sure, when she looked at herself in the mirror, whether she could continue to find the energy within herself to do just that. Never in her life had she felt so isolated, so entirely empty and pointless, as she had in those past few weeks: “We lost our home, which means the familiarity of daily life. We lost our occupation, which means the confidence that we are of some use in this world. We lost our language, which means the naturalness of reactions, the simplicity of gestures, the unaffected expression of feelings. We left our relatives in the Polish ghettos and our best friends have been killed in concentration camps, and that means the rupture of our private lives. If we are saved we feel humiliated, and if we are helped we feel degraded. We fight like madmen for private existences with individual destinies.”[34]

Arendt’s account of her mood serves as an impressive example for those sufferings of the soul that Simone Weil describes as the inevitable consequence of existential “uprooting.” Except that at that moment Arendt was not living in a permanently occupied country, and neither had she herself become the victim of mass deportation. In fact, this passage in her essay “We Refugees” describes the comprehensive loss by which German Jewish refugees in a new world seemed particularly severely affected at the turn of 1942–1943. For weeks she and her husband spent their days staring into the gray nothingness of the New York winter sky. Smoking in silence. Like the last human beings on earth.

NO BANISTERS

Chronically optimistic by nature, Arendt had been both tough and resourceful in her response to her situation over the previous ten years. When it came down to it, she had always found enough fire within herself to forge her journey into yet another new life. From Berlin to Paris, from Paris to Marseille, and from there to where she was now, New York. Always with a view to trying to "get along without all these tricks and jokes of adjustment and assimilation."[35]

In the spring of 1943, the only thing she saw as having been saved from the structure of her private life was her "Monsieur" Heinrich, with whom she shared a furnished room in a shabby apartment building on West 95th Street—and, on the same floor, helpless and ailing in the new world, her mother, Martha Beerwald, the widow Arendt. Certainly, that was more than many other fleeing "displaced persons" had managed to save. But it was a long way from being a self-determined fate worthy of the name.

A former master-student of Karl Jaspers and Martin Heidegger, she had never lost her special knack for placing herself in the exact spot between any number of stools, even during the years of exile. In fact, the number of people on whose benevolence she could truly depend could by now be counted on the fingers of one hand: Arendt's mentor Kurt Blumenfeld in New York, and a scholar of Judaism, Gershom Scholem, in Jerusalem. Her ex-husband Günther Stern in California, and the theologian Paul Tillich, also in New York. Whether the Jasperses were still alive, and if so where, was impossible to find out. The last letter was almost a decade ago. She herself didn't know why contact had been severed so soon—in retrospect he was the only true teacher she had ever had. But her once stormy alliance with Heidegger had been extinguished for quite different reasons in 1933, when he joined the Nazi Party and, in a tailpiece to his Freiburg rector's speech, informed the students, among other things: "The Führer himself and he alone *is* the present and future German reality and its law."[36] She had still not summoned the courage to knock on the door of Ernst Cassirer, who was now teaching at Yale and who knew of her through mutual friends.

THE SPLIT

Since the United States entered the war, it had once again become more difficult to discover the fate of friends and relatives who had stayed behind in Europe—let alone to be of help to them. It was thus a particularly hard blow for Arendt, when, on December 18, 1942, the German-language exile newspaper, for which she herself had been writing columns for a year, published a report about the day of the deportation in the southern French internment camp of Gurs, followed by the long list of names of the deportees.[37] Arendt had been interned there in 1940 and recognized several names.

The article in *Aufbau* was only one of several publications that winter that reported on the start of a new phase in the treatment of Europe's Jews, millions of whom were now imprisoned in concentration camps. Plainly, in line with the "final solution of the Jewish question" announced by both Hitler and Goebbels, the Nazis had begun to murder these people on an industrial scale in extermination camps—to gas them. Neither Arendt nor her husband had ever been in any doubt about the unconditional anti-Jewish hatred of the Nazis, or about their unrestrained brutality in pursuing their declared goals. But it was difficult at first to believe these reports. The procedure described was too monstrous, too senseless as a measure, not least from a logistical and strategic point of view, and precisely now that Hitler's army was suffering one defeat after another. The army was said to have lost a million soldiers that winter in the Soviet Union alone.

It was, however, plainly the case. The reports were too numerous, the sources too diverse. The loss of the world that Arendt felt in the weeks that followed was worse than anything she had ever experienced. It didn't affect any group or community, any concrete place or time, just her sense of humanity in general. As if an abyss had opened in the middle of that world, in the middle of her very being, one that could not be bridged by anyone or anything.

What was it that she hadn't wanted to believe? What had she thought impossible? An entire people—and one scattered all over the world—being declared a deadly enemy was nothing essentially new. The war and its brutal battles weren't, either. History had known such things before; in fact, it scarcely consisted of anything else. But *that* . . . Nothing made Arendt experience her own impotence more clearly than her lasting inability to grasp events in her own words.[38]

BEING PRESENT

Ideally, she would simply have left her old self behind. She would have acted as if she were entirely free to decide who she was and how she would go on living in this world: there were people, even philosophers, who would casually have declared such a thing possible. But she had never been naive enough to succumb to such illusions. In fact, she knew, the creation "of a new personality was as difficult and hopeless as a new creation of the world."[39] No one ever started over again. No one was so free or so unrestrained. However much people might have wished or imagined they were, out of megalomania or deepest despair.

Viewed correctly, this was a way of shedding light on how this infernal spectacle had come about. At its root was the delusional idea of individuals to give the entire world a new form according to their own will, literally to re-create it from a single, solid mold. It was the insane vision of a world that would be defined henceforth by a single face. A world, then, that no longer needed any other people, any physical resistance to re-create itself: the political nightmare of total control.

But if something was a nightmare—this much remained true even in this dark time—it meant that one could wake from it. One had only to find the courage in oneself to open one's eyes—keep them open—to perceive the abysses of one's own time with an alert mind. "To tell the truth, even to the point of 'indecency.'"[40] To bear witness in this way to the terrible depths from which those abysses had entered the world. To succumb, then, neither to the past nor to the future. To blindly follow neither one's own judgment nor that of others. To find the courage to make use of one's own intelligence. To orient oneself freely in one's thoughts.

Right now, at that moment, Arendt gathered new strength—what mattered was "to be entirely present."[41] Or in other words: to philosophize.

II

EXILES: 1933–1934

Arendt leaves her country, Weil her Party,
Beauvoir her skepticism, and Rand her script.

GRID

"Normally when I have someone in front of me, I just have to look up the case in our records and I know what to do. But what am I supposed to do with you?"[1] Plainly her name hadn't yet been recorded in any Gestapo dossier. And even if she had wanted to give the young Gestapo official a helping hand, Hannah Arendt wouldn't have been able to explain fully why, that May morning, while having breakfast in a café near Alexanderplatz, she and her mother had been thrown into a car and taken for interrogation.

There would have been reasons enough. Her apartment on Opitzstrasse had been used as a hiding place for people subject to political persecution. And then there was the request from her Zionist friend Kurt Blumenfeld, who was a generation older, to assemble "a collection of all the everyday anti-Semitic expressions," which brought her to the newspaper archive of the Prussian State Library every day. Even collecting such material was illegal by now.

Possibly, however, they were just putting together lists of names—and lists based on such lists—for the purposes of intimidation. Like Bertolt Brecht's address book, for example. Only a few days after Hitler's accession to power, the Gestapo seized it from his apartment: a Who's Who of the communist-inclined intelligentsia of Berlin, which included Arendt's husband, Günther Stern.

Out of fear of falling into the newly founded Prussian auxiliary police, he fled from Berlin to Paris around the time of the Reichstag fire. For, as if the conflagration on the night of February 27, 1933, had given the long-agreed starting signal, the waves had begun: random arrests, deportations to provisional concentration camps in the surrounding countryside, even urban gymnasiums converted into torture chambers. In Berlin alone there were more than two hundred such places by the summer of that year. Nazi terror had reached everyday life. The number of victims was already in the thousands.

It was more than likely that a Gestapo unit was going through her apartment right at that moment. But what would they find—apart from dozens of notebooks with transcribed quotations in ancient Greek, the poems of Heine and Hölderlin, and countless works about intellectual life in Berlin in the early nineteenth century?

As far as the public records were concerned, she was an impeccable doctor of philosophy with a grant from the Emergency Association of German Science.[2] The classic Berlin existence: academic without an income, journalist without an outlet. Of course, she spent every day in the library. Where else? After all, research never sleeps.

As it turned out, they couldn't even get anything useful out of Arendt's mother. Questioned about her daughter's activities, Martha Beerwald (as she was now) put some words of fine parental solidarity on the record: "No, I don't know what she was doing, but whatever she was doing she was right to be doing it and I would have done the same."[3]

They were both released on the day of the arrest.[4] They didn't even have to call a lawyer. So, lucky for now. But Arendt had made her decision. There was no future in this country. At least not for people like her.

THE CASE OF RAHEL

In that first summer, after Hitler's accession to power, there can have been few clearer illustrations than the example of Hannah Arendt that it wasn't up to individuals to decide who and what they were. Using the example of the Berliner Rahel Varnhagen, she had been researching the complex dynamics involved in the identity of a German Jew and intellectual at the turn of the eighteenth to the nineteenth century. This yielded the psychological portrait of a woman in whose life the fraught history of educated German Jewry was concentrated in exemplary form—and all in relation to the question of assimilation. In a book assembled in large part as a collage of quotations, Arendt draws the consciousness of a woman whose active denial of her Jewish origins for a long time made it impossible for her to construct a stable relationship with herself and the world. As a person of her time, like Arendt herself, marginalized three times over—woman, Jew, intellectual—Rahel refused to acknowledge herself socially as what she inevitably was and had to remain in the eyes of others; this led to a situation of painfully experienced selflessness. "Rahel's struggle with the facts, above all the fact of having been born a Jew, very rapidly became a struggle against herself. She herself refused to consent to herself; she, born to so many disadvantages, had to deny, change, reshape by lies this self of hers. Since she could not very well deny her existence out of hand. . . . Once one has negated oneself, however, there are no longer any particular choices. There is only one aim: always, and at any given moment, to be different from what one is."[5]

For Arendt, the case of Rahel is also exemplary of an entire age in that two forms of necessary courage collide in her situation. On the one hand there is the progressive courage to use one's own intelligence, and so to define oneself as a creature of reason. But there is also the courage required to acknowledge that this attempt at self-creation is always contingent on historical and cultural conditions, from which no individual can fully escape. In Rahel's own time, this is expressed in the tension between progressive and romantic ideals of becoming oneself; between reason and history, pride and prejudice, thought and obedience; between the dream of the complete self-determination of the self and one's ultimately inescapable definition by others.

According to Arendt, progressive reason can "liberate from the prejudices of the past, and it can guide the future. Unfortunately, however, it appears that it can free isolated individuals only, can direct the future only of Crusoes. The individual who has been liberated by reason is always running head-on into a world, a society, whose past in the shape of 'prejudices' has a great deal of power; he is forced to learn that past reality is also a reality. Although being born a Jewess might seem to Rahel a mere reference to something out of the remote past, and although she may have entirely eradicated the fact from her thinking, it remained a nasty present reality as a prejudice in the minds of others."[6]

No human being can escape being subjected to the tension between these forces—and no one should reasonably wish to be able to. And if it were possible, it would mean the loss of everything that deserves to be called world and reality.

ENLIGHTENED

The risk of losing the world in the name of a seemingly rational determination—with this reproach directed at Rahel, Arendt was quite deliberately following in the philosophical footsteps of the two academic teachers who had shaped her the most: Martin Heidegger and Karl Jaspers. Even as a student in Marburg, Arendt had been sensitized by Heidegger, with whom she was engaged for several years since 1925 in a relationship, to the blind spots in the modern image of the world and humanity. Human beings, as described by Heidegger in his seminal work *Being and Time*, were by no means primarily a "subject" gifted with reason, but rather a "Dasein," a "Being-There," thrown into the world for no reason. The human being lived as a thinking and above all as an acting being, not in a mute "reality" that they had to supply with meaningful content, but in an "environment" that had always been meaningful to him. For Heidegger, true human autonomy had barely anything to do with purely rational decisions, calculations, or even prescriptive rules, but was rather about the courage required to take hold of one's own existence at exceptional moments of existential crisis.

In the 1920s, all of these ideas were also floating around the mind of Heidegger's closest philosophical companion at the time, Karl Jaspers, to whom Arendt presented herself as a doctoral candidate in Heidelberg in 1926. Unlike Heidegger's, however, Jaspers's "philosophy of existence" stressed less the power of dark and powerfully isolating states such as fear or the proximity of death, and more the way to a brighter, freer life through communication with and attention to others. This attention was always ideally to be thought of as dialogical, and thus stressed the necessity of an actual interlocutor, which meant that it excluded the faceless "man" ("one"), "the public," or even "humanity."

Having fully absorbed these impulses, from the late 1920s Arendt developed her own interpretation of the human situation, which granted her an extremely independent approach toward the case of Rahel Varnhagen. Could Rahel's situation not have been tailor-made to reveal the pressures that in fact condition every modern existence?

POLYPHONIC

To recognize oneself as a human being through Rahel—for the philosopher Arendt that meant the rejection of all worldless and thus ahistorical conceptions of reason. It meant acknowledging that true self-discovery could occur only through other people, and renouncing any abstract talk of a "human being in itself." It was only logical, then, that Arendt should have preferred concrete case studies to purely abstract analyses and treatises: the philosophy of existence as polyphonic reportage on Dasein.

With the very first sentences of her book on Rahel, Arendt delivers an impressive example of this approach, and sees herself, writing in 1933—exactly one hundred years after Rahel's death—at another crucial turning point in German Jewish history.

Like a Don Quixote who has spent his whole life trapped in false accounts of the world, wandering idealistically through the world in search of himself, on her deathbed the Romantic Rahel Varnhagen also has a moment of true recognition and self-discovery: "What a history!—A fugitive from Egypt and Palestine, here I am and find help, love, fostering in you people. With real rapture I think of these origins of mine and this whole nexus of destiny, through which the oldest memories of the human race stand side by side with the latest developments. The greatest distances in time and space are bridged. The thing which all my life seemed to me the greatest shame, which was the misery and misfortune of my life—having been born a Jewess—this *I should on no account now wish to have missed.*"[7]

When Arendt set these lines on paper, she was facing a deep break in her life. Because just as the protected middle-class daughter Rahel Varnhagen had once been made aware by the event that was Napoleon that "her life also was subject to general political conditions,"[8] so Arendt as a thinker was sensitized to the sphere of the political really only by the event that was Hitler. Like Varnhagen, who in the end could gratefully assert her identity as a Jewish woman, in the course of her work on this book Arendt became increasingly alert and receptive to the specific claims, dangers, and pariah-like opportunities that arose from her Jewishness, which had never before been a major theme in her life.

In fact, her politicization and her sensitization at the emergence of the Nazi regime coincided and led not least to the research project for Kurt Blumenfeld to collect those examples of anti-Semitic insults in Germany, which had become a daily occurrence.

At the same time, who she really was and who she wanted to be in the future remained an open question. All she could clearly see before her eyes was that this definition did not lie in her hands alone, and that the expectations of an unambiguous answer were growing stronger on all sides. As if the police's desire for clear categorization had gripped a whole society overnight.

BEING GERMAN

An exchange that Arendt had with her doctoral supervisor, Karl Jaspers, early in 1933 revolved around these very themes. Like Arendt, he had been inspired by the spirit of the age to develop a psychological portrait of a particular kind. And the question of identity was also in the foreground of Jaspers's mind. After all, he found "so much good will and real vibrancy in confused and misguided chatter in nationalist youth" that he wanted to use the example of a professorial colleague in Heidelberg, the sociologist Max Weber, who had died in 1920, to elaborate the demand "that lies in being a German."

Jaspers had written a study deliberately published by a nationalist press "to reach the readers who need this educational impulse, and who yearn for it,"[9] and had sent it to Arendt as early as 1932 with a personal dedication. The study was titled: "Max Weber: German Essence in Political Thought, Research, and Philosophy."[10] Arendt brooded about a reply for months.

> Berlin, 1 January 1933
>
> Dear Professor
>
> My deepest thanks for the Max Weber, with which you have given me a great deal of pleasure. There is, however, a particular reason why I am only thanking you for the text today: both title and introduction have made it difficult for me to comment on the book. It does not bother me that you portray Max Weber as the great German but, rather, that you find the "German essence" in him and identify that essence with "rationality and humanity originating in passion." I have the same difficulty with that as I do with Max Weber's imposing patriotism itself. You will understand that I as a Jew can say neither yes nor no and that my agreement on this would be as inappropriate as an argument against it. . . . For me, Germany means my mother tongue, philosophy and literature. I can and must stand by all that. But I am obliged to keep my distance. I can neither be for nor against when I read Max Weber's wonderful sentence where he says that to put Germany back on her feet he would form an alliance with the devil himself. And it is this sentence which seems to me to

> reveal the critical point here. . . . In spite of the housework I'm managing to get my work done. Rahel is largely finished.[11]

Apart from the fact that by the end of 1932 and the beginning of 1933 it was becoming increasingly clear what kind of pact with the devil this Germany was prepared to engage in, the genuinely visionary aspect of Arendt's reply lies in her refusal to adopt an unambiguous position. The closest she comes to a declaration involves the fact of her mother tongue and that tradition that first brought Arendt herself to life as a thinking being. Not in the sense of specific attitudes, ideals, or territories, however. Instead, people like Arendt carry their homes around the world in their hearts (and, in the form of books, soon in suitcases as well).

Precisely because it was a matter of repeatedly opening up such a particular "Germany" and bringing it to life through processes of reading and reinterpretation, it cannot be defined by an "essence" fixed for all time. The act of putting it "back on its feet" can, if at all, be done only through acts of understanding and hence benevolent appropriation—and hence through something that, by its very essence, rules out any pact with the devil.

In his immediate reply, Jaspers reminds his former student that one cannot, as a cultural being, "live solely on negations, problems and ambiguities."[12] But at the beginning of 1933, Arendt wanted to hear just as little about Germany's supposed historical-political mission as she did about a one-sided acceptance of a German-speaking Jew into that tradition. As she wrote to Jaspers on January 6 of that year:

> I am of course a German in the sense that I wrote of before. But I can't simply add a German historical and political destiny to that. I know only too well how late and how fragmentary

> the Jews' participation in that destiny has been, how much by chance they entered into what was then a foreign history. . . . Germany in its old glory is your past. What my past is can hardly be expressed in one phrase, for any oversimplification—whether it be that of the Zionists, the assimilationists, or the anti-Semites—only serves to obscure the true problem of the situation.[13]

But how—specifically as a German Jewish woman, or a Jewish German one—could one imagine a life that did not fall into the reactive trap of living "on negation alone" from now on, and at the same time eluded the arrogance of absolute unambiguity? What would a life look like that escaped the Rahel trap without toppling into that of unbridled affirmation and hence also of political acceptance? A life with a foothold but without banisters? Wherever Arendt might find or draft her answer to these questions, it could no longer be in Germany.

BACK DOOR

Together with her mother, Arendt chose the classic route: from the Ore Mountains via the green border into Czechoslovakia. Most of the victims of political persecution remained in Prague, where a strong network of chiefly social democratic resistance had formed in the spring of 1933. Intellectuals, on the other hand, generally carried on via Switzerland to France. By the summer of 1933, about 40,000 people had fled that way, some 20,000 of them to Paris.

As if in a physical embodiment of its newly won "intermediate" position, the border crossing led via the house of a German sympathizer "with a front door in Germany and a back door in Czechoslovakia: they received their 'guests' in the daytime, provided them with dinner and then ushered them out the back under the shelter of darkness."[14]

FURIOUS

The grammar school teacher and trade union activist Simone Weil had also bid definitive farewell to Germany in the summer of 1933. A year before, she had traveled at short notice from Paris to Berlin, to form her own picture of the situation there for a few weeks. After all, as she said in the introduction to her ten-part series of reports for a trade union newspaper, "everyone who has pinned all his hopes on the victory of the working class . . . ought right now to have his eyes on Germany."[15]

What she saw on the ground in Berlin was a nation on its knees: "In Germany you see former engineers who manage to eat one cold meal a day by renting chairs in the public gardens; you see elderly men in stiff collars and bowler hats begging at subway exits or singing in cracked voices in the streets. Students are dropping out of school and selling peanuts, matches or shoelaces on the street. . . . Every worker expects some time or other to be thrown into the compulsory idleness that is the lot of nearly half the German working class."[16]

In other words, the mood in the country with the best-organized and the numerically strongest movement of workers in Europe was clearly revolutionary. Meanwhile, the political left appeared hopelessly split and paralyzed. Instead of putting up a solid front against the Nazis, the German Communist Party and the Communist International, controlled by Stalin and the Russian Central Committee, waged a "sectarian war against Social Democracy as the 'chief enemy.'" The consequences were, to Weil, entirely predictable. "In Germany," she wrote to a trade union official friend in autumn 1932, "I lost all the respect that in spite of myself I still felt for the Communist Party.... All compromise with the party or any reticence in criticizing it is criminal."[17]

Just a year later, it happened exactly as Weil predicted in her articles. Hitler was victorious all along the line, and the purges were in full swing. Stalin's Soviet Union did not even grant asylum to fleeing comrades. Anyone who still believed in the proletarian revolution by the grace of Moscow was in Weil's eyes beyond help.

REVOLUTIONARY

For "Red Simone," as she was already known at the time of her philosophy studies, this was one more reason to intensify her political commitment to aid refugees, trade union education, and journalism.

In the autumn of 1933, after quarrels at her former lycée in Auxerre—only four of her eleven girl students there sat their *baccalauréat* in philosophy—Weil was transferred to teach in the small town of Roanne, northeast of Lyon. The ministry preferred to see the activist working in a rather quieter, more bourgeois area. A small teaching load of twelve hours a week with only five students also left enough time for what seemed to her the important and urgent things. Whenever possible, she took the train to the workers' district of Saint-Étienne, where she taught evening classes and led a lecture series for the miners. Basic geometry, introduction to French literature, "foundations of scientific socialism"—with a view to the coming society, nothing could be left out. Barely four feet eleven, with her hands always deep in her tobacco-filled coat pockets, she hurried from the station to the trade union rooms; she needed merely a few notes for her lessons.

Sometimes she and her comrades also visited a neighboring apartment, where Simone, at the center of a circle of chairs, would go on freely lecturing about the potentially crucial connection between increased output and the means of production, visualizing the temptation of the Cartesian demon, or reciting from memory passages from Homer and Aeschylus. Every now and again she would even join in with very dirty workers' songs. Dancing, however, was beyond her reach. "I don't know how,"[18] she would say, more to herself than to anyone else, and creep from the room.

Once the weekend came, she would march, wrapped in a red flag, right at the front of the protest marches, singing "The Internationale" at the top of her lungs. No, nobody was going to silence "la Simone" as easily as that. Not even the troublemakers of the Stalinist faction who appeared more and more frequently at her events to shout her off the stage.

The struggle continued even at the lycée for girls in Roanne. When a colleague announced she was offering a reading circle that afternoon, studying materials from the Action Catholique youth organization, Weil had the documents sent to her specially from Paris, and then announced at the school after studying them thoroughly: "If that happens, I'll offer a reading circle on rationalism tomorrow." The fight went all the way to the headmistress's office. The result of the arbitration discussion has not been passed down to us.[19]

CAUSE FOR CONCERN

But there is always another Simone, and not only when her headaches return. With her eyes closed and her hands pressed to her temples, she sits alone in her room all night, the thumping headache keeping her awake, trapped in pain. As with her previous teaching posts in Le Puy and Auxerre, her parents accompanied her to Roanne for the first few days, helped the twenty-four-year-old look for a new place to live, furnished her room, made sure she had the basic necessities. Better than anyone else, her mother, "Mime," and father, "Biri," knew about their daughter's genuine fragility, her dangerously self-destructive asceticism and remoteness from the everyday.

Their almost daily letters are filled with the same fundamental concerns: Is the apartment heated? Have you eaten? Can we send you clothes? Questions, however, to which Simone reacts in a tone of aggressive refusal: "My dear Mime, . . . I expressly *forbid* you to buy me anything without my express permission—unless I haven't eaten for more than a fortnight or something like that."[20] Her parents also know how Simone has dealt with her wages for years: for herself she keeps precisely the minimum sum assigned to unemployed factory workers on state support, while the rest she donates to needy or fleeing comrades.

As events develop throughout 1933, Weil's mother increasingly adopts the role of private secretary in Simone's solo refugee charity. Besides their family apartment, the Weils own an empty one on the seventh floor of the building on rue Auguste Comte, near the Jardin du Luxembourg, that now serves as a reception center for refugees.

Every week that autumn, Weil writes to her mother to tell her of the impending arrival of German refugees, who are to be taken in and given financial support without any further questions. Her parents always do as they are told. They capitulated to Simone's will a long time ago, and see their roles—her father is a respected doctor—as principally to support the strange life of their strange daughter the best they can, shaping it as smoothly as possible until the predictable moment of another physical breakdown.

They will have read with a nuanced attention to detail—and a degree of concern—the last sentences of that essay by their daughter, which struck the intellectual landscape of the French left like a meteor in the autumn of 1933: "Nothing in the world," she wrote, "can keep us from being clear. There is no contradiction between this task of theoretical education and the practical tasks of struggle; on the contrary, there is an interrelationship, because one cannot act without knowing what one wants, and without knowing the obstacles to be overcome. Nevertheless, since the time at our disposal is in any case limited, we are forced to divide it between thought and action, or, to talk more modestly: preparation for action. . . . In any case, the greatest misfortune for us would be to perish without being successful and without being able to understand."[21]

THIRD WAYS

Weil's article, published in *La révolution prolétarienne* on August 25, 1933, under the title "Prospects—Are We Headed for the Proletarian Revolution?," could hardly have caused greater offense.[22] In it she establishes the structural similarity between newly fascist Germany and Stalin's Soviet Union. In only a few months Hitler had

> installed . . . a political régime more or less the same in structure as that of the Russian régime as defined by Tomsky: "One party in power and all the rest in prison." We may add that the mechanical subjection of the party to the leader is the same in each case, and guaranteed in each case by the police. But political sovereignty is nothing without economic sovereignty; which is why fascism

> tends to approach the Russian régime on the economic plane also, by concentrating all power, economic as well as political, in the hands of the head of state.[23]

Furthermore, the form of a state completely under the control of a leader, unique in history according to Weil, was also based on a new and technologically supported form of oppression that was due to the monstrous growth in power of a new class of controlling functionaries "that exercises power . . . not in such a way as to bring happiness to those who are subject to it, but in such a way as to increase that power."[24] But in consequence the framework of the Marxist image of class struggle would finally explode.

The new total Hitler- and Stalin-style systems tend in their outward economic form to state capitalism, and in their internal construction to a repressive surveillance state, with the help of a primarily self-serving class of functionaries as well as increasingly advanced surveillance technologies. In these systems, what Weil called a "bureaucratic dictatorship" was installed, for which Stalin's Soviet Union represented by far the most impressive and also the most devastating example.

Consequently, no state could have been further removed from a true workers' democracy. In the end it was of no importance whatsoever whom the means of production nominally belonged to (workers, large-scale capitalists, the state), if nothing changed in the actual conditions of oppression. If anything, under Stalin the brutalization of the everyday working life had increased, accompanied by disastrous new supply shortfalls.

During that autumn of 1933, Weil was partially informed about conditions in Stalin's empire via letters and personal conversations with Russian refugees. In a letter to her mother, she assembled as follows the information she had gathered: "In cities like Magnitogorsk—a city without unemployment—you see how people dig up rotten potatoes with their bare hands and eat them raw, how the workers there, in temperatures of –40, sleep in unheated barracks, that in Ukraine whole villages have been wiped out by starvation, that a special law had to be passed punishing the consumption of corpses with the death penalty... and that for fear of the terror of the secret police no one dared cross anyone's path, there is talk of queues in which people stand in line from eight o'clock in the morning until two in the afternoon at –35 degrees for a ration of potatoes."[25]

Admittedly, Weil had only rudimentary information about the epic horrors of the Holodomor of 1932 and 1933, in which almost four million Ukrainians starved to death in a famine deliberately caused by Stalin's administration.[26] Still, her letters prove that, in 1933, anyone in France who really wanted to know what was happening in the Soviet Union could find out. It was a quiet, secret knowledge that influenced Weil's analyses and judgments.

Weil concluded that in the future these new forms of state, with their "monstrous apparatuses," would inevitably become increasingly socially oppressive, justifying this with propaganda in the name of the people, a people who would have to subordinate the whole of their labor production to a ruthless battle for survival against an external enemy. Only then would the circle of oppression of the individual be closed, under a completely anonymous collective whose sole visible face henceforth would be the face of the leader.

Weil saw no way of halting this dynamic in the future, and neither did she set one out in her essay. As a good socialist, she contented herself in the end with recalling the actual mission of socialism: "That we should assign the highest value to the individual, not the collective. We want to form whole men by doing away with that specialization which cripples us all.... Individuals see themselves brutally stripped of the means of struggle and labour; neither war nor production [is] possible today without a total subjection of the individual to the collective power potential. . . . In the subordination of society to the individual lies the definition of true democracy, and that of socialism as well."[27]

SALVATION ARMY

Excessive bureaucratization, the alienation of the party apparatus from the base, blind unanimity . . . In delivering such critical views of the course of the Russian Revolution, Simone Weil was far from alone in the left-wing camp of the time. In fact, these were precisely the criticisms that Leon Trotsky had leveled against his former fellow fighter Joseph Stalin. Soon branded as a "Jewish conspirator" and "lackey of Fascism," Trotsky first went to Kazakhstan, then fled to Turkey in 1929. Finally, in July 1933, accompanied by his wife, Natalia Sedova, and their elder son, Lev Sedov, he journeyed into exile in Barbizon, a small town south of Paris. In constant poverty, and now stripped of his citizenship by a decree from Moscow, he lived—under severe constraints and in permanent fear of the sleuths of the Soviet secret service—as a freelance journalist. At the same time, he worked in strict secrecy on the organization of a Fourth International whose declared goal remained communist world revolution.

The Daladier government banned him just as rigidly from involving himself in the internal affairs of France as it did from staying in Paris. So his project was very risky, and required both extensive planning and extreme secrecy. Biri resisted for a long time, but gave in as expected to Simone's repeated insistence that they move Trotsky into their rue Auguste Comte apartment.

By the end of the year, the time had come. With a new haircut, a trimmed beard, and his collar covering his face, Leon Trotsky—accompanied by two bodyguards as well as his son and his wife—moved into the Weils' seventh-floor apartment. After a brief visit, it was clear: the Weils' apartment passed muster. There was only a request for an additional armchair for the bodyguards, who kept watch in shifts over Trotsky and Sedova's bedroom, revolvers at the ready.

It was Simone's role as refugee helper and an early contact of Trotsky's son Lev (known to everyone as "the Crown Prince") that would lead to a first meeting—in the Weils' house of all places—of the new high command of the world revolution. Weil and Lev had been in correspondence since July, which had not prevented his father Leon (known in Weil's circles as "Papa") from reacting very personally to the theses Weil had published about the "proletarian revolution." On October 13, 1933, in the journal *La vérité,* he published an article titled "The Fourth International and the USSR," which represents a sharp rebuttal of the analyses and conclusions put forward by Simone Weil: "Disappointed by her experience of the dictatorship of the proletariat," he writes, "Simone Weil has found consolation in a new mission: to defend her personality against society. A formula of the old liberalism, refurbished by a cheaply bought anarchist exaltation. And to think that Simone Weil speaks majestically of our 'illusions'! Many years will have to pass for her and her like before they free themselves of the most reactionary petty-bourgeois [*sic*] prejudices."[28]

So "Papa" was far from amused. Which is also why it isn't hard to imagine the deep reluctance with which he must have accepted the offer of the apartment. But Weil was also in a state of conflict. While this brave man might once have commanded a millions-strong revolutionary army, a good argument was hardly a substitute!

Trotsky's voice carried all the way to the lower floors of the building.[29] He was so agitated that even Natalia Sedova, who was taking tea with Mime and Biri, could only shake her head: "That child actually dares to stand up to Trotsky." As we can tell from Weil's notes made at the time, all the bones of contention that would shape left-wing discourse for years and decades were concentrated in her conversation with Leon Trotsky on December 31, 1933.

What means were permitted—or indeed required—to achieve the end goal of revolution? Especially in reference to the specific question of the presumably unconditional value of each individual human life.

Trotsky—as he had proved, and been forced to prove, many times—was highly flexible in this regard. This was something with which Weil confronted him directly at the beginning of their conversation, referring to the Kronstadt sailors' uprising of 1921, in whose wake Trotsky had personally ordered the execution of 1,500 of the rebellious "counter-revolutionaries." "If that's what you're thinking, why did you put us up? Do you belong in the Salvation Army?"[30]

An almost prophetic question in retrospect, although it was simply the beginning of an argument in which Trotsky increasingly saw himself as being forced into the slightly paradoxical role of defending, in the name of the Revolution, precisely those people who wished to have him killed: "I have no accusations to throw at Stalin (apart from mistakes in the context of his own policies). . . . A great deal has been achieved for workers (women, children). . . . The Russian worker controls the government insofar as he tolerates it, because he prefers this government to a return of the capitalists. That is the seal of his dominion!"

Aha, Weil presses, might we not equally conclude from this that workers elsewhere also control their government via the mode of tolerance, for example in France or Germany? . . . "You idealist! So you are calling the ruling class an enslaved class. . . . Why must you doubt everything?"

At any rate, at the end of this conversation even Trotsky was no longer quite sure of himself: "Not only do I believe that the new left opposition will achieve revolution, I am sure of it!" And that was exactly the farewell message he gave to Weil's parents after a successful conspiratorial meeting with his co-combatants from all over Europe: "We have founded the Fourth International in your apartment!"[31]

TESTAMENT

By early 1934, Simone Weil had also found new certainty for herself, although in a markedly different direction. On February 6 there were serious disturbances and street battles throughout Paris with numerous fatalities and several thousand wounded. In the middle of the deepest economic crisis, a huge banking and stock market fraud had been exposed. As part of a pyramid scheme, a certain Alexandre Stavisky had embezzled several hundred million francs of public funds, his crimes apparently covered up by politicians on the left. It was exactly what the combative right-wing press had been waiting for; they had no qualms about stressing not only the socialist friends of the fraudster, but also his Jewish Ukrainian origins. The day after the disturbances, Prime Minister Édouard Daladier, a member of the Radical Socialist Party, stepped down after only six days at the head of what was now called his "government of murderers." That did little to stabilize the political situation.

A few days later Weil wrote from Paris to her good friend (and later biographer) Simone Pétrement in Switzerland: "Nothing new here, save that the country goes straight to Fascism, or at least to a very reactionary dictatorship; but you must know all that. All the news from Russia is dreadful and hopeless. As for Germany, best not to talk about it. Well, no point in dwelling on all this. . . . I have decided to withdraw entirely from any kind of political activity, except for theoretical work. That does not absolutely exclude possible participation in a great spontaneous movement of the masses (in the ranks, as a soldier), but from now on I don't want any responsibility, no matter how slight, or even indirect, because I am certain that all the blood that will be shed will be shed in vain, and that we are beaten in advance."[32]

Over the coming months, Weil planned to devote her entire intellectual energy to an essay that she described to friends as her "intellectual will and testament." Weil was twenty-five years old at the time. The title of the essay also served as a prophetic headline for the whole of the coming decade: "Reflections Concerning the Causes of Liberty and Social Oppression."[33]

THREATENED

On February 12, 1934, when Simone de Beauvoir's teacher colleagues, like four million other French people, followed the trade unions' call to a general strike, she was, she said, "such a stranger to all practical political activities that it never occurred to me that I might join them."[34] After all, striking means showing solidarity with the interests of other working people. But Beauvoir felt no inner impulse to do so. Neither was she willing "to act as the teacher I was,"[35] nor could she understand at that point in her life what any other person's existence was good for. "The existence of Otherness," she wrote in retrospect, "remained a danger to me, and one which I could not bring myself to face openly. . . . I had settled the anomaly of Sartre by telling myself that we formed a single entity, placed together at the world's centre. Around us other people circled, pleasant, odious or ridiculous: they had no eyes with which to observe me. I alone could see. As a result I had the most brazen indifference to public opinion."[36]

For barely five years she and Jean-Paul Sartre had formed a particular kind of couple: united in complete intellectual devotion, while remaining open to other experiences and adventures. In 1929, they had won joint first place in the national final examinations for philosophy teachers (*agrégation*),[37] and were then, in line with the rules of the system, sent for their first teaching years from Paris into the provinces.

In some sense, Beauvoir's move from Marseille to Rouen meant a return to the center of her own existence. At the time, Sartre was teaching in the northern port town of Le Havre, an hour's train journey from Rouen. On weekends Paris was also much easier to get to.

But even this new proximity failed to bridge the abyss that Beauvoir felt her life was shaped by, particularly since her literary writing was not coming together. Again and again she came up with novels in the cafés of Rouen, but threw away her initial efforts after only a few weeks; her intention was to describe the social pressures suffered by the women of her milieu as soon as they sought a truly free existence.

THE OTHER

The situation of this twenty-six-year-old highly intellectual philosophy teacher could also at first be described in a distinctly more prosaic way. Despite her deep and unique relationship with Jean-Paul Sartre, two years her senior, she had not yet found her own position in life, not in a professional or a literary sense. Not politically or philosophically. Not even erotically.

Plainly a new self was fermenting inside her. It hadn't yet seen the light of day. She was suffering. Particularly in the milieu of women her own age, there were some who seemed far more advanced. One of these was Colette Audry, strongly committed to communist groups and the only local colleague with whom Beauvoir sought anything like a friendship. Another was Audry's closest friend:

> Colette Audry sometimes spoke of Simone Weil, to me; and though I felt no great sympathy for her, this unknown woman's existence was forced upon my consciousness. She was a university teacher... it was said that she lived in a truck-drivers' hostel, and on the first of every month would put her entire salary packet out on the table and let anyone help themselves. . . . Her intelligence, her asceticism, her total commitment, and her sheer courage—all these filled me with admiration; though I knew that, had she met me, she would have been very far from reciprocating my attitude. I could not absorb her into my universe, and this seemed to constitute a vague threat to me.[38]

Even at the age of nineteen, when Beauvoir began her studies at the Sorbonne, she described the opposition between "self and others" as the actual driving question.[39] And just as Sartre, deep within his own creativity, became the exhilarating "great equal" in their student days, during that time her fellow pupil Simone Weil assumed the position of the "great other."

The sparks of absolute difference flew at their first meeting:

> She intrigued me because of her great reputation for intelligence and her bizarre get-up; a great famine had broken out in China, and I was told that when she heard the news she had wept: these tears compelled my respect much more than her gifts as a philosopher. I envied her having a heart that could beat right across

> the world. I managed to get near her one day. I don't know how the conversation got started; she declared in no uncertain tones that only one thing mattered in the world: the revolution which would feed all the starving people of the earth. I retorted, no less peremptorily, that the problem was not to make men happy, but to find the reason for their existence. She looked me up and down: "It's easy to see you've never been hungry," she snapped. Our relations ended right there.[40]

Weil's will to absolute identification with the suffering of all others, even those farthest away from her, coincides with Beauvoir's absolute identification of her ego with her own self and that of her closest partner—against all others. For Beauvoir, behind the challenge "to find a meaning for human existence" there lay a twofold problem. First: What is a meaningful existence based on? And second: What role should the existence of other people play in that? In other words: What meaning, if any, does their obvious existence have for one's own existence?

Where she and her meaning of life in the world were concerned, the existence of Sartre was quite enough. The rest could be met with indifferent irony; but where it could not, other people did one thing above all: they bothered her mightily.

ISOLATED

The reluctance, which shaped Beauvoir's life so far, to imagine herself empathetically in others, or even to acknowledge their existence, goes far beyond a mere psychological peculiarity. After all, the entire edifice of modern philosophy—beginning with René Descartes—was burdened with the doubt of how and upon what basis one might know, as a subject entirely isolated within one's own thoughts, that other thinking subjects existed. One could not, in the end, literally creep inside other people. All that remained regarding the conscious life of other human beings were the conclusions drawn from one's very own experiences. Entirely according to the motto: "In their place I would now be experiencing, thinking, feeling the following . . ." But as Descartes seemed to have demonstrated once and for all in the *Meditations*, these conclusions could be false—indeed, in an extreme case they could dispense with any explicable foundation. For one sufficiently practiced in the art of philosophical skepticism, nothing and nobody could provide any certainty about the revealed behavior of other people, or could prove that those others were thinking, feeling beings. In the end they might be mere automata or robots without any real inner life. In Descartes's words from the seventeenth century:

> [I] glance out of the window at people walking along the street. Using the customary expression, I say that I "see" them. But what do I actually see apart from hats and coats, which could be covering automata.[41]

This is literally the attitude that Beauvoir and Sartre, a couple intellectually very much on the same wavelength, shared in the cafés of Rouen, Le Havre, and Paris. Other people do not really exist for them as people. The two of them are the only beings who truly feel. The rest of humanity serves solely as a backdrop to stimulate their own thought games. As Sartre and Beauvoir sensed quite acutely, this imagined uniqueness was both attractive and ultimately damaging: they paid for it with a loss of immediacy and perhaps even of the plenitude of their own reality.

As a philosophical couple fully in tune with the times, they were therefore troubled during this phase by the questions: How could this fading of reality be prevented without affecting the unimpeachable sovereignty of their own consciousness? How could one escape being isolated in one's own cranial cavity without being dictated to by the world of others? How could one take the world and its demands literally without ceasing to maintain an ironic distance?

MAGIC POTION

At the beginning of 1933, the pair arranged to have a drink with a former fellow student, Raymond Aron. Aron was just back in Paris after his study year in Berlin. At their meeting in the Bec de Gaz bar on rue du Montparnasse, the returning traveler told them about an entirely new German trend in philosophy called "phenomenology." As Beauvoir remembered: "We ordered the specialty of the house, apricot cocktails; Aron said, pointing to his glass, 'You see, my dear fellow, if you are a phenomenologist, you can talk about this cocktail and make philosophy out of it!' Sartre turned pale with emotion at this. Here was just the thing he had been longing to achieve for years—to describe objects just as he saw and touched them, and extract philosophy from the process. Aron convinced him that phenomenology exactly fitted in with his special preoccupations: by-passing the antithesis of idealism and realism, affirming simultaneously both the supremacy of conscience [consciousness] and the reality of the visible world as it appears to our senses."[42]

All of a sudden Sartre and Beauvoir were presented with a possibility they had been seeking for so long: a third and entirely new way of thinking about everyday life as freely experienced, which did not involve losing either the quicksilver swiftness of one's own intellectual life or undistorted contact with so-called reality. But what exactly did its principles consist of?

Sartre and Beauvoir soon discovered, via their own original readings, the works—as intense as they were linguistically demanding—of the mathematician and philosopher Edmund Husserl. In Göttingen and Freiburg before World War I, he really had established a new form of philosophical inquiry. Under the slogan "Back to things themselves," Husserl required that his students provide as precise, undistorted, and, most important, unprejudiced a description as possible of what appeared to consciousness as given. How do things really show themselves to consciousness?

Husserl called this almost meditative attitude of concentration on the purely given, avoiding any addition or deviation, "reduction." And one of his first central insights from this consisted in the following: Consciousness, however it is concretely shaped or whatever it may be concerned with, is always consciousness of or about something! We taste the sweetness of liqueur, we are disturbed by the noise of a car that rattles by, we have memories of our vacation in Spain, we hope for good weather. To the extent that consciousness can be grasped at all, it must be grasped as consciousness of something. To this essential directedness toward or action of consciousness Husserl gives the name "intentionality." In fact, an apricot cocktail in the middle of Paris was enough to explain this reality.

Closely related to this, Husserl identified a second characteristic quality of consciousness: By virtue of being directed (intentional), consciousness is always also about things that are essentially external to and different from itself (liqueur, a car, the landscape, the weather). To be itself, consciousness therefore always forces its way out of itself into the open and into other people. In other words, it has an essential urge to go beyond itself—or, to quote Husserl, to "transcend" itself.

Aron had correctly explained it to Sartre and Beauvoir, he had fully grasped the philosophical explosiveness of this approach: Phenomenology opened up a radically new way of understanding one's own existence. In Husserl's world, consciousness did not take its bearings passively from things (realism), nor was consciousness a compass toward which things were directed (idealism). It was rather that realism and idealism were unshakably related to each other without ever really becoming one. The world does not entirely disappear into consciousness, but neither does consciousness dissolve entirely in the world. As in a perfect dance, they are both entirely themselves, and yet one is nothing without the other.[43]

WALLS

It says a lot about the enthusiasm unleashed in Sartre that, only six months later, in the summer of 1933, he enrolled in a one-year residency at the Maison de France in Berlin to study the new theory in the country and the language of its origin. Into the eye of the new intellectual storm, into a new reality, he went. Beauvoir too, still in Rouen, immersed herself that autumn in her philosophical investigations. She took German lessons from a refugee, studied Husserl in the original, and engaged in an intense exchange of reading matter with Sartre. At the same time, she was carrying out literary experiments in the footsteps of Virginia Woolf, examining phenomenologically inspired narrative techniques such as the "stream of consciousness."

Something was moving, not least in their relationship. Gone was the time of absolute unity and dialogical intimacy. Particularly from Sartre's point of view they had come to know each other sufficiently. True to their new philosophical premises, they now needed to explode each other in a physical sense as well. Sartre started first and, in the winter, informed Beauvoir—as their 1929 pact of intimacy had explicitly required—in detail about his relationship with the wife of one of his fellow grant-holders in Berlin. Beauvoir showed no sign of jealousy, but the event was enough for her to have herself signed out sick for two weeks by a Paris psychiatrist in late February 1934 (reason: mental exhaustion), and to take the next express train to a wintry Berlin. False alarm. Sartre's "moon woman," as they both called her, was not actually a serious threat. And Berlin, indeed Germany in general, was entirely worth the trip. Or at least it was in 1934.

Beauvoir's descriptions of their time in Germany are impressive examples of how uncomplicatedly remarkable philosophical alertness can go hand in hand with almost complete blindness to political realities—particularly if one compares these notes with the reports that Simone Weil had brought back from the same Berlin eighteen months before.

The real-world consequences of Hitler's accession to power go largely unmentioned in Beauvoir's records. Together she and Sartre visit the Leibniz House in Hanover ("very pretty, with bull's-eye windows"), Dresden's Old Town ("even uglier than Berlin"), and Hamburg's Reeperbahn ("where made-up whores with curly hair displayed themselves behind spotless window panes").[44] Her notes focus on architectural and culinary impressions and images of nightlife, as in the following passage: "Cantin took us into some incredibly debauched night-spots around the Alexanderplatz. One notice hung on a wall amused me: 'Das Animieren der Damen ist verboten,' which means 'It is forbidden to encourage women.' . . . I drank beer in enormous beer halls. One consisted of a whole sequence of rooms, and three bands were playing at the same time. At eleven o'clock in the morning every table was full, people were embracing one another and rocking to and fro as they sang. 'That,' Sartre explained to me, 'is Stimmung [atmosphere].'"[45]

Back in Rouen, by the summer, Beauvoir's mood had reached a new depressive low. Rather than feeling liberated, she could see only "walls to block my vision."[46] The time of the great "we" was gone, just as much as the years of an uncomplicatedly enjoyable adolescence. At this point, she was largely politically uninterested, and bored with her work; her private life was in crisis and her literary activity stagnant, and the sole emotion that she could honestly feel about her social surroundings was a vague hatred of "bourgeois order." Meanwhile, her own superego's glance in the mirror produced only negative thoughts: "No husband, no children, no home, no social polish . . . When you reach this age you want to have your feet on the ground."[47]

In Berlin, Sartre was opening up a new world every day, while for Beauvoir, the monotony of everyday life was threatening to rob the world and herself of meaning. She was more than just alone. She was lonely. As if the universe itself wanted to make fun of her, she was staying in a hotel called La Rochefoucauld and teaching in a school called Jeanne d'Arc, and all in a city whose provincial claustrophobia Gustave Flaubert had chosen as the perfect setting for the suicide of his Madame Bovary. A long way from the story, and above all the reality, that had once been her dream. A long way from the salvation that she had hoped would come through philosophy.

A WRITING ENGINE

By the spring of 1934, the Great Depression had reached even the Rands. As with the façade of their house, copied from a Loire château, from the outside everything seemed still to be in full working order. But in fact, the financial resources of the young artists—he a film actor, she a screenwriter—had been largely used up. For a long time,

Frank O'Connor's Hollywood career had been stagnating. The thirty-seven-year-old son of a steelworker from Ohio—tall, dark-complexioned, slender, and elegant—had, according to Rand's biographer, enjoyed his greatest success as a bit-part player in a sequel to *King Kong*.[48] For Ayn Rand, too, a gulf between her private ambition and any genuine recognition still yawned.

In her case it certainly wasn't due to a lack of will. "From now on—no thought whatever about yourself, only about your work. You don't exist. You are only a writing engine. The secret of life: You must be nothing but will. Know what you want and do it. Know what you are doing and why you are doing it. . . . All will and all control. Send everything else to hell!"[49] she had sworn to herself in her diary in 1929. Since then not a single day had passed without some progress. Via short stories and treatments, she felt her way around the great literary forms—drama, script, novel—in what was still a foreign language to her.

As an author, the crucial question for her remained: How can works of fiction deal with philosophically demanding questions without losing the interest of the wider public? The certainty that, at least in principle, this was possible was something she had absorbed with her mother's milk. What, in the end, were the novels of Dostoyevsky and Tolstoy but metaphysical blockbusters that brought delight to an entire cultural circle? Or Chekhov's dramas? Now this same miracle had to be performed for the twentieth century, and ideally in that century's actual medium of the future: cinema.

After seven years in Hollywood, she had a clear vision of how to be accepted: the plot had to have several different layers. "This must be done," she wrote to the producer and director Kenneth McGowan on May 18, 1934, "in such a manner that one and the same story can stand as a story without any of its deeper implications, so that those who do not care to be, will not be burdened with any intellectual or artistic angles, and yet those who do care for them will get those angles looking at exactly the same material."[50]

For example, a romantic triangle, in which a woman must give herself to a second man to save or win the man she really loves. This kind of thing is already quite exciting enough at the level of the pure development of the plot—you want to know how it's all going to turn out. On a second level, however, the same plot provides deeper insights into the emotional life and the specific challenges of the protagonists. Treated on a third, philosophical level, finally, such a plot deals with the fundamental existential tension between "duty" and "inclination," "sacrifice" and "happiness," or indeed "means" and "end."

Certainly, Rand admits in the same letter, that sounds odd at first, "an attempt at philosophy in a motion picture. But if that philosophy is there only for those who want it, if it does not intrude for a single moment to bore those who do not care for any thinking in their entertainment... well, why not?"[51] Rand had a clear vision of her artistic goal: philosophy for all, at the highest level—captured in the form of screenplays and novels with the potential to be bestsellers! That was what she wanted. And she would never rest until she saw it turned into reality.

AIRTIGHT

Her battle for this ideal had not been entirely successful. In 1932, several studios had shown an interest in her first complete screenplay. Titled *Red Pawn,* it tells the story of an American who is both pretty and brave, and has herself taken to a remote island gulag to liberate her imprisoned husband—a Russian engineer, who has been traduced in the Soviet system because of his special talent and his excessive sense of initiative. The heroine's plan is to start a relationship with the camp leader, win his heart, and finally open his eyes to the unconditional value of each individual human being, especially, of course, her imprisoned husband.

Everything according to Rand's recipe: a classic romantic triangle, with a philosophical and ideological emphasis on the inhuman nature of the Soviet system as well as the liberating power of the dream of the "pursuit of happiness"—all pepped up in a thoroughly American style. When Rand finished the screenplay in 1932, she was still employed full time in the props department of RKO's film studio: fourteen hours of brainless logistical work every day. She wrote at night and on Sundays.[52]

In the end, the script for *Red Pawn* went to Universal for $700, plus a further $800 for a finished version that was to be produced by the author. Rand would rather have seen her work in the hands of Metro-Goldwyn-Mayer. Marlene Dietrich, who was under contract there, had been enthusiastic about the material, while her former mentor and director Josef von Sternberg had been firmly dismissive. A few months before, a Russian film he had made had been a total flop.[53]

In the week before she was due to sign the contract, Rand resigned from her hated day job and, at the height of the economic crisis, dared to make the leap into the life of the freelance writer. Now or never!

But two years later, *Red Pawn* was still waiting to be filmed. And Rand's first big novel, into which she had put almost all her creative energy, didn't find any takers. *Airtight*, the working title of the book that would become *We the Living*, a good half of which was already written by the spring of 1934, was once again about the efforts of strong-willed individuals to find self-realization, love, and happiness. This time the location of the total loss of freedom was not a Siberian gulag, but the young Soviet Union as a whole. The very title powerfully expresses the work's atmosphere of economic scarcity, everyday drudgery, constant anxiety, and the institutionalized abuse of power.

Rand presented *Airtight* as the first work from the pen of someone who had experienced conditions in the young Soviet Union firsthand but described them from a distinctly American perspective and attitude. Surely there must be a publisher for it! All the more so in that it would be a mistake to imagine that the American reader, as Rand wrote to her literary agent Jean Wick in New York, quoting the editor Barry Benefield, "'has a fair knowledge of existence in Leningrad during the time covered by the novel.' The American reader has no knowledge of it whatsoever. He has not the slightest suspicion of it. If he had—we would not have the appalling number of parlor Bolsheviks and idealistic sympathizers with the Soviet regime, liberals who would scream with horror if they knew the truth of Soviet existence. It is for them that the book was written."[54]

Basically, however, the novel is about much more, and much deeper matters than conditions in Russia or a fight for love and freedom by its heroine: "'Airtight' *is not* the story of Kira Argounova. It is the story of Kira Argounova *and* the masses—her greatest enemy. . . . The individual against the masses—such is the real, the only theme of the book. Such is the greatest problem of our century—for those who are willing to realize it."[55]

These apparently didn't include editors at New York's leading literary publishing houses. And if they did, in 1934, on the key issue they were more likely to be on the side of the masses than that of the individual.

The American dream had turned gray in the years of the economic crisis, even in the land of the free. When the Democrat Franklin Delano Roosevelt won the 1932 presidential election against the Republican Herbert Hoover, the unemployment rate in the country was 25 percent. Roosevelt put his election promises of a New Deal into action: strict regulation of the financial markets, state employment programs, redistribution through higher taxes, and a prohibition on private ownership of gold to stabilize the dollar.

No one had to tell Ayn Rand how closely interwoven her own life had always been with the surrounding political and economic conditions. In light of the traumas that she and her family had suffered at the beginning of the revolution in Saint Petersburg, the new parcel of presidential measures with their accompanying rhetoric seemed suspiciously familiar. Soon she feared the worst. The fact that her manuscript was being rejected on top of everything else she took as another sure sign of the extent to which the East Coast creative elites had already been infiltrated by communists.

Did no one here want to understand the global scenario that was right in front of her eyes: the subjection of the individual to the diktat of the rebellious masses, the mob? All of this had long ceased to be fiction, you just had to open the paper: in Moscow, Berlin, Paris, and now in Washington, too, every day collectivism was winning another battle! As never before since arriving in the United States, she felt disappointed in her deepest hopes and yearnings. In the dramatic words of her heroine Kira: "It was me against 150 million."[56]

IDEALS

Thrown back on her own resources like that, in the crisis-ridden spring of 1934, Rand began a "philosophical journal."[57] It would deal quite explicitly with the pervasiveness of the questions that constitute the foundation or, in their absence, the abyss of every human life: the problem of freedom of the will, the relationship between emotion and reason, the essence of language, the existence of unconditional values, the ethical tension between egoism and altruism.

The first two entries in the journal testify to the particular confidence with which she planned to address these human questions:

> These are the vague beginnings of an amateur philosopher. To be checked with what I learn when I have mastered philosophy—then see how much of it has already been said, and whether I have anything new to say, or anything old to say better than it has been said.
>
> The human race has only two unlimited capacities: for suffering and for lying. I want to fight religion as the root of all human lying and the only excuse for suffering.
>
> I believe—and I want to gather all the facts to illustrate this—that the worst curse on mankind is the ability to consider ideals as something quite abstract and detached from one's everyday life. The ability to *live* and *think* quite differently, thus eliminating thinking from your actual life. This applied not to deliberate and conscious hypocrites, but to those more dangerous and hopeless ones who, alone with themselves and to themselves, tolerate a quick break between their convictions and their lives, and still believe that they have convictions. To them, either their ideals or their lives are worthless—and usually both.[58]

NIETZSCHE AND I

A distinct hatred of religion; undisguised elitism; a rejection of any idea of the necessity of suffering; the call to integrate accepted ideals of development into one's day-to-day life . . . Rand's first tentative systematic steps clearly reveal the influence of Friedrich Nietzsche, the only philosophical writer to whom she devoted herself with any intensity.

Nietzsche's *Thus Spoke Zarathustra*, the first book she bought in English, became something like her house Bible over the years. In her darker moments, she would keep returning to it to raise her spirits and assure herself of her own mission. Long before she began to keep an actual "philosophical journal," phrases like "Nietzsche and I think" and "as Nietzsche has said already" accompany her personal notes.[59] In fact, Rand had first encountered Nietzsche's writings during her youth in Saint Petersburg, where the German thinker's writings about the Übermensch were very popular among entrepreneurial and avant-garde circles, not least in the progressive Jewish milieu of the metropolis.

As with millions of other young people who found their way into philosophy through the champion of the Übermensch, not to mention Nietzsche's rebellious content and stylistic brilliance, the psychological element had been crucial for Rand. Nietzsche's writings give young people who are intellectually alert but largely isolated in that critical phase of their development an existential justification for being social outsiders: a kind of matrix of understanding for their own difference, which also has the seductive effect of allowing them to see their experience of exclusion as making them part of an actual elite.

The impulse has its dangers, because it also has a narcissistic aftertaste. Even twenty-nine-year-old Ayn, as her philosophical journal proves, was aware of that apparent tendency toward elitism.

> Some day I'll find out whether I'm an unusual specimen of humanity in that my instincts and reason are so inseparably one, with the reason ruling the instincts. Am I unusual or merely normal and healthy? Am I trying to impose my own peculiarities as a philosophical system? Am I unusually intelligent or merely unusually honest? I think this last. Unless—honesty is also a form of superior intelligence.[60]

Words of astonished self-interrogation, which could fundamentally also have come from the pens of Simone Weil, Hannah Arendt, or Simone de Beauvoir. All of them were tormented from an early age by the same questions: What could it be that makes me so different? What is it that I clearly can't understand and experience like all the others? Am I really driving down the freeway of life in the wrong direction—or is it not perhaps the mass of wildly honking people coming toward me flashing their lights? A doubt underlying every life lived philosophically.

SOCRATIC TENSION

The philosophizing person seems to be essentially a pariah of deviant insights, the prophet of a life lived rightly, whose traces can be found and deciphered even in the deepest falsity. At least this is one way to understand the role that Ayn Rand as well as her contemporaries Weil, Arendt, and Beauvoir assumed with ever greater confidence. Not that they had expressly made a choice. They simply experienced themselves as having been placed fundamentally differently in the world from how other people had been. And deep inside they remained certain of who or what the problem needing treatment was: not themselves, but the Others. Possibly, in fact—all the Others.

If one were to pursue that view, the actual impulse of astonishment at the beginning of all philosophizing is not the surprise that there is "something and not nothing," but rather, honest bafflement that other people live as they do. In other words, the decoupling of philosophical thought from its original impulse is not ontological or epistemological, but social. It affects not the relationship of the self with the mute world, but the self with speaking Others.

For the historical moment of 1934, when Roosevelt introduced his New Deal, we may imagine Ayn Rand being just as troubled by the behavior of her compatriots as Hannah Arendt was at the police station in Berlin, Simone Weil during discussions with her communist circles, or Simone de Beauvoir as a respectable member of the staff of the Lycée Jeanne d'Arc in Rouen.

Obviously, there was something fundamentally wrong with that world—and with the people in it. Perhaps there always had been. But what exactly could it be? And how, in the early 1930s, was it possible for an individual to heal that increasingly oppressive malaise?

III

EXPERIMENTS: 1934–1935

Rand is drawn to Broadway, Beauvoir to Olga, Weil to the factory, and Arendt to Palestine.

ACCUSED

They were all there. The director Frank Capra, Pola Negri, Gloria Swanson, and Marlene Dietrich—as well as all of L.A.'s Russian aristocrats in exile sitting in the front row, led by the former tsar's general Ivan Lebedeff. Obviously, he was not going to miss out on the opportunity to bolster the new prodigy on this most crucial of days. In Rand's honor, Lebedeff had arranged a party later that evening at the White Eagle Café, the regular haunt of the Russian diaspora.[1]

But first it was the turn of the jury. Would they acquit the heroine and prove that there was still a genuine sense of freedom in this country? A saving remnant of goodwill for people with their own center, their own ambition, romantic daring, and thrilling independence? Or, in the imminent verdict, would the conventional morality of the majority, the "far too many," emerge victorious, with their petty rules and anxieties, their empty formalism and learned respectability, their surreptitious dislike of anything truly grand and daring?

The tension in the hall was palpable. Only Ayn Rand, the actual main character of the plot, seemed strangely uninvolved, as if it had nothing to do with her. With considerable skill she had arranged the clues in such a way that it would be impossible for the jury to make their judgment based on the facts alone. What do facts say, in the end? Is the crucial question in life not primarily how one approaches the given facts?

For Rand, the human ability to make autonomous decisions fundamentally depended on something that she called the "sense of life," and that she took to mean a sense, more felt than argued, of what mattered to each individual: a sense of their own place in the world and hence also of their own goals and ideals. What was the deal with that sense of life? How was it distributed and stored in her new homeland "of the free"? And how could it be effectively encouraged? Those were her questions, that was her actual experiment.

As early as 1933, she dreamed up the drama as an almost perfect crime. The courtroom drama in three acts was having its world premiere that evening in late October 1934 at Los Angeles's Hollywood Playhouse under the title *Woman on Trial*. Her first American publication of any kind!

FACING JUSTICE

She had arrived in this city less than eight years before, without adequate knowledge of the language and with nothing but a suitcase in her hand. Now her own name shone out in big glowing letters onto the boulevards of Hollywood! Just as she had prophesied, even promised, to herself and her family back in Leningrad. Anyone else would doubtless have been bursting with pride to have achieved so much. Rand, though, who dreaded the impending premiere party even more than the performance itself, felt a curious mixture of honest fatigue and nausea. Still: the main actress, the former silent film star Barbara

Bedford, was convincing in the leading role of the accused secretary Karen Andre. And even if it was painfully obvious that the low-budget production left a lot to be desired in terms of props and execution, at least its director and producer had stuck strictly to Rand's script. Above all, the gimmick with the jury seemed to be very successful: before the play began, twelve volunteers were chosen from the audience, and then, as part of the performance, just before the end of the drama they would deliver their verdict onstage in the name of the people. Nothing like that had ever been done before. It was quite new, and it was Rand's idea.

The play *Woman on Trial* (original title: *Penthouse Legend*), which Rand had written in only a few weeks, was originally inspired by the real and much-discussed case of the Swedish match magnate and speculator, Ivar Kreuger. With extremely risky business and credit practices, this man had built up a global conglomerate of more than one hundred companies and accumulated what must have been fantastic wealth. Confronted in the spring of 1932 with bankruptcy and a likely conviction for financial fraud, Kreuger chose suicide and shot himself in a luxury hotel in Paris. Because of his outgoing, playboy lifestyle, his case was also closely followed by the tabloids.

In Rand's slightly fictionalized transposition, Kreuger became the unscrupulous businessman Björn Faulkner. The crucial question of the drama is whether, and if so for what reason, Faulkner's secretary of many years, his partner and, not least, passionately devoted lover Karen Andre, is responsible for his fatal fall from the balcony of his luxury penthouse. On the witness stand, the young widow of the deceased and his banker father, deeply implicated in Faulkner's business dealings, claim that Faulkner was killed in cold blood over an unhappy love affair. The accused, on the other hand, vehemently disputes the accusation, although she was without any doubt involved in Faulkner's fall at the scene of the crime, as witnesses confirm. During her impressively confident appearance before the court, she also denies any kind of disappointment or jealousy toward the man she deeply loved and admired, whose criminal business dealings, affairs, and sham marriage she had covered up for years.

A classic trial, then, with contradictory statements and inconclusive evidence. The drama was based on Rand's preferred plot recipe—the traditional love triangle, surface tension along the lines of "Who committed the murder?" On a deeper level, however, the issue to be assessed by each individual audience member was the fundamental conflict between "passionate self-assertiveness" and "conventionality," "independence versus conformity."[2] The jury had to decide which side they believed, and where their sympathies lay. In the absence of clear evidence, everything hung on the "sense of life" of the jury members. So they would be the ones who delivered the judgment, as in a real court case.

SELFISH

As to her own feelings, Rand would have had no hesitation. Inspired by the Nietzscheanism that she had internalized early in her life, she was particularly fascinated by uncompromising men of action, whether they were in real life criminal dodgy financiers or even murderous sex offenders. If the conventional morality of the envious masses is identified as the actual enemy, anyone who unrepentantly resists those norms immediately becomes an ally. The guiding principle behind this superhuman sense of life is simply: Anything but mediocrity! Anything but modesty!

The disappointment the next morning was correspondingly great. The play had a largely good reception, however, and the considerable talent of its author was stressed. But the critics were mostly delighted with the gimmick of the live jury. Not a word about what Rand considered to be the true subject of the play. Not a word about what she saw as the global struggle between "heroic individuals" and the "far too many."[3] What was gained by achieving the recognition of the broad masses if it happened for the wrong reasons? Only people without true self-worth could really be satisfied by success of that kind. And Rand was certainly not among them. In fact, the obvious inability to value works of art for the right reasons was, in her view, deeply embedded within the country—and with devastating consequences, not least for the creative self-confidence of artists themselves.

A few months previously, she had written in her philosophical journal on the basis of an intense reading of Ortega y Gasset's *Revolt of the Masses*:[4]

> The so-called "selfish" man of today uses "ideas" only as means to attain *his* own end. But what is that end? What is accomplished if the man attains power and prominence at the cost of playing down to the masses? It is not he that triumphs, it is not his ideas and standards. It is only his physical frame. Essentially, he is only a slave to those masses. This explains my meaning when I consider the "selfish," ambitious man of today as essentially *unselfish,* or rather *selfless.* The true selfishness is that which demands the right to *its own* higher ideas and values. The "supreme egoism" is that which claims things for their *essential,* not their secondary values.
>
> An example from my own experience, which, at the present time, affects me most, is the fact that few men have the ability or *the desire* to judge literary work by its *essential* worth. To most men, that work becomes valuable only after it has been recognized as such by someone else. They themselves do not have any standards of their own (and they do not feel the lack).[5]

Only someone who can call a solid, independent self his own can be a good egoist. The vulgar egoism of a sneaky mass manipulator, on the other hand, who is potentially willing to do anything and everything to attain success, prominence, or power, is in fact too hollow and unfocused within himself to be able to claim the title of a supreme egoist.

Furthermore, she argued, societies that unconditionally idealized such empty heroes had lost any supporting criterion for their own value, and hence manifestly placed their own existence under threat. This was particularly true in the case of a democratically accepted dictatorship having at its head an individual with a gift for manipulating the masses. That was Rand's nightmare for her land of the free.

SECOND HAND

But what actually lay behind the urge to voluntary self-abandonment in the name of the "far too many"? What mechanisms were psychologically and socially crucial here? An everyday conversation with her neighbor was an enlightening experience for Rand in this respect. The young woman, who, like Rand, worked in the film industry, and who was a highly successful executive assistant to David O. Selznick, had for some time struck Rand as particularly ambitious and career-oriented. One day Rand asked her very directly what she considered her actual goal in life. The woman, Marcella Bannett by name, didn't have to think for long: If nobody owned an automobile, she didn't want one either. If some people owned one automobile and others had none, she wanted one too. If some people owned two automobiles and others only one, she wanted two. She was also keen that people should know she had more than they did.[6]

Rand could barely grasp what she was hearing. This woman's personal intentions were clearly measured solely against the goals pursued by other people around her, and with the aim of surpassing and outdoing those people where possible. Everything she considered desirable depended on the wishes and hence the chosen goals of other people, so in fact it was secondary in nature.

But what if the people who inspired the desire of this secretary were also impelled by nothing but the desire that they perceived in other people? Rand found herself confronting the abysmal image of a supposedly free society whose ambition and individualism were inspired by nothing but derivative self-determination and a perverted urge for acceptance. She didn't want to, couldn't live like that. And she didn't think anyone else should have to, either.

STRAIGHT OUT OF THE MOVIES

Still, so-called success was there now. The film rights to the play were also soon sold, and in the shape of Samuel "Sam" Grosvenor Wood, she had one of the most successful directors of the day offering to produce her drama on Broadway. If he had permission to make personal interventions into the text. And if Rand agreed to work with him on the spot to bring the material onto the screen.

What was there to keep her in Hollywood? Certainly not the climate in California. And certainly not the obvious noncareer of her husband, Frank O'Connor. Barely a week after she signed, their old life in Hollywood was wound up, and the couple set off for the East Coast in an old pickup truck. On this trip Rand caught her first glimpse of another America: that of the impoverished towns, the indigent farmers, the deepest, blackest poverty, and, not least, a ramshackle infrastructure.

When Frank had to swerve to avoid an overtaking truck in Virginia, their car rolled over and came to rest in a roadside ditch. Uninjured but completely broke, they continued the trip on a Greyhound bus to New York, where things developed in the worst imaginable way after their arrival. The financing for the planned Broadway production of *Woman on Trial*, titled *Night of January 16th*, unexpectedly collapsed, and early in January 1935, Rand found herself in a state of helpless waiting. To save money, the couple moved in with Frank's brother Nick, who was also living hand-to-mouth in New York. The three of them now sat squashed in the kitchenette of a tiny apartment, waiting for better times. If Rand was honest, her circumstances differed marginally, if at all, from those of her family in Leningrad. To judge from their letters, her father, once so proud and still without a job or an income, walked the streets of the city for days to get hold of something like a lightbulb. If there was a kilo of apples in the house it was cause for celebration. Rand's mother and sisters, fluently multilingual and with an excellent education, had to be careful not to miss events thrown by the Communist Party, to avoid endangering their jobs as tour guides.

What kept the Rosenbaum family going more than anything was the fabulous success of their absent Alisa. So that their father could also enjoy her works, her mother had translated the text of *Night of January 16th* with her own hand. Her father, Zinovy, was not sparing in his praise and compared her work to Shakespeare's in terms of the beauty of its language. Her sister Nora added pictures of huge neon signs featuring Ayn's name to her letters. Her mother, Anna, expressed herself satisfied that even in Hollywood, defined though it was by superficiality, it was impossible to avoid reaching the conclusion that "white is white."[7] All of them had always known: Where freedom reigns, outstanding talent will out. Albeit indirectly. Very indirectly.

During this phase, the producer's weekly reassurances were joined by further rejections of the now completed manuscript of *Airtight*. In order not to collapse into complete passivity, Rand fired her agent. Without any income of her own—and in recession-hit New York, Frank, too, looked in vain for paid work—Rand had to be glad to be allowed to work at starvation wages as a script editor at her former studio, RKO. So all back to the beginning. Almost like a movie.

PROVINCIAL MANNERS

A particularly charged drama was also beginning in Rouen, northern France, in autumn 1934. It was played out again and again every weekend in the cafés, bars, and even brothels of the provincial city. The central parts were played by a scandalous twenty-six-year-old philosophy teacher at the local girls' boarding school and her long-term lover, just back from Berlin a few weeks previously, also a philosophy teacher and based during the week in the port town of Le Havre. The other part was played by a sensuous eighteen-year-old former pupil named Olga Kosakiewicz, with family roots in the Russian aristocracy, who had explored the city's nightlife with the Ukrainian and Polish refugees who were arriving in ever greater numbers.

Since both the resident teacher and her remarkably diminutive partner vied with various degrees of success and skill for the favors—not least, sexual favors—of the youngest member of the team, this was first and foremost a romantic triangle. On another level, however, tensions were building up within this configuration, which would affect life as consciously lived: freedom against necessity, present or future, subject versus object, authenticity or inauthenticity.

These tensions were all introduced explicitly into the development of the plot, especially by the two philosophers, originally from Paris.

That autumn, its opening can be described as follows: Standing on the threshold of adult life, Jean-Paul Sartre and Simone de Beauvoir had to admit that they were far behind their own hopes and expectations. Once the best in their year at the most prestigious university in the country, now they were just two out of several thousand philosophy teachers in the French provinces. Jean-Paul's disappointment, in particular, dragged him down into a permanent depression, which was all the more stubborn because his intoxicating scholarship year in Berlin had opened new horizons to him, in both intellectual and sensual terms.

His thoughts and statements around this time revolved around barely anything other than the foreseeable monotony of his existence: his life, firmly anchored with Simone's; their few true friendships, already made; his professional career clearly mapped out. "We were both still the right side of thirty, and yet nothing new would ever happen to us!"[8]

Sartre's hair was visibly starting to thin. As when he was a five-year-old—when his golden curls were cut off during a visit to the barber's and, looking in the mirror, he suddenly had to identify with a new and far from lovely appearance—the loss of his hair again became a trauma, doubly violent because it hinted at the last and insurmountable insult to his existence.

If Simone could summon the strength, she vehemently contradicted Sartre's diagnosis of decay, repeatedly praised his philosophical originality, and, convinced of his unique gift, counseled patience, persistence, and realism. In this she had no discernible success, not least because she, too, was reflecting more and more frequently, tears streaming down her cheeks, on the profound incompatibility between the happiness of the moment and the unavoidable nothingness of all striving. Particularly when she had once again had too much to drink.[9]

The everyday life they shared in the provinces had grown stale. And if they were honest with each other, the same was true of their diminishing sex life. Jean-Paul seldom showed any initiative, and for all their mutual openness he often left her on her own for long periods. Was it just that they were intellectually too close? Or was the unanimity of their thought, so frequently evoked in conversation as a sound basis for their relationship with the world, only one more illusion?

That winter of 1934–1935, the cracks that had appeared the previous year finally threatened to become an abyss. With several interrupted novel projects in her drawer, Beauvoir had put nothing down on paper for a year, while Sartre's production continued unabated, with an intensity and a speed that clearly had something compulsive about it: in the previous months alone he had written a manuscript several hundred pages long about the human psyche. He was also still, or once again, engaged in rewriting a fragment of a novel that at that point bore the working title *Melancholia*.[10]

The two projects were closely connected by Sartre's conviction that it was the pitfalls of mankind's own imagination that sent him into a permanent state of despair. Particularly when the ideas that individuals have about themselves are in open conflict with their actual existence. At the same time, the ways of fundamentally missing the outline of one's own identity are as rich and diverse as the power of the human imagination itself. To imagine this, the couple had only to look out of their café window and observe the good citizens of Rouen or Le Havre drifting by in more or less silent despair. Just a little more bad luck and in a few years' time they, too, would be among them.

Still, they all had goals that went considerably beyond the mere performance of everyday chores. But was that actually a good thing? Or wasn't it the actual problem?

THE OLGA PRINCIPLE

How different for Olga. It was only toward the end of her final class that she had come to Beauvoir's attention with a brilliant essay on Kant. This explosion of ideas, apparently from out of nowhere, was exemplary of the unpredictable willfulness of Olga's approach to the world, which oscillated in a barely intelligible way between unprejudiced clear-sightedness and profound disorientation. With a single glance she seemed to grasp the most complex connections, but above all the inner lives of other people, while remaining almost blind to her own goals and impulses.

Beauvoir explained this with reference to the particular tension that defined Olga's parental home and upbringing. Olga's French mother had gone to Russia as a nanny and fallen in love with an engineer from an aristocratic family. In the wake of the October Revolution, the young family had to flee to France, where, like so many others, they led a largely reclusive social existence, which was further intensified by the isolation of the provinces. One was not a part of it and did not strive to become so.

While aristocratic etiquette and an elite sense of self reigned within their own four walls, in their everyday lives they experienced deep downward mobility and exclusion. Homeschooling followed the free cultural ideal of people who would never have to work for money, while the actual impoverishment of the family meant the children were forced ambitiously into careers that would bring in an income. This was true of Olga, whose parents insisted that she was to study medicine, while in her first year after leaving school she found nothing within herself to connect her with that goal, nor anything that expressly contradicted it. "Olga . . . had been convinced since childhood that she did not belong to her society or environment, and she did not envisage future time in such a context; tomorrow scarcely existed for her, and next year not at all."[11]

As she was for so many pupils in her class, the unconventional philosophy teacher Beauvoir had become an admired model for Olga, while Beauvoir understood Olga's obvious forlornness and depth of thought as a pedagogical challenge. At first, they drank coffee together, went for walks, got to know each other, and soon spoke more openly to each other. With growing fascination Beauvoir observed that all the claims that others made on Olga, and all the expectations they had of her, bounced off her without any effect whatsoever, without producing anything like pressure, shame, or even penitence. While the twenty-six-year-old Beauvoir was still deliberately fighting to emancipate herself from the demands and expectations of her parental home, Olga, who had just turned eighteen, seemed to have achieved that goal almost by sleepwalking. Olga simply threw herself into life without a plan. She was no one other than who she was, nor did she give anyone to imagine that they could take her over. "I got along very well with Olga, yet we were totally different types. I lived for my future plans, while she denied the future altogether. All striving she regarded as merely contemptible; in her eyes prudence was synonymous with pettiness, and perseverance with self-deceit. She only valued her emotions; cerebral concerns left her cold. . . . For Olga, the present was all-sufficient, and words of definition, limitation, promise or anticipation—especially the last—seemed wholly irrelevant."[12]

If one wished to give it an intellectual charge—and Sartre and Beauvoir had been striving to achieve that discipline, the psycho-philosophical authority over their social life, for years—Olga was a prime example of the utopia of a philosophical immediacy of life, the principle of pure vitality surrendering to the moment.

SORCERERS

Sartre also noticed, after their first few meetings, how unusually stimulating it was to be with the "little Russian," how perfectly suited she was to act as a screen for all the attitudes and desires that offered him a way out of the mind-numbing tedium of his existence. Because by the spring of 1935, Sartre was not only very depressed, but also increasingly convinced that he was heading straight for insanity. Not least because of the legions of human-sized crustaceans and insects who followed him everywhere he went. His academic interest in the essence of the human imagination had led him to participate in the mescaline experiments of a Paris psychiatrist friend. Contrary to the doctor's assurances that the hallucinations resulting from the drug would last for no longer than thirty-six hours, in Sartre's case they returned even weeks and months after he had taken the drug, in clusters and with undiminished intensity. It was not just that he was plainly getting older and that he would one day die like everyone else. No, now madness was taking hold of his mind on top of everything else.

Again and again that spring, he made Beauvoir promise not to leave him alone on the clearly irrevocable journey into lunacy. Doctors spoke of overexertion and prescribed rest and writing breaks. Meanwhile Beauvoir, very familiar with Sartre's hypochondria over the years, came to another diagnosis. What Sartre needed to get him through this crisis was a new object of desire. Ideally one complex and independent enough to keep him permanently busy both physically and intellectually. Distraction as a survival strategy: "I much preferred the idea of Sartre angling for Olga's emotional favours to his slow collapse from some hallucinatory psychosis."[13]

That was how it came about that the one solid and necessary relationship, the dyadic pact of their life, would develop quite officially into a triad throughout the course of 1935, thanks to the wild card Olga. The young woman found stability and acceptance in this pair of thinkers and assumed the function of a thrust of vitality urgently needed particularly by Sartre. Or, to give a more flowery account of the same state of affairs: "Caught by the magic that sparked from our eyes as they met, each of us felt [ourselves] playing a double role—enchanter and enchanted at once."[14]

ROLE-PLAY

Since it was impossible with no plan at all, a system of head-to-head meetings and quorate gatherings was developed under Beauvoir's direction, which was to allow each of them to claim their rights. Especially at the start of the experiment, Beauvoir felt healingly liberated from the permanent destructive pressure that Sartre's existential crisis had placed on her over many months. In fact, her sense of herself and the world was entirely different during this phase.

While the teacher's life must have looked to Sartre, who had always been coddled and financially well taken care of by his family, like an unworthy cul-de-sac, in which he saw "his freedom trickling away," for Beauvoir, in spite of all its impositions, the profession meant a way into genuine self-determination—particularly at a time when women in France did not even have the right to vote. In the provinces Sartre felt like someone who was being remotely operated in a role that he had been thrown into, but Beauvoir proudly felt that she had chosen her fate there by herself and fought for it.[15] For Beauvoir, the welfare of her "most dear little being"[16] still provided a core of meaning for her own life, too, while Sartre's genius for relationships consisted of remaining entirely fixed upon himself and the development of his thoughts and writings. At least in that sense Beauvoir remained trapped in a classic relationship dynamic: he came first!

However, Sartre felt truly comfortable only when Beauvoir remained intellectually effervescent. The writer's block that she had suffered over the previous year seriously worried him too. Again and again, he asked about the progress of her literary experiments; sometimes concerned, then demanding, but also occasionally playful: "You used to be full of little ideas, Beaver."[17]

But here, at the supposed center of her existence, writing, another categorical difference appeared, one based less on intelligence, talent, or understanding and more on the actual goal of thought. Beauvoir describes it as follows:

> If a theory convinced me, it did not remain an external, alien phenomenon; it altered my relationship with the world, and coloured all my experience. In short, I possessed both considerable powers of assimilation and a well-developed critical sense; and philosophy was for me a living reality, which gave me never-failing satisfaction.
>
> Yet I did not regard myself as a philosopher; I was well aware that the ease with which I penetrated to the heart of a text stemmed, precisely, from my lack of originality. . . . It would be more useful to explain *how* certain individuals are capable of getting results from that conscious venture into lunacy known as a "philosophical system," from which they derive that obsessional attitude which endows their tentative patterns with universal insight. As I have remarked before, women are not by nature prone to obsessions of this type.[18]

Beauvoir recorded this memory, remarkable in every respect, in the late 1950s, and thus at a time when her work *The Second Sex* (1949), which would be fundamental for the future feminist movement, was already ten years old. The passage is a prime example of Beauvoir's lifelong conviction that the intellectual dispositions of men and women are generically different. And in a way that Beauvoir interprets along the axes "plasticity versus rigidity" and "relationship with reality versus delirium." This categorization, if one looks closely enough, does not argue in favor of the supposedly fundamental male system. Even a *planned* delirium in the end remains precisely what it is: a delirium—and hence a form of loss of reality.

Beauvoir's way of philosophizing, on the other hand, was that of a concrete relationship with life and the everyday, to go on to see the things that everybody thinks they know, by redescribing them, in a light that makes them appear more clearly, more vividly, and finally more freely. The starting point for this art of redescription lay primarily in her own experiences and events that are elaborated through narrative. Philosophy as semi-fiction on a biographical foundation.

After many attempts and several false starts, in 1935 Beauvoir tried again. This time not in the form of another novel, but different, loosely connected short stories inspired by the "multitude of crimes, both small and great, which hid behind a veil of spiritual hocus-pocus"[19] of religion.

In her deeply felt dislike of, indeed revulsion for, the bourgeois Catholic milieu of the French upper middle class that she came from, Beauvoir's stories had the following goal: to present religious ideals—and, bound up with these, religiously based everyday norms—as the chief culprits for a self-abnegation that forced young women in particular into a persistent inauthenticity, lack of freedom, and not least sexual frustration. "I would limit myself to the things, the people that I knew; I would try to convey a truth that I had experienced myself. It would define the unity of the book whose subject I had borrowed ironically from Jacques Maritain: *Primauté du spirituel* (The Ascendancy of the Spirit)."[20]

FLOWERS OF SPIRITUALITY

It is easy to guess in which respects Olga—as will and idea—must have formed a particularly inspiring object of study within this highly dynamic situation (not least from a philosophical point of view). Because on the one hand Olga, being gloriously free of plans, seemed to embody the desired directness and hence vitality of an entirely undistorted approach toward the world in its pure form. Especially in the eyes of Sartre, who, with and through Olga, experienced "the intoxicating spell of naked, instant consciousness, which seemed only to feel, with violence and purity. I placed her [Olga] so high then that, for the first time in my life, I felt myself humble and disarmed before someone, felt that I wanted to learn."[21]

Beauvoir, too, was inclined to transfigure Olga, "with [her] rebellious upheavals and intransigent emphasis on freedom," into a "myth"[22]—the myth of the pure, entirely undistorted, and blossoming consciousness of the now. At the same time, she was soon seriously concerned about Olga's extremely strong influence on Sartre's world: "His determination to conquer Olga meant that he set great store by her. Suddenly I found it impossible to take his opinions or tastes or dislikes casually."[23]

Beauvoir's growing detachment may have had something to do with her heightened sense, both literary and philosophical, of the ease with which, particularly for young women, this wonderful, direct openness was nothing other than the deepest confusion of the self, and the constant despair close to instability: a lost state so deep and complete that at the surface level it was practically indistinguishable from direct authenticity. She soon came to see Olga as a chameleonlike figure, giving each of them in turn a different aspect of her shimmering nature, according to which pole of the triad she happened to be playing with (or felt she had to play with). Sartre was still not stable enough for resolute resistance, however: "Both in deed and word I zealously fostered the well-being of the trio; but I did not feel at all happy, either in myself or about the other two, and I looked forward to the future with apprehension."[24]

Things were at least progressing in literary terms. In the spring of 1935, Beauvoir finished a short story titled "Lisa." It concerns a pupil with philosophical interests in a girls' boarding school. Slight and gaunt, she has been made "barren"[25] by the education she receives there—rather than having her vital spirits awakened.

A small lie grants Lisa permission to travel to the Bibliothèque Nationale in Paris, with a view to bumping into her crush, the brother of her best and only friend, even though he shows no interest in her whatsoever. Instead an older woman at a bus stop accuses her of being her husband's mistress, which has the effect of opening up her image of herself: "Most of the time she loathed her sharp-featured face and her thin, frail body—an absolute grasshopper—but now all at once it seemed to her that her flesh had become soft to the touch, yielding and rich. Could I really be taken for a middle-aged man's mistress?"[26] On a subsequent visit to the dentist, the surgeon in question makes vague erotic suggestions until Lisa's day ends with the vision of an archangel and her library crush merging into a single person, and she pleasures herself in her single room at the boarding school of Saint Agnes.

Flowers of spirituality. Flowers of evil. Let the rest of the world be in free fall. Beauvoir felt an ever more powerful need to follow a trail that led to the goal.

RIGHT AT THE BOTTOM

Whether it was the depressions that led to the weeklong migraines, or whether the headaches led inevitably to a renewed depression—over the course of the year it had become hard to tell the difference. Her medication had ceased a long time before to alleviate the pain. She was barely able to complete the school year. In the summer of 1934, Simone Weil took a year's sabbatical from teaching to put her "philosophical testament" on paper, as she put it. She was twenty-five years old.

She had few doubts at this point that another world war was inevitable, and that nations like France, Spain, and the United States were bound to be drawn into the maelstrom of totalitarian social logic:

> It seems fairly clear that contemporary humanity tends pretty well everywhere toward a totalitarian form of social organization—to use the term . . . the national-socialists have made fashionable—that is to say, toward a system in which the State power comes to exercise sovereign sway in all spheres, even, indeed above all, in that of thought. Russia presents us with an almost perfect example of such a system, for the greater misfortune of the Russian people . . . but it seems inevitable that all of them will approach it more or less in the course of the coming years.[27]

Between September and November 1934, the text, originally conceived as an article, swelled to book length. Under the title "Reflections Concerning the Causes of Freedom and Social Oppression," with its echoes of Jean-Jacques Rousseau, it strives to establish a truly free society of self-determined individuals. The text should be read as a "testament" insofar as it explicitly addresses a generation *after* the disaster. The degradation of her own times seemed so deep to Weil that preventing the coming conflagration was out of the question.

If nothing could be saved in a political sense, there was still the option of integrating insights that she had achieved into life and testing and refining them in concrete practice. Consequently, in December 1934—shortly after the completion of her "testament"—Weil fulfilled a dream she had nurtured since her student days and took an unskilled job in a Paris metal factory run by the Alsthom company.

She wanted to experience firsthand the oppression that she sought to remedy as a thinker. Out from the ivory tower of theory, into the everyday suffering of the workers! Neither Marx nor Engels, Trotsky nor Stalin had ever really experienced a factory from inside. And that, Weil said, was also clearly apparent in their analyses and measures.

In the sealed echo chambers of both camps, the bourgeois and the proletarian, ignorance of other ways of life arose from a lack of concrete experience. This in turn generated truly monstrous worlds based on false assumptions and suspected conspiracies. According to the fantasies of the proletariat, it was the demonic powers of "finance," "industry," the "stock markets," or "banks" (and of course, in France as elsewhere, "the Jews") that ruled in the realm of the bourgeois entrepreneur. And the propertied class in turn assumed that the proletarian activists were nothing but "provocateurs," "paid troublemakers," or simply "looters."[28]

ON THE CONVEYOR BELT

In the winter of 1934, Weil risked a definitive reality check, and in her factory diary she even speaks of her desire finally to make "direct contact with life."[29] Upon further reflection, it may not have been easy to explain why the everyday life of a person stamping out metal shapes with a single motion of the hand ten hours a day, for what was barely a living wage, was in some way more "real" than that of a philosophy teacher in the French provinces or an exiled Russian working in the film business in United States.

Weil's desire for the factory stands in a respectable tradition of philosophical experiments whose declared objective was to turn one's back on a presumably alienated world and attain greater intellectual clarity by stepping into a way of life or environment that was supposedly closer to reality. Like the Buddha fleeing the palace, or Diogenes in his barrel, or of course Thoreau building his hut on Walden Pond.

Weil left her parents' apartment near the Jardin du Luxembourg for a rented room near the suburban factory, but admittedly Mime and Biri's safe haven was not far away and was always accessible, even for having dinner *en famille*. An offer that Simone accepted only on condition that she left the exact value of an equivalent visit to a restaurant on the dinner table for her mother, a charade that Weil's mother countered in her own way. During her not infrequent visits to Simone's chronically untidy worker's accommodation, she hid small amounts of money in clothes and drawers to give her daughter the feeling of having made a chance discovery.[30]

The project also had a clear time limit (she would work for not even twenty-four weeks), and, in fact, her acceptance into the factory had been made possible through the intervention of Weil's old trade union comrade. He was personally acquainted with the relevant decision makers in the Alsthom factory, and informed them in advance of Weil's investigative project, as well as of her total incapacity to assume anything like a productive role in the labor process. He also made them promise to keep a protective eye on the noble apprentice with two left hands throughout her predictably short stay.

On Monday, December 17, 1934—only two weeks after she began her employment—when Weil arrived for dinner at her parents' house on rue Auguste Comte in her oil-smeared overalls, her condition was already a cause for concern. Simone spoke even less than she ate: always a big warning sign. She barely had the strength to sit upright on her chair. This was something she really hadn't reckoned with: the deep fatigue that penetrated all her limbs and didn't even leave her with enough energy to record her daily experiences carefully in her factory diary and reflect upon them, as she had planned. The entry for December 17—she probably wrote it in the Métro—reads as follows:

> Afternoon—*stamping press*: pieces very difficult to position, at .56 per hundred (600 from 2:30 to 5:15); 1/2 hr. to reset the machine, which was out of adjustment because I had left a piece in the tool. Tired and fed up. Feeling of having been a free being for 24 hours (on Sunday), and of having to readapt to slavery. Disgust at being forced to strain and exhaust myself, with the certainty of being bawled out either for being slow or for botching, for the sake of these 56 centimes . . . Augmented by the fact that I am having dinner with my parents—Feeling of slavery.
>
> The speed is dizzying. (Especially when in order to throw yourself into it you have to overcome fatigue, headaches, and the feeling of being fed up.)[31]

An entirely typical day in the life of the factory worker Simone Weil. Not once during those six months would she manage to achieve the prescribed minimum quantity. Instead, with miserable regularity, she produced rejects: machines refused to obey her will; bits dropped to the ground or came out wrong; she confused essential pieces, forgot about them, put them in the wrong way, or, very often, simply left them in the machine once they were finished.

Again and again, the monotony of the assignment led her into an accident-prone absentmindedness, which because of her constant fatigue was in the end free of ideas: a kind of inner death, which extended after a few days to her entire existence. Fear of failure crept into her uneasy dreams, crying fits were her only relief. Even those did not alleviate the murderous headaches underlying everything.

KNOWLEDGE AND INTEREST

It should have come as no surprise or special insight that Weil was not made for this kind of life. But what human being was, or would be? Were there sentient beings who could maintain their self-respect and dignity under such conditions?

These were the questions addressed by her now complete philosophical "testament." They had been among the leading questions in the analyses of Karl Marx. Except that he, as Weil says in her *Reflections*, provided essentially mythical answers, with fatal consequences for the proletarians of all countries, who were to be liberated in the course of a revolution.

For all its clear-sightedness and aspiration to scientific status, Marxist analysis was burdened with a pseudo-religious philosophy of history. The central mistake lay in Marx's own assumption, neither explained nor examined, that all progress in humanity's productive forces allowed people to advance along the path to liberation. Accordingly, the process toward a communist society of true individual freedom is reconstructed by Marx as the history of the technologically and mechanically achieved increase in productive forces. If the arc of suffering of the proletariat was long and harsh, it bent in the end inexorably toward their liberation. Thanks to the "increase of productive forces" the history of humanity was fired by an intrinsic goal that could not be missed.

It's worth quoting Simone Weil's critique of this dogma at length. Not least since this passage on the Marxist fetish for the growth in productive forces reveals the common but hidden roots of both a capitalist and a communist conception of history. Both ideologies, in Weil's view, under the auspices of the myth of infinite growth, dreamed up the end of history. Both dreamed of a global systematic victory on an ultimately economic basis. Of a liberation of humanity not only from the yoke of work but also from the yoke of a reality that contradicted our desires. In other words, under the cloak of science both finally revealed themselves as caught up in glaringly unscientific, plainly nonsensical fundamental assumptions.

> Marxists . . . believe that all progress in productive forces causes humanity to advance along the road leading to emancipation, even if it is at the cost of a temporary oppression. It is not surprising that, backed up by such moral certainty as this, they have astonished the world by their strength.
>
> It is seldom, however, that comforting beliefs are at the same time rational. Before even examining the Marxist conception of productive forces, one is struck by the mythological character it presents in all socialist literature. . . . Marx never explains why productive forces should tend to increase. . . . The rise of big industry

> made of productive forces the divinity of a kind of religion.... This religion of productive forces, in whose name generations of industrial employers have ground down the labouring masses without the slightest qualm, also constitutes a factor making for oppression within the socialist movement. All religions make man into a mere instrument of Providence, and socialism, too, puts men at the service of historical progress, that is to say of productive progress. That is why, whatever may be the insult inflicted on Marx's memory by the cult which the Russian oppressors of our time entertain for him, it is not altogether undeserved.[32]

LIMITS OF GROWTH

Weil's critique of the myths of Marxism leads directly to a critique of modern belief in growth. This in turn necessarily goes hand in hand with the dogma of increase in productive forces as a universal panacea. The constant promise of healing, by both capitalists and socialists, is based on the assumption that the incredible increase in productive forces over the past three hundred years could continue in the same way and with the same intensity in the future—indeed, that it could be accelerated.[33] If we take it seriously, this expectation leads directly to the question of the energy needed and the sources of energy in a finite world.

Because even if it were difficult to predict the energy sources that would one day be available, it remains the case that "nature does not give us this energy, whatever may be the form in which it offers itself—animal power, coal or petroleum; we have to wrest it from her and transform it through our labour so as to adapt it to our own ends."[34] Consequently, Weil refines her observations from 1934 into the paradox of an infinite belief in growth in a world of finite resources. Their imagined vanishing point was like a perpetual motion machine, something that does not and cannot exist.

The development toward the final communist idyll according to Marx, in which the human being of the future is as self-determining as possible, able "to do one thing today and another tomorrow, fish in the afternoon, rear cattle in the evening and criticize after dinner without ever becoming a hunter, fisherman, shepherd or critic"[35] is an utter fantasy. Far more plausible is a situation in which exploiting and using natural energy sources, because of increased scarcity and geological inaccessibility, "involves more labour than the human expenditure of energy one is seeking to replace."[36] From this perspective the yoke of the workers would be more inclined to become heavier in the future.

For Weil, then, there can be only one relevant question in the name of a (proletarian) revolution worthy of the name:

> It is a question of knowing whether it is possible to conceive of an organization of production which, though powerless to remove the necessities imposed by nature and the social constraint arising therefrom, would enable these at any rate to be exercised without grinding down souls and bodies under oppression.[37]

But this question cannot be explored and answered from the comfort of an armchair. It needs experience of the production process itself. It must be understood and grasped from within. Although Weil's factory adventure might have been motivated by the ethical impulse of active solidarity with the workers, her primary interest was theoretical. She had wanted to find illustrative material for the solution of a single problem, which struck her as relevant to the objective of the progressive emancipation of working people.

WORLD TURNED UPSIDE DOWN

Under the imperative of a constant increase in production, the labor process was subject to a logic of machine-centered and hence thought-free "rationalization." One was not supposed to think for oneself, but to serve thoughtlessly. Not to question, but to obey proactively. Not to create, but to labor monotonously. And not for oneself—which given the barely subsistence-level minimal wages would have been senseless in any case—but for the good of the great collective (people, nation, class, etc.) that felt permanently threatened by external enemies in the competitive struggle for survival. From the perspective of this collective, which numbered in the millions, individual human beings were so infinitely small and insignificant that they lost any sense of the potential infinity of their own thought—as well as any feeling for the concrete consequences and meaning of their actions. For this reason, far from being the expression of a true striving for emancipation, Weil saw the rhetoric of the collective and of collectivization as the clearest expression of an ideologically embellished oppressive endeavor:

> Never has the individual been so completely delivered up to a blind collectivity, and never have men been less capable, not only of subordinating their actions to their thoughts, but even of thinking. . . . We are living in a world in which nothing is made to man's measure.[38]

Weil's sketch of the social life of her present culminates in diagnosing the decay of a world that has its priorities completely upside down. The world must therefore spin faster and more destructively around its own now purposeless hunger for power: "The scientist does not use science in order to manage to see more clearly into his own thinking, but aims at discovering results that will go to swell the present volume of scientific knowledge. Machines do not run in order to enable men to live, but we resign ourselves to feeding men in order that they may serve the machines. Money does not provide a convenient method for exchanging products; it is the sale of goods that is a means for keeping money in circulation. Lastly, organization is not a means for exercising a collective activity, but the activity of a group, whatever it may be, is a means for strengthening organization. . . . The dispossession of the individual in favour of the collectivity is not, indeed, absolute, and it cannot become so; but it is hard to imagine how it could go much farther than at present."[39]

MODERN TIMES

In order to truly liberate humanity from this planetary nightmare, a comprehensive cultural U-turn would be necessary. When it came to the forces of production, ideas would be needed to rethink the rationalization of labor not as a collectivization, but as a process of individualization. In Weil's view, that would inevitably have to happen in conjunction with smaller companies as well as a "progressive decentralization" of planning and the control of the entire production process. A human scale could be regained by locally based companies organized as cooperatives, whose size would not necessarily overtax an individual's judgment.[40] The ideal worker in such an enterprise would be a person who kept a complete overview of all the relevant procedures in the company and felt that a "community of interests would be sufficiently patent to abolish competitive attitudes; and as each individual would be in a position to exercise control over the collective life as a whole, the latter would always be in accordance with the general will."[41]

Weil was only too well aware that in describing this goal of a global network of medium-sized cooperatives of intellectually, technically, and empathetically gifted experts, she was presenting an ideal far from anything that could actually come into being; nonetheless, "perfect liberty is what we must try to represent clearly to ourselves, not in the hope of attaining it, but in the hope of attaining a less imperfect liberty than is our present condition."[42]

The experiences of her time in the factory confirmed this conviction. There, the suppression of thought and the monotony of the activity required were joined by a hierarchical regime based on constraint and control. Everything that is supportive of life is impossible there: attention, a sense of measure, autonomous thought, open dedication. Modern times are a nightmare that has become reality.

EXTINCTION

With each new day in the factory, Weil felt "humiliated to the core of her being." At Alsthom, she writes in the closing words of her factory diary, "I almost only rebelled on Sundays." And there was something very important that she gained in this experiment, which was the firsthand experience of absolute oppression, the feeling of comprehensive disenfranchisement and outsiderdom. She experienced the horror of being so dependent on external circumstances as a thinking being that it would be enough for "circumstances to force me to work at a job without a weekly rest—which after all is always possible—and I would become a beast of burden, docile and resigned (at least for me)."[43]

What Weil actually came into direct contact with for the first time during her "factory year" was thus less "reality" as such than a concrete possibility in her life and in every life: the experience of a lasting extinguishability as a thinking being while still alive, accompanied by the feeling that "I do not possess any right whatever, of any kind."[44]

The crucial thing, however, was the recognition she sensed firsthand. Not only was she able to bear that total disenfranchisement, but she saw it as a kind of paradoxical thrust of liberation. She felt it like a passageway into another sense of self. Like a step into a realm that essentially exceeds and transcends pure human will and determination.

When Weil says that the "dispossession of the individual" cannot be total, it is because of the factory experiences of 1934–1935. That experience of something beyond the purely social, whose healing effects reveal themselves only when one's own value has been reduced to zero, had shown itself to be liberating. In her own words: "The feeling of self-respect, such as it had been built up by society, is *destroyed*. It's necessary to forge another one for oneself (though exhaustion wipes out consciousness of one's ability to think). Try to hold on to that one."[45]

It was precisely the experience of that "other" emotion, a sense of self-worth behind all the acknowledged self-worth, that was deeply transforming for Weil, and thereafter would become part of her journey as a thinker.

In a critical state of physical exhaustion, she ended her "factory year" in the summer of 1935, a broken woman. But she had never felt more free, more certain of herself and her mission.

BEFORE THE LAW

Largely without being personally involved, in 1934–1935 Hannah Arendt also experienced a life beyond the prevailing ideas of law and human dignity: like most of her fellow refugees, the majority of them German Jews, she soon found herself threatened in her Paris exile by a situation that national legislations had not anticipated. Because of the racial laws passed in Hitler's Germany in 1933, and constantly tightened thereafter, as well as the Law on the Revocation of Naturalizations and the Deprivation of German Citizenship of July 1933, Jews fleeing the country and critics of the regime could be summarily stripped of their German citizenship. This was increasingly happening. Arendt and her family were thus threatened with becoming *stateless* refugees in France, and hence people who were legally impossible to place. Even the temporary solution of a *carte d'identité* provided by the French—as the last state-recognized identification paper—was increasingly difficult to obtain given the rise in refugee numbers. This was even more serious because these documents soon became officially necessary for work (although the identity card itself required possession of an existing work contract).

Most of the German, and particularly German Jewish, refugees lived as a miserable advance party of a predicted stream of millions more, in a constantly accelerating swirl of acquiescence, whose drift and dynamic could change by the week. It often left those affected unclear, in an almost tragicomic way, about whether they still had a nationality and if so what it was; whether they were in France legally or illegally, and if so how; or whether they were married or no longer married, and if so to whom.

In those first years after Hitler's assumption of power, countless thousands of German-speaking refugees wandered the streets of the City of Light in search of documents, work, and lodgings. It would have been observed in Arendt's circles at the time, not without some dark amusement, that it was that year, of all the years, that the works of Franz Kafka appeared in the bookshops.

The cafés of the city, between Montparnasse and the Latin Quarter, became a kind of living room for the German intellectual diaspora—not with an existentialist lifestyle, however, but with an existential threat. That happened with all the beauties and tensions imaginable, when formerly affluent and highly regarded authors and thinkers—who hadn't necessarily been wild about one another even in the cafés of Berlin—crossed paths daily in a new context of downward social mobility and speechlessness. For these people the language barrier was the truly limiting one, and affected their acceptance into French intellectual circles. Even those who, like Walter Benjamin, spoke fluent French remained at best outsiders in the Paris milieu, invited along to occasional soirées and receptions more out of pity than genuine interest. If it had been possible to convert German doctorates directly into francs, what parties they could have had! But as things were, what was missing was money for the most basic necessities.

Even in French exile, of course, not all differences in status were abolished. Figures of the rank and solvency of Thomas Mann or Lion Feuchtwanger, who had been stripped of citizenship as early as August 1933, moved into villas on the Côte d'Azur. The town of Sanary-sur-Mer, in particular, would establish itself henceforth as a center of the exiled German literary aristocracy. In the summer of 1933, the Manns, along with their housekeepers, moved into the six-bedroom Villa La Tranquille. From there, Thomas Mann visited his neighbor Lion Feuchtwanger every day for "mourning tea"[46]—eyed critically by Aldous Huxley, also a resident, who described the somewhat snooty newcomers as a "rather dismal crew, already showing the fatal effects of exile."[47] Even in French exile, then, people saw themselves only as equal before the law. They were nobodies in no-man's-land.

PLACES OF ORIGIN

Lucky were those who were able to connect with already established networks and contacts right at the beginning. Newly arrived in Paris and still firmly determined "never again to touch any intellectual history,"[48] as the then twenty-six-year-old Hannah Arendt said, resolutely shaking off her life as a scholar and throwing herself into the practical work, which in this situation could only be "Jewish work."[49]

She landed her first job, still without a *carte d'identité*,[50] as secretary to a Zionist organization, Agriculture et Artisanat. Under the direction of Senator Justin Godart, it "offered young émigrés training in farming and crafts to prepare them for a future in Palestine."[51]

The arrival of the Jewish refugees from Germany and Eastern Europe caused considerable tensions, not least within the long-established Jewish community in Paris. Apart from the fear of political infiltration by the often distinctly left-wing new arrivals, there was also concern that German-speaking Jews might further encourage and intensify anti-Semitism in France, since they were the perfect enemy for the French fascists who were also bolstered by Hitler's and Mussolini's successes. Walter Benjamin sums up the mood: "The Parisians are saying: '*Les émigrés sont pires que les boches*' [The émigrés are worse than the Krauts]."[52]

That was not to say that a noble consensus existed among the new arrivals, since the German emigrants—most of them part of a former cultural elite—often viewed the usually rather rural and less liberal Jews from Eastern Europe as contemptuously as the French Jews viewed the German Jews. And not only that. As Arendt would remember, "French Jewry was absolutely convinced that all Jews coming from beyond the Rhine were what they called *Polaks*—what German Jewry called *Ostjuden*. But those Jews who really came from Eastern Europe could not agree with their French brethren and called us *Jaeckes*."[53] Quite ordinary people, then. Each with their own locally rooted identities, properties, preferences, and, not least, prejudices.

For these refugees, far more urgent than the question of where one actually came from was that of where they could go. Precisely this had been the foundational question of the Zionist movement. Even at the First Zionist Congress in 1897, where some two hundred delegates from around the world took part, a guiding charter had been drawn up under the auspices of the Vienna journalist Theodor Herzl:

> Zionism seeks to establish a home for the Jewish people in Palestine secured under public law. The Congress contemplates the following means to the attainment of this end:
>
> 1. By fostering the settlement of Palestine with farmers, laborers, and artisans.
>
> 2. By organizing the whole of Jewry in suitable local and general bodies, in accordance with the laws of their respective countries.
>
> 3. By strengthening the national Jewish feeling and national consciousness.
>
> 4. By taking preparatory steps to attain any Governmental consent which may be necessary to reach the aim of Zionism.[54]

If one had, like Arendt, said yes to oneself as a Jew in the early 1930s, and if one had, like Arendt, acknowledged the strategy of assimilation as a fake solution to the "Jewish question" and hence also to the problem of anti-Semitism, Zionism would inevitably have seemed like the only possible path to take, precisely against the background of recent developments. During this period, what made the émigré German Jews stare more deeply and more cruelly than all the others—such as Russian or Ukrainian refugees—into the abyss of statelessness was ultimately the fact that their sole "crime" against the laws of the country in which they were born and where they had grown up consisted in "being" Jews, without the possibility of adopting a different citizenship. The problem was thus, or this is how Arendt saw it, primarily a political one. And one for which there could be only a practical solution.

CONTRADICTIONS

The credo that Arendt had come to at this time was: "If one is attacked as a Jew, one must defend oneself as a Jew. Not as a German, not as a world-citizen, not as an upholder of the Rights of Man."[55] This assertion becomes more controversial with the second sentence: "Not as German, not as a world-citizen, not as an upholder of the Rights of Man." In the end, the defining experience of the early years in Paris was one of falling through all the nets that might have preserved her human rights.

It was not until more than a decade later that she would express with complete clarity what she had viscerally intuited in Paris in the early 1930s: that the concept and conception of human rights since the French Revolution contained a crucial mistake of birth. It became apparent in the fact that

> the moment human beings lacked their own government and had to fall back upon their minimum rights, no authority was left to protect them and no institution was willing to guarantee them.[56]

This essentially contradictory character of an unconditional right to protection, imagined and conceived for precisely the cases in which it could *not* be imposed, was nowhere more striking than in France. After all, it was there, as a consequence of the French Revolution of 1789 (and also shortly before this, the American Revolution), that a first binding declaration of universal human rights had come about—rights that applied to all human beings, regardless of origins or status.[57]

The human being as such was its source and its actual goal.[58] For Arendt the long-hidden paradox of this lies in the fact that

> this right reckoned with a "human being as such" that exists nowhere, because even savages live in some form of human community, and this right seemed to formally contradict nature itself, because we know "human beings" only in the form of "males" and "females," while the concept of "human being," if it was to be politically useful, always had to include human plurality. That plurality could only be recognised, in the conditions of the 18th century, by identifying "the human being as such" with the member of a people. . . . Given that the French Revolution conceived humanity as a family of nations, the concept of "the human being" underlying human rights was oriented towards the people and not the individual.[59]

In Arendt's view, the first contradiction in these natural "innate rights" lies in the fact that the idea of the "human being as such" (singular) conflicts with the notion of the human being as essentially part of a community of human beings (plural!), and hence locally and historically rooted. The contradiction could in turn be broken down only if an individual *unconditionally* protected by those rights was tacitly imagined as a member of a people—and hence during the nineteenth century as part of a "nation" making sovereign decisions over its own laws. The extent to which that solution must necessarily contradict the spirit of human rights itself appears in the early 1930s above all with the French mass phenomenon of the "stateless person."

QUESTION IN HUMAN FORM

Even by 1934–1935, it cannot have escaped Arendt that the figure of a Jewish woman expelled from Germany embodied all the implicit contradictions affecting the concept of human rights: namely, as the essential part of a *people* that had not had its own *national state* for thousands of years, but that because of its membership in that people was particularly in need of protection as a persecuted *individual.*

In this context Arendt's own biographical case represented a further complication, since she was a Jewish woman who explicitly said yes to Jewishness, because of her de facto exclusion from the community with which, culturally, she sought primarily to identify: "the tradition of German-language writing and thought." As early as 1930, Arendt had explained to her doctoral supervisor Karl Jaspers, describing her Varnhagen project, that it seemed to her as if "certain people are so exposed in their own lives that they become junction points and concrete objectifications of life."[60] She herself had now become one of those "concrete objectifications"—the question in human form of the actual basis of human rights.

The consternation was commensurate. It would preoccupy Arendt throughout her life, principally in the role of a persistent questioner "who doesn't know what human rights actually are," and who also knows that "no one else seems to know."[61]

True to the instruction that Socrates once received from the Delphic

Oracle—Know thyself!—Arendt's way of thinking can be interpreted as recognizing herself, standing in for everyone else, as someone whose mere existence as a refugee exploded and fundamentally called into question the political theory of her time and her cultural sphere. How was the most fundamental of all rights—the right to have rights at all—even imaginable within a conceptual framework that renounced the abstraction of "the human being as such"? And indeed in one who resisted the temptation to view the individual as inevitably part of a collective—a people, a nation, a class? How could the very existence of this question have eluded the entire philosophical tradition?

VIRGIN TERRITORY

During her Paris years, Arendt absorbed like a sponge the original contradictions of classic concepts that were now coming to light. That applies not least to her practical experiences in the Zionist movement and in the aid work she was involved with. In 1934, she switched to a welfare organization for Jewish children's homes maintained and financed by Baroness Germaine de Rothschild. Classic humanitarian patronage, then, carried out by an influential member of the most powerful religious association of Parisian Jews, the Consistoire de Paris. Arendt's chief task as personal assistant to the baroness consisted of coordinating and monitoring the streams of donations to the various homes and relief organizations.[62]

This was without a doubt very valuable and useful work on behalf of the "Jewish cause," but given that the charity it provided was privately funded, it can hardly have had Arendt's deep approval. Putting the cause and protection of the Jews in the hands of powerful patrons, however thoughtful and benevolent, was to her mind a hopeless and possibly even a counterproductive strategy. In the end it was part of the nature of political questions that they did not have private solutions.

Arendt didn't feel that she was quite in the right place until she started working for the office of the Zionist Youth Aliyah, which took her on early in 1935. The name of the organization, founded by Recha Freier, a German poet and the wife of a rabbi, was already its actual program: Aliyah in Hebrew literally means "rise," and according to the Bible also means the return of the Jews from Babylonian exile to Eretz Israel. It was a matter of providing young Jewish émigrés who were embarking on a settler's life in Palestine with the necessary knowledge, as well as logistical help, for their move to the Promised Land. In 1935, as general secretary of this aid organization established two years previously, Arendt had the opportunity to travel to Palestine, still a British protectorate, and get a picture for herself of developments in the Zionist project.

EXCLUSIONS

Since 1933, about ten thousand immigrants had arrived in Israel from Germany alone—a considerable challenge for the Jewish community, which was still under construction. And the flow of arrivals showed no signs of drying up. In this situation, the Berlin religious scholar and Judaist Gershom Scholem, who had already immigrated to Jerusalem in 1923, became the chronicler of the German Jewish intellectual elite escaping to the Promised Land.

Like migrating birds whose networks stretch across the whole of the world, these small circles remained closely connected across the continents through kinship and rumor, but above all through old customs. In a letter to Walter Benjamin of August 25, 1935, Scholem told his best friend from his Berlin days, now in Paris: “Some weeks back, I saw your cousin’s wife, Hannah Stern, who is now in Paris, preparing children for life in Palestine, but I did not get the impression that she could have been in close contact with you or else she presumably would have conveyed greetings from you, and so I refrained from inquiring about you. She was at one time a prize student of Heidegger’s.”[63]

In fact, Günther Stern (alias Günther Anders) was the son of an uncle of Benjamin’s, William Stern, who had studied as a developmental psychologist in Hamburg. As Arendt had already formed a close friendship with Benjamin in Paris in 1934, the real reason for her silence to Scholem may have had something to do with the rocky state of her marriage to Günther. And perhaps also with the predictably divergent estimations and feelings about the progress of the Zionist settlement projects, which Arendt had now seen with her own eyes in the form of the working villages and, above all, the kibbutzim.

The kibbutzim, in particular, represented a social experiment in which, with an eye on the true reasons for the suppression and unfreedom of the Jewish people of the world, the analyses of Simone Weil and Hannah Arendt seemed to flow into one another: these were middle-sized, largely egalitarian agricultural cooperatives in which, ideally, every worker could take on any task that might arise. According to Weil, on a small scale these communities therefore exercised those forms of organization and cooperation, which at least promised a global-local, socialist way of working without oppression. As part of the project of establishing a Zionist state, however, the constantly expanding network of these kibbutzim was essential to the policy of settlement and appropriation by the Jewish minority over the still-overwhelming Arab majority of Palestine.

It is probably in these terms that we should understand Arendt’s impressions of that first visit, recorded later, when she wrote: “I still remember my first reaction to the kibbutzim very well. I thought: a new aristocracy. I knew even then . . . that one could not live there. 'Rule by your neighbours,' that is of course what it finally amounts to. Still if one honestly believes in equality, Israel is very impressive."[64]

What forms of collectivization resist leveling and the imposition of conformity? And which, if any, could be turned into reality without the construction of a group of Others threatening the survival of one's own community?

It was with these questions in mind that she returned from Palestine to Paris in the autumn of 1935, at once excited and somewhat disillusioned. When she arrived there in September of that year, the Nuremberg Laws had just been passed in Germany. Apart from the Blutschutzgesetz (Law for the Protection of German Blood), which prohibited marriage or intercourse between "Jews" and "non-Jews," the new laws distinguished between "citizens of the Reich" and mere "nationals," which meant that from now on, Jews were quite officially downgraded to second-class citizens even within the Reich territory. Another step toward dehumanization, including the dehumanization of Arendt's life. By no means the last.

IV

NEAREST AND DEAREST: 1936–1937

Rand loves a superman, Arendt a pariah,
Weil the Republic, and Beauvoir her new family.

WE THE LIVING

"My only excuse for my long silence is that of a person who has just emerged from Hell. The year which has passed has been so terrible, with the constant disappointments, the indefinite waiting and the struggle, that I did not want to let anyone hear from me, for all I could say would have been complaints. I had to reach some success before I could feel like a human being again—and write like one."[1]

The words with which Ayn Rand begins a letter to her Californian fellow screenwriter Gouverneur Morris on November 29, 1935, could have been committed to paper with equal aptness by Simone Weil, Simone de Beauvoir, or Hannah Arendt. On the brink of turning thirty, they had all found themselves, both professionally and privately, put in passive rather than active roles. Not to mention the maelstrom of global politics that seemed to be threatening to suck everything and everyone deeper and more palpably into its swirl.

"I am just beginning to raise my head—more or less," Rand continues. "Not because of my play—although that is doing rather nicely—but because of my book. Selling it has been the greatest thing in my life so far. I had been so bewildered and discouraged by the long delay on the book, that I felt I would never be able to write again. Now that's over. Whether the book fails or succeeds, it will at least have been published."[2]

A week before, the manuscript of *Airtight* had been accepted by a publisher. The advance for the work was $250. The following spring, the famous New York publisher Macmillan was due to publish it, under the title *We the Living*. Meanwhile, *Night of January 16th* had been enjoying considerable success on Broadway since its premiere in August. For Rand alone, throughout the late autumn of 1935, it was bringing in royalties of up to $1,200 a week—the average annual income in the United States at the time.[3] This did nothing to diminish Rand's fury over the director's planned mutilation of her work into a "terrible burlesque," but at least financially she would have little to complain about for the time being.

In December, she now sat once more, in a new and more spacious apartment, at the only piece of furniture she had had shipped from Los Angeles, her walnut writing desk. She prepared sketches for her next project: a novel that was to outdo in scope and complexity, but above all with philosophical heft, everything that came before it. In the shadow of the Statue of Liberty and the recently constructed Empire State Building, Rand saw beneath the working title *Second-Hand Lives* the actual purpose of the book: *"A defence of egoism in the true meaning of that word."*[4]

RECONQUEST OF "I"

Rand was particularly concerned to show how the always shared premises of Christianity and communism had led to the hopelessly self-denying cynicism of modern consumer capitalism. Without a doubt, the true reason for the crisis of these "Modern Times"—and here Rand agreed with her philosophical primary sources, Friedrich Nietzsche, Oswald Spengler, and Ortega y Gasset—was not material but spiritual:

> We have developed technically—oh yes!—but spiritually we are far below Renaissance Italy. In fact, we have no spiritual life in the grand manner, in the sense it used to be understood. Is it the fault of machines? Is the twentieth century incapable and unfit for my spiritual exultation? Or—is it only that little word "I," which, after twenty centuries of Christianity's efforts, has been erased from human consciousness, and along with it took everything that was human consciousness?[5]

In its intense focus on wanting what other people already possessed, achieved, or valued, the supposed individualism of contemporary capitalist society showed itself to be just as deeply morally corrupt as collectivist approaches to society. Neither system had the faintest idea of what truly distinguished a human individual and might guide them in their decisions. At a time when human beings supposedly based their value judgments and their principles on those of others, the sacred word "I" had forfeited any meaningful function: aesthetically, morally, politically. Against this background only one path leads out of the cave: the reconquest of "I" must be accomplished through a radical negation of the relevance of others, all other people!

But what form might the existence of an individual take that consistently trod that path based on an unconditional *yes* to their own powers of judgment and creativity? Would such a person be able to exist, let alone succeed, under the conditions of the present day? Or would the person necessarily fail and fall victim to the resentment of the "far too many"?

Open questions, of which there was no shortage in this early planning phase. But what Rand could already see with absolute clarity was the hero of her novel. This unique creative force would strive for realization in the art form that had been seen both as socially conditioned and as pointing into the future of the twentieth century: architecture. By February 9, 1936, she had gotten it. Rand captured the profile of the new superman down to the last detail.

HOWARD ROARK

> Attitude toward life. He has learned long ago, with his first consciousness, two things which dominate his entire attitude toward life: his own superiority and the utter worthlessness of the world. He knows what he wants and what he thinks. He needs no other reasons, standards or considerations. His complete selfishness is as natural to him as breathing. He did not acquire it. He did not come to it through any logical deductions. He was born with it. He never questions it because even the possibility of questioning it never occurs to him.[6]

Rand's hero Roark has neither acquired nor developed the predispositions that characterize him, but has simply preserved them from the threatening contamination of others. Later in the novel, in fact, he is introduced as an orphan without any identifiable past. The problem associated with this persists, however. For human beings, the journey to acquiring that true autonomy Rand imagines, demonstrated by Roark's example, as a universally valid ideal of existence, is undeniably socially conditioned. At first thrown into existence as entirely helpless beings, and largely free of instinct, we—each and every one of us—come to know the world and ourselves via the laps and hands of others. It is the voices of others that call us into life as thinking beings. To that extent, the ideal that Rand imagines is only the climbing of a ladder that, once one has reached the heights of one's own autonomy, one knowingly pushes away. Rand places her hero on this lonely summit from the very beginning:

> Indifference and an infinite, calm contempt is all he feels for the world and for other men who are not like him. He understands men thoroughly. And, understanding them, he dismisses the whole subject. He knows what he wants and he knows the work he wants. That is all he expects of life. Being thoroughly a "reason unto himself," he does not long for others of his kind, for companionship and understanding.[7]

So Roark does not dispute the *existence* of other people but only their *relevance* for the shape and direction of his own life. Precisely because he understands how (entirely deficiently!) most other people think and live, he pushes them aside from his lofty height. It is logical to imagine this new and completely antisocial redemptory figure as a cheerful and active person. Instead of forgiving others their sins, Roark, the ideal human, lives in an active present of the mind, in which the sole possible sin for him consists in missing his own creative targets. As a clear opposite of the Christian redeemer Jesus Christ (a carpenter by profession), the architect Roark does not strive to redeem all others forever by his suffering, just himself through his own actions:

> He does not suffer, because he does not believe in suffering. Defeat or disappointment are merely a part of the battle. Nothing can really touch him. He is concerned only with what he does. Not

> how he feels. How he feels is entirely a matter of his own, which cannot be influenced by anything and anyone on the outside. His feeling is a steady, unruffled flame, deep and hidden, a profound joy of living and of knowing his power, a joy that is not even conscious of being joy, because it is so steady, natural and unchangeable. . . . The world becomes merely a place to act in. But not to feel in. . . . He does not even have to ponder about it—it is his very nature to be clear, consistent and logical about everything.[8]

Roark's resistance to frustration is thus a direct consequence of the ability to subject his entire emotional life to the control of thought. Just as Roark doesn't see his body as a possible source of stubbornness and resistance, neither does he allow his emotional life to get in the way. The consistent exclusion of difference that penetrates the whole of his existence does not begin with the existence of other people, but in relation to his own physical qualities, states, and drives.

SENSORY EGOCENTRISM

The constant serenity and joy that Rand's ideal human being finds in existence feeds on the certainty that this world is one in which his own desires and goals are completely accessible by means of thought and logic. (Rand soon comes to speak of the idea of a "benevolent universe.") It is this joy or serenity that typifies the hero Roark in every respect: life as constant success solving problems for the accomplishment of self-imposed goals.

Here the whole realm of nature appears merely as the means to an end. Roark the architect is interested in stone solely as material, a hillside as a building site, the sun as a provider of light and shade. In other words, nature has no intrinsic value for him—just for him and his projects. The only obstacles standing in the way of a "pursuit of happiness" described in these terms remain: other people. Roark has understood that. And he draws logical conclusions from it.

> Politics—interested only in not being interested in politics. Society as such does not exist for him. Other people do not interest him. . . . His main policy in life is to refuse, completely and uncompromisingly, any surrender to the thoughts and desires of others. . . . Because the rewards of success as such—money, ease and fame—mean nothing whatever to him; his life has to be real, his life is his work, he will do his work as he wants it done, the only way he can enjoy it—or not at all, and perish in the battle.[9]

Even a person like Roark can fail. But, if he plays his cards right, neither he himself nor the world of objects will be to blame, which is why even in that failure he can never be robbed of his dignity and his worth. And that dignity—as an uninterrupted sense of his own value and status in the world—is more important to him than anything else, more important even than the actual realization of creative plans. In the end, this self-worth is the actual foundation, or rather the source that allows him to utter the word "I" with confidence.

For that reason, the source must be kept free of all contamination by others. A verdict that applies even to those all-too-human states of extreme joy and ecstasy that even Roark, an entirely earthly person of flesh and blood, does not want to escape:

> Sex—sensuous in the manner of a healthy animal. But not greatly interested in the subject. Can never lose himself in love . . . His attitude . . . is not: "I love you and I am yours." It's: "I love you and

> you are mine." It is primarily a feeling of wanting her and getting her, without great concern for the question of whether she wants it.[10]

In normal terms, then, a person like Roark does not know and learn what love is. His love of himself, the only unconditional love, remains forever in the way of that. As long as he can experience and enter into solid relationships, the binding power must therefore come from people prepared to devote themselves to him entirely—which according to Rand is imaginable only through the mode of permanent admiration and, not least, sexual submission. There is always a sadomasochistic note to this element of pleasurable submission. In the novel this is illustrated by Roark's relationship with Dominique (as is always the case in Rand's works, the name here is telling). And, in fact, the first sex between Roark and Dominique in the novel (although framed, paradoxically, as consensual) is indistinguishable from rape—a recurring motif in Rand's work, with an entirely calculated potential for scandal.

Roark, the ideal human being, was fixed in terms of his fundamental features. The novel itself was anything but. In the spring of 1936, the plot and structure were still in the dark. Only the original conception of the work as a bildungsroman was gone. Instead the course of the plot would have to derive its tension from the obstacles that put themselves in Roark's way in the form of other second-rate people. Since her hero consistently rejected any kind of bootlicking, Rand wrote at the conclusion of her first thorough sketch, he will, "as a consequence, [endure] economical hardships, years of struggle with obscure jobs, poverty, silent, grim, relentless work. Every economical humiliation that society knows how to inflict."[11]

TOGETHER AND APART

Roark was the embodiment of Rand's very own ideal existence—and he was supposed to be. Not an entirely uncomplicated direction to take. Either for her—or for her husband. Certainly not in their shared everyday life. By 1936, in fact, Rand had definitively assumed the classic "male position." She was the male breadwinner, she brought the money in, received outward recognition, worked creatively, and defined and assessed things. Admittedly the publication of *We the Living* in April 1936 was a bitter disappointment from a commercial perspective (the surprise bestseller of that spring was by a certain Margaret Mitchell and bore the title *Gone With the Wind*), but the book received appreciative reviews. Not least, the Soviet focus of the book put Rand in the role of a political commentator whose views were in demand in the media—a function that she accepted in numerous interviews and opinionated evening talks, with increasing joy and commanding ease. Her husband Frank supported her the best he could—above all in the role of the cautious homebody and emotional support. With the move to New York, the goal of a big film career for him had finally become a fantasy. Rather than go on being humiliated by further refusals, he stopped applying for parts. A decision that Rand, given the experiences of her father, fully understood. After all, there are circumstances and times in which a person's only alternative if he is to preserve his dignity lies not in struggle against the prevailing conditions, but in an active boycott, a refusal to take part in them. Regarding the themes that preoccupied Rand, Frank contributed best in the role of the patient listener, as well as occasionally being a sharp commentator whose dry wit found its way immediately into Rand's otherwise largely humorless work.

After seven years of married life in New York, the two newcomers had nothing that could have been called a social life, or indeed a circle of friends or even acquaintances. This was largely because of Rand, who was not tormented by any great social longings, and who also didn't feel more displaced anywhere than in American small-talk parties. Only Frank's brother Nick, a lover of both life and ideas, brought occasional relief to the couple, who were now losing interest in anything remotely sensuous or erotic.

In the years that followed, Frank's sole engagements, more as a hobby than a profession, consisted of acting in male roles in summer stock productions of Rand's play *Night of January 16th*. When he set off for Connecticut to take part in one such performance, it was the first time in years that the couple had been separated for more than a few hours. Once Frank was gone, Rand sat down at her desk:

> 19 August 1936
>
> Cubby Sweet!
>
> Well, here is the first love letter I ever had a chance to write. And I have nothing to say, except that I miss you terribly. As a matter of fact, I don't really miss you, it's the funniest feeling: on the one hand, I feel so blue that I could cry any minute, and on the other hand I feel very proud and virtuous that I've actually done it: let you go away and stayed to do "my duty."
>
> The worst thing was coming home from the station. It was terrible and I enjoyed it, because it was a completely new feeling, something I've never felt before: the whole city seemed empty, and that's not such a cliché as it sounds, it was

> the certainty that no one, not anywhere, on any street, really mattered to me. I felt free and bitter and I wanted to cry. I didn't look back at your train once. How did you feel?
>
> There's one good thing, however: the absence of my "inspiration" inspires me more than anything else. I've really done grand work and I feel like working.
>
> Do I have to tell you that I love you? . . .
>
> Good night, Tweet!
>
> XXXXXXX
>
> Your Fluff[12]

A Howard Roark, we can say with some certainty, would never have set such things down on paper. Just as one does not need to have the eye of a trained couples therapist to detect considerable potential for tension in these lines. The role-play is still intact, while the roles themselves shifted long ago.

What part—Frank aside—other people played in Rand's life and thought will remain an enthralling question. Only alone, Rand was convinced, can a person think. And the same is true of the supreme form of thought: creative work and the elaboration of worlds in which it is worth living and loving.

FRONTAL

Hannah Arendt also had to struggle with herself to commit the sentence "I love you" to paper without reservation. On August 24,

1936, from Geneva, where, as an observer, she was attending the meeting to found the World Jewish Congress, she wrote to the new man in her life: "That I love you—you knew already in Paris, as I did too. If I didn't say it, it was because I was afraid of the consequences. And the only thing I can say today is: Let us try—for our love's sake. Whether I can be your wife, will be your wife, I do not know. My doubts have not been brushed away. Also not the fact that I am married."[13] What Arendt was afraid of was the loss of independence that went hand in hand with the experience of love. Even as a young student in Marburg, Arendt had encountered this with a force that had almost undone her standing in the world. The shadows of those years still went with her. Heinrich Blücher still knew nothing about her affair with her then philosophy professor Martin Heidegger, author of *Being and Time*, who joined the National Socialists in the spring of 1933. Just as Hannah Stern—whose de facto husband Günther had immigrated to the United States in the spring of 1936—knew nothing of Blücher's still extant marriage to the Russian Natasha Jefroikyn, who was also living in Paris. After all, they had known each other for only a few months. And a little bit of secrecy has never hurt a love affair. Especially a very new one. So there were reservations. Particularly since political developments around the world were taking an ever darker turn.

As if in response to a secret signal, over the course of 1936, tensions mounted around the word, leading to the formation of fronts and warlike conflicts. On August 26, Gershom Scholem writes to his old philosopher friend Walter Benjamin in Paris: "We've been living under a state of siege in Jerusalem for three months, every evening you hear more or less incessant shooting. . . . You become accustomed to a certain measure of fatalism, since nobody knows whether or not a bomb will be thrown at him at the next corner. . . . In the long run you become fairly unflappable. . . . That sort of thing accustoms a person to a large share of fatalism. . . . Life in the cities is still ideal compared to the open country. There, pitched battles are being fought, partly between the army and groups of Arab partisans, and partly between those groups and the Jewish colonies, whom they attack ceaselessly."[14] While in Palestine, a British protectorate, the first great resistance movement of Palestinian Arabs was breaking out, Benjamin reported from Paris with dry disenchantment that he did not "view the European situation—in terms of its latent structure—any more confidently than the Palestinian one."[15] And not only from the point of view of a German Jew who had emigrated to Paris.

DARK PROCESSES

In 1936, Hitler placed German industry on a war footing, laying claim to the freedom to arm; the economy and the armed forces were to be fit for war again within four years. A massive rearmament project started, whose first public sign was the invasion by German troops of the demilitarized Rhineland in March 1936—a blatant contravention of the treaties of Locarno and Versailles, but one that went unsanctioned by the victorious powers of World War I. Regarding Germany, now brought completely under Nazi rule, their line was: Anything as long as there's no more war. Meanwhile the left-wing opposition in Germany was so weak and broken that the number of political prisoners in concentration camps had dwindled to about three thousand.[16] On the basis of the regime's logic, new internal and external enemies had to be dreamed up and persecuted. With even greater intensity than before, this placed the Jews at the center of National Socialist hate propaganda.

After six months of defensive war and with more than a quarter million fallen soldiers, in May 1936, Ethiopian troops capitulated to Mussolini's armed forces. Il Duce then proclaimed a reawakened Italian

"Imperium."[17] Meanwhile, in Moscow, Stalin was once again stepping up his fight against high-ranking opponents within the party, including many former associates of Trotsky. The first big show trials were scheduled for the summer of 1936. All the accused—and usually their close relatives—were executed. By now the number of political prisoners interned in the gulags had risen to 180,000.[18] Deliberately planned as the prelude to numerous "cleansings" across the Soviet empire, the trials led left-wing intellectuals in Central Europe to distance themselves for the first time from Stalin's empire and its ideals.

Thus 1936 can be seen among other things as the year of a European left resurrected as a "popular front." As the result of a change of strategy in Moscow undertaken in 1934,[19] social democrats in countries such as France and Spain were no longer attacked by the Communist International as "social fascists." Instead, Stalin encouraged the communist parties in those countries to join forces with the social democrats and assume power that way.

The new strategy enjoyed its first success in Spain, where in February 1936 a popular front (largely from the bourgeois middle class) of Republicans, communists, separatists, and trade unionists won the elections against the right-wing Catholic government coalition by a small margin. With nine million votes in total, the popular front had a lead of only 150,000 votes.[20]

Three months later a left-wing popular front triumphed in France as well. The actual dividing line was less between nationalism and internationalism and more between a nationally inclined Catholicism and popular communism. In these elections there was no longer any room for a politically liberal middle, or indeed for the idea of democratic opposition rather than enmity. Just as Simone Weil had predicted, the remaining European democracies—except for Britain—were being drawn into the pull of irreconcilable hardline collectives.

Under the new prime minister, Léon Blum, the first socialist and also the first Jew at the head of France's government, the prospect was raised of a large package of reforms, which included old-age pensions and the shortening of the workweek, as well as unemployment insurance (but not, as were also promised: votes for women, paid vacation, or codetermination in the workplace).

As soon as the measures had been introduced, in June and July, France was gripped by the worst wave of strikes in its history.[21] With thousands of spontaneous and entirely peaceful actions, from work slowdowns to sit-ins and factory occupations, public life came almost to a standstill. Revolution was in the air, a menacing backdrop that was used by Blum to make further demands of private business. Better to bend now than be dispossessed in the future. Admittedly, France was still in a deep crisis whose clearest sign was an army of two million unemployed as well as a franc propped up by massive state intervention. As popular as the measures looked, they were, it would turn out, barely sustainable.

On July 14, when euphoric crowds processed through Paris to celebrate France's national holiday, Spain was on the brink of civil war. Three days later, on July 17, 1936, General Francisco Franco launched a military uprising, with the aim of toppling the new government. The two fronts thus became opposing sides in a civil war. The ideological split in society became a front line that passed through every city and every village. Within a few days the tensions escalated into mutual murder, looting, arson, rape, and execution that cost tens of thousands of Spaniards their lives, even at this early stage of the conflict.

As national teams entered the newly erected Olympic Stadium in Berlin, and both the Italian and the German teams resolutely honored Adolf Hitler with the fascist salute, Franco's troops were already receiving huge logistical support from both Mussolini's and Hitler's armed forces. The Spanish Civil War threatened to become a proxy war for both large totalitarian blocs.

There was a great clamor from the left across Europe. But neither the young Blum government nor the United Kingdom nor, at first, even Stalin had any interest in intervening directly in this conflict. In Paris this was denounced as a "betrayal" of the socialist brothers. From the end of August, tens of thousands of people enrolled voluntarily as an International Brigade to support the Spanish Republic in the fight against Franco's Phalange. Thus, the civil war also became in part a war of intellectuals and literati.

TRIBES

The situation in Spain was a topic of fierce discussion among Arendt's circle of friends in Paris. It was hardly to be assumed that its members were considering joining the International Brigades to fight on the ground. Aside from the fact they were all stranded in Paris, what connected these people from a great variety of professions and backgrounds, who met more and more often from 1935 onward for evening discussions, was their skepticism toward any kind of default assumption of political ideologies or movements—whether communism, anarchism, or Zionism. This Paris "tribe," as its members soon ironically called themselves, was defined more by the will to preserve the last and most precious space in their new pariah lives: the will to think for themselves.

That applied equally to the philosopher and critic Walter Benjamin, to the lawyer Erich Cohn-Bendit, from Frankfurt, to the Polish poet Chanan Klenbort, to Käthe Hirsch, to Lotte Sempell Klenbort, to the painter Carl Heidenreich. But it also applied to a particular degree to Heinrich Blücher, born in Berlin in 1899—and hence to a man who was living so illegally in Paris at the time that he "didn't know where he lived."[22]

Active as a young man in the labor movement and, in the early 1920s, also in the Communist Party, Blücher would go out in Paris by day dressed as a bourgeois tourist, with suit and walking stick and impeccable manners, and in the evening stay with friends in hotels and apartments. When asked what he did for a living he liked to say *Drahtzieher*—string-puller, one who gets things done. That had also been his code name in the party, from whose ideological strings he had increasingly disentangled himself during the 1930s.[23]

Blücher, who had grown up without a father in the Wedding district of Berlin, was an autodidact. Besides his manly habits and the accent of his original milieu, he had preserved a typical Berlin skepticism of highfalutin intellectualism. A classic self-made man, who stood firmly on his own two feet without any kind of safety net and whose intellectual independence was matched only by his poverty. A pariah par excellence, then, and hence entirely to Arendt's taste, refined as it had been by life.

Because of his always elegant appearance and his middling knowledge of French, Arendt ironically called Blücher "Monsieur"—and sometimes, in intimate contexts, "Stups" (meaning "nudge"). If the couple had taken each other by storm, Arendt, as a letter of August 20, 1936, testifies, was by no means inclined to allow the fact to "blow her away." Her reservations were particularly a result of her doubt as to whether she would be able to reconcile the experience of love with the preservation of her own identity and integrity. A concern that she took all the more seriously because it represented the question at the heart of her

Heidelberg doctoral thesis, supervised by Karl Jaspers, "The Concept of Love in Augustine,"[24] which dated from 1928 and thus from a phase of her life during which she was still secretly meeting Martin Heidegger.

LOVE THY NEIGHBOR

With reference to the church father Saint Augustine's (354–430) concept of love, Arendt pursues the question of the "relevance of the Other" for one's own relationship with oneself and the world in her first independent work. But nowhere is this question more urgently posed—and perhaps more clearly answered—than in love. Love is, in the words of a letter from Heidegger to Arendt written in 1925, "the break-in of the presence of the other."[25] Those who love are not alone in the world. And they no longer experience the meaning of the world and themselves from their isolation.

It is even more surprising, then, that in Augustine's concept of love the agency of another human being—the irreplaceable, individual Other—does not play a major role. The reason for that lies in the fact that Augustine's powerfully Christian philosophy has its origin in God—and finds its true aim in God. And the same is true of every form of any dependable meaning of life, as well as any kind of shelter in this world.

What is in truth loved and what should be loved as a neighbor is for Augustine only the fact of the Other's origin in God, as well as their membership in a community of all beings that are afflicted with original sin and hence mortal. Before God—the actual source and goal of love—all are ultimately equal, however. Which is why God's love, even among human beings, applies not to their individuality but to their fundamental equality.

In Augustine, this equality is assured by the fall of Adam and Eve, as an earthly origin of our finitude and ineradicable depravity. In the closing chapter of her 1928 dissertation, which tellingly bears the title "Vita Socialis" (social life), Arendt therefore maintains:

> The explicitness of equality is contained in the commandment of neighborly love. The reason one should love one's neighbor is that the neighbor is fundamentally one's equal and both share the same sinful past.[26]

> I never love my neighbor for his own sake, only for the sake of divine grace. This indirectness . . . puts an even more radical stop to the self-evident living together in this earthly city. This indirectness turns my relation to my neighbor into a mere passage for the direct relation to God himself. The other as such cannot save me. He can only save me because the grace of God is at work in him.[27]

The question of whether and how one's own individuality can be lovingly preserved or acquired in the first place is not posed, cannot be posed, against the background of Augustinian philosophy. Arendt had exposed this as a genuine scandal in Western thought as early as 1928, when the question of love was treated only as an existential intensification of the question of whether *other* people exist at all (and not, for example, fundamentally identical by nature). And above all what their Otherness might mean for one's own existence. Even woman as woman, according to the original fiction of the Old Testament, is not imagined as merely Other, but only as an identifiably inadequate version of the original man. Consequently, according to the story, she is formed from a body part that humanity does not need for naked survival—the rib.

Where purely earthly conditions are concerned, the equality of human beings in the philosophy of Augustine (and hence also in his concept of love) is assured by a shared kinship origin, namely the "common descent from Adam," which no human being can escape.

> This kinship creates an equality . . . of situation. All share the same fate. The individual is not alone in this world. He has companions-in-fate (*consortes*), not merely in this situation or that, but for a lifetime. His whole life is regarded as a distinct fateful situation, the situation of mortality. Therein lies the kinship of all people and at the same time their fellowship (*societas*).[28]

The individual as part of humanity—a single "community of fate" consisting of mortals, of those destined for death: in the interpretation of this student of Heidegger and Jaspers, this is the true critical point of church father Saint Augustine's theory of love, and also of politics. It is no coincidence that he was also the author of *City of God*.

ARENDT CHANGES DIRECTION

The future author of *The Origins of Totalitarianism* must have seen with great clarity, as early as 1936, how the apparently long-outmoded motifs of Augustinian thought further unfolded and played out their totalizing and equalizing effect with an almost uncanny continuity—behind the backs of the geopolitical players, as it were—in the name of different collectives.

To interpret the political present, in fact, Arendt had only to move from the transcendence of almighty God to the immanence of the almighty Führer, to reveal the actual devaluation of the individual as one whose isolated contingency was reduced to the relationship with that Führer. In this totalitarian vision of the world, the individual had no essential significance. Individuals might exist, but there was no need for them to. The sacrifice of the individual did not really mean the end of the world.

But in Arendt's political present under Hitler, the mythical origin narrative of the human community as the community of those exiled from Paradise was consistently replaced by supposedly historically established origin narratives of people and, where appropriate, nations. And here, too, the desired total conformity was affected in the sense of a national collective belonging. Love your national comrades as yourself! And if necessary, sacrifice your life for theirs in the name of that same national community. It is only logical that under such an arrangement, love of the representative of the national body should become identical with love for its Führer in the same way as, in Augustine, love of one's neighbor becomes identical with love of God.

Within this intellectual framework there is no longer any plausible answer to the question of the "relevance of the Other"—world-guaranteeing and hence to be preserved at all costs—as a single and unique human being. To put it in even more extreme terms: it cannot even be made intelligible as a question. That question acquired plausibility, if at all, in so-called purely interpersonal relationships in the private sphere and hence relationships that, according to the ideal of a total state, should no longer exist. The private coupledom of lovers as a first and last outpost of resistance to a society threatened by total conformity—how had Arendt so nicely put it in her letter to Heinrich from Geneva: "Let us try—for our love's sake."[29] Not for the sake of any other love. Not even that of a god. Or in other words: purely for the sake of ourselves, our happiness and status in the world, and above all for the sake of the freedom from anxiety, typical of love, concerning our own finitude.

Viewed from a purely philosophical perspective, the idea of how one might imagine a love that allowed the Other as Other to penetrate one's own existence, without finding oneself dispossessed and permanently under siege, was by no means resolved for Arendt. But at least in the experience of a lovingly shared everyday, there were soon several concrete reference points, as Hannah revealed to her Stups a year later, again from Geneva, and without holding anything back:

> 18.9.37
>
> My dear, beloved, one-and-only dearest,
>
> I am very proud and very happy that I was with you in the night. You see, dearest, I always knew, even as a kid, that I can only truly exist in love. And that is why I was so frightened that I might simply get lost. And so I made myself independent. And about the love of others who branded me as cold-hearted, I always thought: if you only knew how dangerous love would be for me.
>
> And when I met you, suddenly I was no longer afraid—after that first fright, which was just a childish fright pretending to be grown up. It still seems incredible to me that I managed to get both things, the "love of my life" and a oneness with my self. And yet, I only got the one thing when I got the other. But finally I also know what happiness is. . . .
>
> Today my divorce decree came through. I'm going to have a lot of running around to do. But to some extent I'm glad—you can laugh, I'm being childish—to get my old name back.[30]

With the acknowledgment of the divorce Arendt also lost her German citizenship. Let the world go to hell in front of everybody: with

"Monsieur" by her side, the stateless Hannah felt safe for the first time—like a wreck. Heinrich's experience was much the same. As early as autumn 1936 they had moved in together—which meant in concrete terms that they shared a room in a hotel on rue Servandoni whose most important furniture consisted of two camping stoves and a gramophone and records: a true picture of earthly and hence finite happiness in a dark time.

PARIS IS FOR LOVERS

Two people in a shabby Paris hotel room where the only personal bits of furniture are the bookshelf and the record player. In the autumn of 1936 that is a precise description of Simone de Beauvoir's situation. Like a real-life answer to an era-defining question, whether there was still a "corner of the world left on which we could pin our hopes,"[31] Beauvoir and Sartre clung above all to each other. However, they had not fled from Berlin to Paris, but had come back from the tedious provinces of the north to their hometown. Their hotel room lifestyle is not the result of financial constraints or a lack of legitimation, but the freely chosen nonconformism of two tenured lycée teachers. The same is true for the choice of cafés in Montparnasse and the Latin Quarter as their actual sitting rooms and studies. What Beauvoir particularly liked about the multilingual chatter of the refugees at the next table was not its news or survival value, but the narrative space given to her by the presence of people who were "so near, yet so distant, so busy fumbling after the lost remnants of their lives."[32]

To an even more striking extent this applied to prostitutes, dropouts, and drug couriers, as well as the Americans drinking themselves into a stupor again every evening, who completed the crowded picture of the smoky café at night. Because of the reforms by Blum's Popular Front government, which were going way over budget, the value of the franc against the dollar had fallen strongly again. This gave the myth of Paris as the party capital of Europe, firmly anchored in the works of such Roaring Twenties icons as F. Scott Fitzgerald, Ernest Hemingway, and Gertrude Stein, a further boost.

When Beauvoir opened the annual assignment letter from the ministry in August 1936, she could hardly contain her happiness: a job at the Lycée Molière in the 16th arrondissement. A comfortable Métro journey from the center of the city. Sartre's posting to Laon, 150 kilometers away, also enabled him to spend considerably more time in Paris. "Twice a week I would go and meet Sartre at the Gare du Nord. . . . We would make our way down towards Montparnasse. We had set up our GHQ, as it were, in the Dôme. On those mornings when I was not due at the *lycée* I used to have breakfast there. I never worked in my hotel room, but preferred one of the booths at the far end of the café. All around me were German refugees, reading the papers or playing chess."[33]

By November, Olga, without her parents' permission, had followed the couple, and now lived a floor above Beauvoir. In the meantime, she had given up any idea of pursuing her studies. She spent the day working irregularly in a tearoom, and at night, depending on arrangements and availability, they would go out on the town as a duo or a trio. What had changed for Beauvoir since Rouen was the radius but not the shape of her circle of hell.

Sartre was by now thirty-one, Beauvoir twenty-eight. Almost all their friends and former fellow students, such as Maurice Merleau-Ponty, Paul Nizan, or Raymond Aron, were in steady relationships or married, and hence settled in a bourgeois sense. It was not without a certain irritation that they observed Sartre's and Beauvoir's deliberate acceptance of chaos in their lives. Their way of life also caused consternation at the family home. For fear of infecting herself with a disease, her mother refused to set foot in Simone's hotel room, while her father, at their increasingly rare Sunday dinners, made no secret of what he thought and expected of his older daughter: "You are too old to think anymore, never mind to write a decent book. You'll never amount to more than the Worm's whore."[34] And as if her father weren't annoyed enough already, Simone's younger sister, Hélène, an aspiring painter, was ever more clearly drawn to her sister's example.

A SHAKY PACT

What troubled Beauvoir's view of her life more than anything was the permanent challenge that Olga represented to her bond with Sartre. It was not primarily a matter of erotic supremacy or physical jealousy. As a couple, Sartre and Beauvoir, in the seventh year of their pact, were far beyond the stage where shared sex represented a foundational pillar of their relationship. Particularly because during this early phase of the return to Paris, Sartre began to reveal—and satisfy—the full extent of his gigantic sexual appetite. His many and varied trysts ate deeper and deeper into his Paris timetable. He barely had time to meet Beauvoir for a coffee at Le Dôme or even at the station, to hand her the latest manuscript pages of his novel in progress, *Melancholia*.

No, what Olga Kosakiewicz—more a cipher than a real person—stands for in Beauvoir's world is in fact the question of the nature of her bond with Sartre—the actual essence of their pact. To what extent, particularly from Sartre's point of view, was it really the only "necessary relationship" in their lives? And upon what exactly was that necessity based?

From Beauvoir's perspective, the essential core of a lasting bond lay in the prospect of a shared future, based on an accepted past.[35] With Olga's appearance as a third party in the union, however, a principle of total immediacy arose that undermined any expectation of commitment: "Olga was furiously sceptical concerning all 'voluntaristic' interpretations, which by itself was not enough to unsettle me; but in the face of her opposition Sartre, too, let himself go, to the great detriment of his emotional stability, and experienced feelings of alarm, frenzy, and ecstasy such as he had never known with me. The agony which this produced in me went far beyond mere jealousy: at times I asked myself whether the whole of my happiness did not rest upon a gigantic lie."[36]

Beauvoir's suspicion that she was by now (or possibly forever) experiencing not a necessary bond, but a monstrous lie, fed on the question of the understanding of freedom with which Sartre viewed their relationship. Did he find the constancy and stability that Beauvoir granted him a guarantee of freedom or a restriction of it?

If the "Olga principle" came to dominate, Beauvoir would in the end become just one out of many—her privileged status would prove to be mere illusion. An illusion that preserved its permanence only in the fact that Beauvoir's action was directed toward a different understanding of freedom. The tug-of-war between her and Olga had nothing at all to do with the struggle of two women over erotic primacy in a man's life. And not just because Olga, who found Sartre intellectually stimulating but physically repellent, wasn't pulling—was refusing to pull—at the other end. It was in fact an issue that went to the heart of Sartre's and Beauvoir's understanding of love. It concerned the conditions of a loving relationship based on mutually granted freedom—not least sexual freedom.

FREE LOVE

Beauvoir's philosophical love worries are almost the polar opposite of Arendt's. For Arendt, if the paradox to be resolved lies in asking how it's possible, in the words of her letter to Blücher, "to be the love of my life and a oneness with myself."[37] For Beauvoir, the miraculous mystery of her love of Sartre lay from the start in the fact that in their coupledom they had acquired a single unbroken identity as "we." Arendt saw the actual challenge as being that of becoming part of a loving dyad without at the same time abandoning one's own identity. For Beauvoir in 1936, however, it lay in acknowledging the obvious fractures within her own unified and necessary bond of love, without at the same time endangering or sacrificing the identity of her own person, essential as it was to the existence of that dyad. In answer to the question, who was she as a person without Sartre, she would not with the best will in the world have been able to present a compelling answer. After all, she loved Sartre. Beauvoir summed up her situation in the winter of 1936–1937 as follows:

> What disturbed me even more was the way I sometimes found myself in opposition to Sartre. He always took great care not to say or do anything which might change our relationship; our discussions were extremely lively, as always, but free from any hint of rancour. Yet all the same I was led to revise certain postulates which hitherto I had thought we were agreed upon, and told myself it was wrong to bracket myself and another person in that equivocal and all-too-handy word "we." There were some experiences that each individual lived through alone. I had always maintained that words could not fully express the physical essence of

> reality, and now I must face the consequences. When I said "We are one person," I was dodging the issue. Harmony between two individuals is never a *donnée*; it must be worked for continually. This I was quite prepared to admit.[38]

Reluctantly, Beauvoir was obliged to admit the irreducibility of each person's own experience. Nothing in the world—no word, no oath, no companionship, however intimate—can fully bridge the separation of one existence from another. There is always a crack, if not an abyss. An insight so fundamental and decentering that Beauvoir had placed it, after due reflection, on a level with the loss of her faith in God in her youth. Just as, according to Kant, God's existence was a postulate of practical reason, and faith in his existence had a morally supporting function in the world, for Beauvoir it had been faith in the unifying principle of the loving word "we" with Sartre that had given her a secure foundation. Because of the "Olga" experience she had lost that faith.

What might it in fact mean to love one another freely? Could even the deepest of all imaginable bonds be understood as a truly open project that had to be constantly renewed and preserved in a shared existence? And if so, was that really such a bad thing?

ELECTIVE AFFINITIES

Apart from the liberating clarity of those false assumptions on which their own existences might have been passed, in the winter crisis of 1936–1937, Beauvoir and Sartre revealed new ways of stabilizing their relationship. What argument was there against bringing in other people besides Olga? Like the bright and confident Jacques-Laurent Bost, a former student of Sartre's, who had already come every now and again from Le Havre to Rouen the previous year? Or Olga's sister, Wanda, two years her junior, who also yearned for escape from the drudgery of the provinces, and who was easily a match for her sister in terms of openness and hunger for experience? Bost, the younger brother of the Parisian writer Jean Bost, was taking up his studies at the Sorbonne that autumn. Wanda also followed her sister to Paris. Of course, Sartre bestowed the nicknames: Bost was just "Little Bost," and because Olga had been christened "the little Russian," Wanda could only be "the very little Russian."

Half joking, Sartre and Beauvoir were soon talking about "the family" and created a way of life based on everyday shared familiarity that harmonized entirely with their philosophical principles, which were assuming ever more concrete form. In the end what bonded that "family" together was played out beyond innate qualities or a long-shared past. The responsibility they accepted for each other was much more due to the act that, in Beauvoir and Sartre's belief, constitutes the core of all human existence: the radically free choice for or against something, for or against a value, for or against a project, an existing norm, a way of life, or membership in a community. And the decision for that freedom of choice—the decision, effectively, to make one's own decisions—in a given situation, particularly for the younger members of the family, meant a significant break from the way of life that their families had set out for them.

Even if, as Olga would recall, the younger ones were "all like snakes, mesmerized" by the sheer presence of Beauvoir and Sartre, and "did what they wanted because no matter what, we were so thrilled by their attention, so privileged to have it,"[39] the free spaces thus gained were immeasurably greater than anything imaginable in the milieu that they came from. From now on, Sartre and Beauvoir's "family" developed as an experiment on a philosophical basis, in which theory and practice, entirely as the pair of thinkers wished, fed into and powered each other. As an open experiment in existence.

MELANCHOLIA

Regardless of one's moral view of this setup, it was above all extremely draining, particularly for the person who was the meeting point for all the threads, namely Simone de Beauvoir. "What with Olga, and Sartre, or the two of them together, I tended to stay up late at night; Sartre could rest at Laon, and Olga had the daytime to recover in, but I never made up for the sleep I lost. . . . While waiting for Sartre in a café near the Gare du Nord I sometimes closed my eyes and lost consciousness for several minutes."[40]

Sartre was once again in need of exclusive attention early in spring 1937, not only because of the painful partial loss of Olga to young Bost. In spite of the advocacy of Paul Nizan, his friend from his student days who was already established as an author, Sartre's novel *Melancholia* (later *Nausea*), on which he had been working intensely for more than four years, had been turned down by the publisher Gallimard. That was difficult to digest, not least for Beauvoir, who had accompanied the creative process from the outset, as its first reader and editor.

As a couple, they had put much of their energy, both creative and philosophical, into this philosophical project. They both saw the book as the successful literary expression of their analysis of and ideas about human existence. Now they were failing at the very beginning. The reason Gallimard gave for its rejection was not so much the actual execution as the conception of the work as a plainly metaphysical novel.

Beauvoir's deep concern about her partner's psychical equilibrium—

at least the man-sized crustaceans had disappeared from Sartre's perceptual world for the time being—had much to do with the content of the book that had now been rejected. The actual plot of the novel, after all, uses diary entries to follow the journey of the red-haired hero Antoine Roquentin, strolling slightly crumpled through the world into a total loss of meaning and the self.

Roquentin looks like the dizygotic twin of Ayn Rand's superhuman redhead Howard Roark—although a twin that sprang from a different and considerably less cheerful egg. All the questions and doubts, of which Rand's hero Roark is happily unaware, dog Roquentin's every move. Nothing is obvious to him, least of all his own existence. He feels nothing more painfully than the eyes of others upon him. Rather than energetically building skyscrapers that point to the future, Roquentin spends his days in the French provinces writing the biography of a not particularly noteworthy French diplomat from the previous century. A project that he soon recognizes as completely pointless and shelves, just as any kind of plan and goal he might have comes to nothing in the course of the book. His life descends into an outwardly inactive maelstrom of doubt. Nothing is solid. Everything dissolves into an abysmal, shapeless void, including his so-called "self."

In the end, even the existence of such supposedly consciousness-free objects as stones and plants is swept into Roquentin's whirl of meaninglessness:

> So I was in the park just now. The roots of the chestnut tree were sunk in the ground just under my bench. I couldn't remember it was a root any more. The words had vanished and with them the significance of things, their method of use, and the feeble points of reference which men have traced on their surface. . . .

> But that all happened on the surface. If anyone had asked me what existence was, I would have answered, in good faith, that it was nothing, simply an empty form which was added to external things without changing anything in their nature. And then all of a sudden, there it was, clear as day: existence had suddenly unveiled itself. It had lost the harmless look of an abstract category: it was the very paste of things, this root was kneaded into existence. Or rather the root, the park gates, the bench, the sparse grass, all that had vanished: the diversity of things, their individuality, were only an appearance, a veneer. This veneer had melted, leaving soft, monstrous masses, all in disorder—naked, in a frightful, obscene nakedness.[41]

This irruption into the true essence of things was based on an experience that Sartre had had in person at the peak of his depressive phase in Le Havre, at the turn of 1934–1935, and written down in the form of his philosophical journal entry. According to this, nothing that existed was anything in and of itself or necessarily there. And so—at least this was a possible conclusion to be drawn from it all—everything was as nothing in the end. That is the abyss that opens up effectively as an illumination in Sartre/Roquentin's experience in the park, to plunge him from exhausted melancholy into a state of profound nausea over the "soft, monstrous mass" of being. A nausea that Roquentin will go on to feel all the more deeply and despairingly because his consciousness—quite simply because it is a human consciousness—cannot, even when presented with a sound insight, help tormenting him with the illusory experiences of the solidity of the self, objects in the world, and what is known as meaning.

Fundamentally irresolute, for the rest of the novel Roquentin oscillates between the almost euphoric feeling of unconditional liberation and a sense of being hopelessly imprisoned in the near-nonsensical loops of his stream of consciousness:

> Lucid, static, forlorn, consciousness is walled-up; it perpetuates itself. Nobody lives there any more. A little while ago someone said "me," said *my* consciousness. Who? Outside there were streets, alive with known smells and colours. Now nothing is left but anonymous walls, anonymous consciousness.[42]

> I am free: there is absolutely no more reason for living, all the ones I have tried have given way and I can't imagine any more of them. I am still fairly young. . . . But do I have to start again?[43]

This novel had been rejected precisely for being what it was and wanted to be: the experiment of expressing new metaphysical truths and feelings in literary form. The couple were very disconcerted by the book's rejection. In Beauvoir's words: "How could there be such a discrepancy between other people's views and our own?"[44]

By the spring of 1937, this consternation transferred directly to the advance of political developments. The Popular Front government under Blum was on the brink of internal collapse. And counter to all hope and initial euphoria, with the fall of Málaga the Spanish Civil War also seemed to be turning in Franco's favor once and for all. Everything could be different, but they could change nothing. Sartre, if he was being honest, hadn't even voted. How much more eccentric the idea must have seemed to copy so many others from their milieu and go to Spain, to fight with their last strength for the freedom of another Republic: "There was no question of our going off to Spain ourselves; nothing in our previous background inclined us to such headstrong action," Beauvoir later recalled. "In any case, unless one got into some clearly defined technical or political job, there was a danger of being a nuisance rather than a help. Simone Weil had crossed the frontier determined to serve with the infantry; but when she asked for a gun they put her in the kitchens, where she spilt a bowl of boiling oil all over her feet."[45] That at least was the story that was told in the "family" about Simone Weil. It even corresponded almost to the truth.

HEADACHES

The chief source of joy during those days, for Simone Weil as well as the others, was a gramophone. During her stay at a Swiss sanatorium in the spring of 1937, the record collection of a medical student on an internship there was the only effective therapy. Her suffering had gotten so bad that when the attacks, which came in waves, were at their worst, she even wondered whether the moment of her death had arrived. Only music was able to free her momentarily from her pain, and particularly recordings of Bach's Brandenburg Concertos.[46]

Apart from "severe headaches" and anemia, her father noted on December 15, 1936, when she had once again been signed off from her teaching post, Simone's "left leg, which had a very extended burn . . . still pains her a great deal."[47]

The injury dated from her deployment in the Spanish Civil War, but not, as people might have whispered to one another in the cafés of Paris, as the consequence of an accident while working in the kitchen. It happened on the front, when Simone, with her twenty-person unit, was camping in the forests of Aragon and, very late at night, stepped in a pot of boiling hot oil that her comrades had placed in a hollow in order to avoid smoke and covered with leaves.[48] Her scalded skin hung in strips and led to burn wounds that, once she had been successfully transported back to base, made amputation appear necessary. Her fellow fighters were rather relieved despite everything. Even before setting off along the River Ebro, they had voted unanimously in Barcelona against issuing comrade Weil a rifle, let alone letting her load it. After all, given her extreme shortsightedness, there was no guarantee that she could have focused on the nearest tree. Weil still insisted on being issued a rifle. She was the only one who didn't need to use it.

Just a month after her accident, her unit was attacked by enemy forces and most of its members executed in the village of Perdiguera. By then, Weil was already back in Paris. As if suspecting something, her parents had followed her to Barcelona and tracked down the wounded fighter to a military hospital. All in all, Simone's Spanish adventure—from crossing the border in Portbou on August 8, 1936, until her return to France on September 25—lasted a total of six weeks.

Disguised as a journalist, she traveled to Spain, immediately enrolled with POUM troops—members of the Workers' Party of Marxist Unification set up by communists in opposition to Stalinism—and requested permission for a solo special deployment. She wanted to set off on a secret mission to Galicia to find the founder of this group (a brother-in-law of her fellow French trade unionist Boris Souvarine), who had disappeared without a trace, and liberate him. A suicide mission without any prospect of success or even survival, as her commander had to make clear to her over hours of argument.

Still resolved to do anything, Weil joined an anarchically inclined trade union group within the militias. She sent her parents, by now almost dying of worry, postcards telling fabulous tales of a generally relaxed atmosphere, a lack of combat, and excellent weather. Not a word of the airplanes dropping bombs over her head, which the brigade rifles were powerless to bring down. Not a word about the deadly fear she felt with each new hill that needed to be taken. Every house a possible nest of enemies, every woodshed a final ambush. Being taken prisoner meant execution. That applied to both camps.

Shortly after her arrival in Catalonia, Weil witnessed her comrades planning to take a Catholic priest to execution. In her war diary, she reports on the spiritual battle she faced during those minutes. Was she prepared to step in at the critical moment, protect her brother in faith, and thus provoke her own execution? Would she find the courage to do that? For some reason that was not further explained, the shooting was postponed. But what would happen the next day? Is one less guilty of a crime because one does not witness it directly? Her experiences of the war preoccupied and tormented Weil ever more seriously in the winter of 1936–1937, although that didn't keep her from proudly wearing her brigade uniform when she strolled along the boulevards. No, she regretted nothing; in fact, she spoke several times of returning to the front as soon as possible.

Meanwhile, in a way that even her best friends and acquaintances found confusing, in her articles and essays she argued energetically *against* the French government offering any military support to Republican forces. A convinced pacifist in the volunteer uniform of the International Brigades—what was that about?

MORAL HINTERLAND

In a subsequent letter to the conservative Catholic writer Georges Bernanos, author of the influential antiwar novel *Les grands cimetières sous la lune* (*The Great Cemeteries under the Moon*),[49] Weil justified her attitude: "I do not love war; but what has always seemed to me most horrible in war is the position of those in the rear. When I realized that, try as I would, I could not prevent myself from participating morally in that war—in other words, from hoping all day and every day for the victory of one side and the defeat of the other—I decided that, for me, Paris was the rear."[50]

Consequently, there was a way out of the situation! Particularly since the International Brigades operated on a quite different basis from a national army. The latter is based, in the event of war, on compulsory state conscription, while the former was an army of volunteers.

Weil was convinced that the criteria for entering a war were vastly different, and more intense than for individuals who could make their own decisions. As a Frenchwoman, Weil therefore fully rejected the idea of involvement, let alone the deployment, of the army in Spain. As the moral being that she was, however, there was no alternative for her but to fight. Just as there are people who refuse military service for reasons of conscience or belief, and who are instead willing to accept any sanction and any sacrifice, for Simone Weil in the summer of 1936, it was indispensable for moral reasons to fight for the Republic and thus accept any sacrifice that needed to be made.

It is worth contrasting this pattern of justification with Simone de Beauvoir's at the same time. About the Spanish situation in winter 1936–1937, Beauvoir writes:

> The farce of "nonintervention" struck us daily as more criminal. For the first time in our lives, because the fate of Spain concerned us so deeply, indignation per se was no longer a sufficient outlet for us: our political impotence, far from furnishing us with an alibi, left us feeling hopeless and desolate. And it was so absolute: we were mere isolated nobodies. Nothing we could say or do in favor of intervention would carry the very slightest weight. There was no question of our going off to Spain ourselves.[51]

Both thus felt with great clarity that in this situation there were no longer any moral alibis, just different ways of shaping one's own impotence. And Weil was only too aware of her powerlessness as an individual, as she was of her inadequacy as a fighter. At the same time, her decision to go to Spain was anything but impulsive; in fact, it was fully thought through. It had nothing to do with the illusion of making any decision that would affect the outcome of the war through her own presence. It was simply the case that Simone Weil—in response to the question: What might an ethical reaction to one's own powerlessness and isolation in this situation be?—believed that she must react in a fundamentally different way.

From Beauvoir's vantage point, the only appropriate response lay in demanding, as a citizen, a state-authorized intervention by her own country. For Weil the answer was to volunteer in a spirit of solidarity. In her case, the impotence and isolation she felt was a mood that she assumed was similarly experienced by people in Spain. And above all by those who found themselves amid the conflict through no fault of their own. Those were the people with whom Weil wanted to stand shoulder to shoulder in the name of a complete identification with the victim. That was how closely her self-regard was involved with her unconditional willingness to fight for other suffering human beings. The only alternative for Weil was to give in to that powerless cynicism that Beauvoir perceived as an inner threat in the same situation.

In her self-determination, Weil was also following a distinctly Christian understanding of love that sees the neighbor in the suffering Other and requires one to love them as oneself. Love as a will to passion in the name of the guiltlessly humiliated. Entirely as one with this, as far as we know, is the renunciation of any kind of romantic love or physical intimacy that defined her whole existence. Ultimately, for her nature, romantic love was one thing above all: manifestly unjust and morally entirely random. It picks an individual out of all the others as "the one"—and not even as a conscious choice. For her deeply moral identity, that is not a living option.

As what was doubtless only a random detail of the invisible threads that seem to keep these two careers together, in April 1937, both Weil and Beauvoir were ruled *hors de combat* for health reasons. Whereas for Weil it might have been her unconditional altruism that had taken her beyond the limits of her resilience, in Beauvoir's case it was her hedonistic hunger for experiences. In March 1937, she had a breakdown in her Paris hotel room and was taken to the hospital in an acute, life-threatening condition. One of her lungs had already given up and the other was inflamed. Unconditional peace and quiet was prescribed and, as for Weil, a cure lasting many months.

SPIRALS OF DEHUMANIZATION

By the spring of 1937, the boundary between civil war and proxy war had definitively been crossed. Anyone who was still actively involved—as Weil never tired of stressing—was involved for reasons that had barely anything to do with the original causes of the war. More precisely, those people were guilty of pointless murder. What deeply disturbed both Weil and other observers of the Spanish case was the unbridled brutality and the indifference to what was going on, violating even the most elementary norms of protection. Where were its reasons and causes? Was it only fear of one's own death that led both sides to such blind and comprehensive cruelty?

Weil didn't believe that. To her mind, slaughter on this scale necessarily required a blockage of the human imagination. Or more precisely a blockage about the question of who still belonged to the camp of humanity:

> My own feeling was that once a certain class of people has been placed by the temporal and spiritual authorities outside the ranks of those whose life has value, then nothing comes more naturally to men than murder. As soon as men know that they can kill without fear of punishment or blame, they kill; or at least they encourage killers with approving smiles. . . . The very purpose of the whole struggle is soon lost in an atmosphere of this sort. For the purpose can only be defined in terms of the public good, of the welfare of men—and men have become valueless.[52]

Civil wars are more susceptible to this spiral of dehumanization and hence violence than classic conflicts between nations. After all, the combatants in them are people who lived next door to one another only a few weeks before—which means that the degree of repression required must be particularly large and uncompromising. Especially with regard to the question of how they are to live together again once the war is over. Against this backdrop, the will to extermination easily defeats reconciliation, which is held to be impossible.

Added to this is the fact that for the German and the Italian military, the Spanish front was more and more clearly coming to be seen as a testing ground for new tactics and technologies. As a country that had no great strategic significance in terms of the other wars that were appearing on the horizon, Spain was useful to them as a laboratory of future cruelty. In war, too, the limits of what is doable can be tested only by crossing them.

Given this grim state of affairs, and given her own experiences at the front in 1937, Weil increasingly turned her attention to the threat of military conflict between Germany and France. Rather than intervention, aid, or voluntary call-up, for the student of Alain (the sobriquet of Émile Chartier—still the most defining pacifist voice in France), the question of the legitimacy of a war to defend one's own country was defining. Was there such a thing as a just war, and did it follow that there were also just aims of war?

EMPTY WORDS OF POWER

Following the theory that the cruelest conflicts in history were all distinguished by their lack of any precise definable goal (and that it was the actual absence of a defined goal that spurred on the cruelty still further), Weil, in an essay of April 1937, concentrated on the keywords and terms that were mobilized across the whole of the European context to legitimize a war. Philosophical linguistic criticism as concrete peace work. Because

> to clarify thought, to discredit the intrinsically meaningless wars, and to define the use of others by precise analysis—to do this, strange though it may appear, might be a way of saving human lives.[53]

As the prime example in the West for the bloodiest imaginable war (and the richest in sacrifices), waged over a pure chimera, Weil chooses the Trojan War. Hence the title of her essay, "Ne recommençons pas la guerre de Troie"—"Let's Not Start the Trojan War Again":[54]

> The Greeks and Trojans massacred one another for ten years on account of Helen. Not one of them except the dilettante warrior

> Paris cared two straws about her. . . . For the clear-sighted, there is no more distressing symptom of this truth than the unreal character of most of the conflicts that are taking place today. They have even less reality than the war between Greeks and Trojans. At the heart of the Trojan War there was at least a woman and, what is more, a woman of perfect beauty. For our contemporaries the role of Helen is played by words with capital letters. If we grasp one of these words, all swollen with blood and tears, and squeeze it, we find it is empty. . . . This is illustrated by all the words of our political and social vocabulary: nation, security, capitalism, communism, fascism.[55]

In Weil's analysis, these terms are stripped of any identifiable meaning particularly through their absolutist use in political speech, and their potential for meaning is thus limited to the point of unrecognizability. "Each of these words seems to represent for us an absolute reality, unaffected by conditions, or an absolute objective, independent of methods of action, or an absolute evil; and at the same time we make all these words mean, successively or simultaneously, anything whatsoever."[56] Words and people educate (and displace) one another. For Weil, the actual conditions of such completely unlimited violence as marked the Spanish Civil War therefore lie in forms of escalating speech, in which words that govern action are first removed from their traditional contexts of use and then converted into an absolute form that allows them to degenerate into mere phantoms of meaning. In language of this kind, when words take a warlike holiday, the concepts distorted for propaganda purposes lose all connection with the reality of which they previously gave a nuanced account.

In other words, the secret that lies behind the violence of both the past and the present is that of speech freeing itself from normal use and assuming a total value in its own right. That precise form of speech is the one to which Adolf Hitler and his kind brought a new diabolical mastery during the 1930s. It is also that form of speech with which a Soviet delegate, at a congress of French trade unions in 1937, justified Stalin's show trials and the major purges that were beginning across the Soviet Union as necessary blows against the "vanguard of fascism." Also that form of speech which—according to a trade union anarchist by the name of Simone Weil (who was fighting on the side of the Republic in Aragon)—in the eyes of the military doctor who treated her in Barcelona (who was involved with the Communist Party), was also nothing but another "fascist." In this way of speaking, the overcoming or indeed the defense "of capitalism" comes to mean the same thing as the salvation of the whole of mankind. But as Weil sets out in her text, no one can say what that salvation may consist of in concrete terms, or what the "capitalism" charged with such a mission or its "system" as a root of evil might actually mean:

> Apparently it is easier to kill, and even to die, than to ask ourselves a few quite simple questions like the following: Can the laws and conventions which control our present economic life be said to constitute a system?[57]

In this analysis of April 1937, as sarcastic as it is proclamatory, Weil is concerned not only with the relationship between speech and warlike actions, the one making the other possible. For her it is equally serious that the conflicts and wars born of such unbounded discourse are inevitably false conflicts and false alternatives.

> Another good example of murderous absurdity is the opposition between fascism and communism. The fact that this opposition

> constitutes today a double threat of civil war and world war is perhaps the gravest of all our symptoms of intellectual atrophy, because one has only to examine the present-day meaning of the two words to discover two almost identical political and social conceptions. In each of them the State seizes control of almost every department of individual and social life; in each there is the same frenzied militarization, and the same artificial unanimity, obtained by coercion, in favour of a single party which identifies itself with the State and derives its character from this false identification, and finally there is the same serfdom imposed upon the working masses in place of the ordinary wage system. No two nations are more similar in structure than Germany and Russia, each threatening an international crusade against the other and each pretending to see the other as the Beast of the Apocalypse. . . . In these circumstances it follows, of course, that anti-fascism and anti-communism are also meaningless.[58]

FALSE OPPOSITIONS

It may be due to Weil's training in the trade union milieu that her analyses of the Soviet regime, here again, appear significantly more cogent than her rather favorable view of the German Reich. It remains remarkable, however, that in this essay neither the name Hitler nor the term National Socialism is mentioned. But how much discrimination can we attribute to an analysis that makes no significant distinction between Mussolini's Italy and Hitler's Germany? This gap in the analysis fits only too consistently with the complete absence of any mention of the centrality of anti-Semitism to Hitler's system. At the same time, the continuing spread of the term "Jew"—alongside the passing of increasingly harsh legal measures against this group—remains a prime example of the diabolical vagueness of word and language in the name of violence that Weil identified. The supposed differentiation in the vocabulary concerning first-, second-, and third-class Jews, for example, served only to conceal the elimination of meaning from these terms, which was unsupported by any scientific theory or real-life evidence. What remained was a term for all those who had stood up or "conspired" against the "historic mission" of the German people and their Führer. This development in public speech was also apparent in the show trials saturated with anti-Semitic stereotyping in Moscow during the great "purge years" of 1937 and 1938.

All military conflicts in the 1930s, Weil believed, were based on a purely false opposition, compared with which—the author observed dryly—even the Trojan War was revealed as "a flash of good sense."[59] Precisely because the supposed goal of the war proved on closer inspection to be empty and meaningless, it must be replaced by the goal of complete extinction of the group that has been declared the enemy. The boundlessness of the violence thus becomes visible as a function of those concepts most likely to incite a war, precisely because they have lost all meaning. That leads to the point where the dynamic of war makes both sides so like each other, even in their ways of living and acting, that no difference is discernible between the two. In this final stage the conflict becomes a sham conflict.

When that happens, the goal of war can be only murder itself, to the point of total extinction. The only thing that can halt the orgy of violence at this stage is the exhaustion of the resources needed for killing—the raw materials, the factories, the structures—or in the end, human beings themselves, now the raw materials for murder.

PROPHETIC

The diagnosis of the age could not have been gloomier. In a letter to the editor of a trade union newspaper, Weil hones her analysis into a prognosis, or perhaps a prophecy, of the horrors to come:

> I predict—and we can both take note of this—that we shall enter a period in which one will see throughout the country the most incredible absurdities—and they will appear natural. There will be less and less civilian life. Military preoccupations will more and more dominate the everyday aspects of existence. . . . Capitalism will be destroyed, but not by the working class. It will be destroyed by the development of national defence in each country, and replaced by the totalitarian state. That is the revolution we shall have.[60]

That was how Simone Weil saw the political state of the world in the spring of 1937. There can be no doubt about which side she would unequivocally be on in that struggle: for the most oppressed of the oppressed; for those who had always struggled the hardest in wars. They were her neighbors, whom she wanted to love as herself—in the name of her own wounds and those of others. That was her *passion*. All analyses and learned theories aside, by that spring Weil already had deeper reasons for believing that her stations of the cross had just begun.

V

EVENTS: 1938–1939

Weil finds God, Rand the solution,
Arendt her tribe, and Beauvoir her voice.

IN THE CUL-DE-SAC

The only thing that can be said with any certainty about Simone Weil's persistent headaches was that the symptoms resonated quite weirdly with the political developments of the time. In the late autumn of 1938, the state of her health had reached a new low. Teaching was out of the question. When she and her parents sought out a tumor surgeon, Weil delivered a bombshell in the waiting room. "If he advises an operation, I want it done as soon as possible."[1] Her mother advised giving such a decision a considerable amount of thought. But Simone's patience was finally at an end: "Then you would rather I gradually decay intellectually!" In fact, because of her endless pain, Weil was now concerned about her rational mind—a prospect that led her to consider suicide at around this time.

In one of the few outlines for an article that she could still summon strength for, she summed up the whole political situation under the title "The Disorder of Our Time."[2] "The total absence of security, above all when the calamities one fears are so out of proportion to the resources that can be furnished by intelligence, activity, and courage, is surely harmful to the health of the soul."[3]

There seemed to be no way out, and throughout 1938 the cul-de-sac leading to war grew narrower by the month. The Anschluss of Austria by Nazi Germany in March was followed by the definitive failure of the Popular Front under Léon Blum. In May, the new laws concerning foreigners were intensified once again. In September, the International Brigades in Spain, almost as a formality, announced their dissolution. By now about half of their fighters, 40,000 in all, had lost their lives. With the Battle of Ebro in the summer, Franco was heading for clear victory. Meanwhile, Hitler was busy taking the Sudetenland and risking another war between the major powers of Europe on grounds of mutual defense. At the last minute, in late September, the outbreak of conflict involving Germany, France, the United Kingdom, and Italy was prevented once again, by the Munich Agreement.

Finally, on the night of November 9, 1938, state-organized pogroms raged across the whole of Germany in what came to be known as Kristallnacht. Five days later the legal situation of Germans who had fled to France was aggravated once again. Hitler's troops were preparing to march on Prague and, contrary to the most recent agreements, present the world with yet another fait accompli.[4]

The time of conferences, as Weil stated in her outline, was over for good. The only remaining questions were in what way war would come, and with what intensity. "The sense of security has been profoundly undermined. . . . There can be no security for man on this earth, and beyond a certain measure the feeling of security is a dangerous illusion."[5]

NOTES OF MERCY

Weil's mood of general resignation and intellectual introversion is apparent in the titles of her few essays from this period. Rather than witty references or evocative imperatives, the texts are presented as "reflections" or even "meditations."[6] But intellectual work is in any case almost out of the question for now. The search for the physical causes of her suffering, even in Dr. Clovis Vincent's office, remains fruitless. At any rate it isn't a tumor. And where palliative care was concerned, Weil had already decided on her own course of action.

Dismissed from her teaching job on grounds of poor health, in the summers of 1937 and 1938, she undertook extensive travels around Italy, based largely around sacred music. On trips to Florence, Bologna, and Rome she attended up to three masses and concerts a day. Wherever liturgical song or organ playing sounded in a church, the pain faded into the background and even allowed her to feel, in her deep devotion, removed from the realm of the physically restricted here and now. As if, behind this world of absolute pain, there lay another, healing world.

In April 1938, the yearning for this experience led Weil to the Benedictine abbey of Solesmes on the Sarthe River, famed for its Gregorian chant. Her intention was to attend Easter Mass there with her mother. During her ten-day visit Simone did not miss a single one of the many religious services. Looking back, she would remember what happened to her there during the solemnities as a crucial phase in her life: "I had intense headaches; each sound was as painful as a blow; only through extreme concentration could I escape this wretched flesh to let it suffer alone, curled up in its corner, and find a pure and perfect joy in the ineffable beauty of the song and the words. This experience allowed me by analogy to have a better understanding of the possibility of loving divine love through misfortune. It goes without saying that in the course of that service the idea of the Passion of Christ entered me once and for all."[7]

GOD'S KINGDOM

As early as September 1935, weakened by the experiences of her "factory year," Weil had been similarly "touched by faith" while on vacation with her parents. One evening when she was strolling along the alleyways of the Portuguese fishing village of Viana do Castelo, she found herself caught up in a procession. Beneath the full moon, the fishermen's wives were carrying a statue of the Madonna to the boats in the bay. Under the impression of what Weil called the "doubtless ancient chants," it was there that she first understood with total clarity that "Christianity is a religion for slaves par excellence, that slaves cannot help but belong to it—and me among them."[8]

Of far greater weight, once again, was the experience that Weil had in the summer of 1937 near Assisi, in the church of Santa Maria degli Angeli, which housed the Porziuncola, where Saint Francis was said to have withdrawn to pray. The only visitor in that "incomparable miracle of purity," as if having a fit, she was "forced for the first time in my life by something stronger than myself to kneel."[9]

So there were precursors. Nonetheless, where the question of the existence of God was concerned, until November 1937 she had never considered the possibility of "real contact, person to person, here below, between a human being and God. I had vaguely heard tell of things of this kind, but I had never believed in them."[10]

Aside from immersing herself in music, Weil had over the years also taught herself another healing attention-building technique. It consisted of reciting poems like a mantra in times of the greatest pain ("The poem teaches us to contemplate thoughts instead of changing them"[11]). In Solesmes, an English novice to whom she would later give the name "Angel Boy" had drawn her attention to the work of the English poet George Herbert (1593–1633). She was almost magically drawn to Herbert's religiously and metaphysically charged poem "Love," which ends with the words: "You must sit down, says Love, and taste my meat. / So I did sit and eat."[12]

A few days after her visit to the doctor in November 1938, when, tormented by pain, Weil sat down again and recited this poem, she experienced something she had not known before. She experienced herself, in the form of Jesus Christ, entirely imbued with divine love, and in the form of an immediate presence, in which, in her words, "neither my senses nor my imagination had any part; I only felt in the midst of my suffering the presence of love, like that which one can read in the smile on a beloved face."[13]

It was as if her eyes had been opened—or closed—for the first time. From her perspective, it was an experience that barely left room for doubt or skepticism. According to her interpretation, in November 1937, she had been filled with the presence of divine love, and hence a form of presence that was "more real than that of a human being."[14] Behind the certainty of the "face-to-face," then, according to this experience, there was another level—the kingdom of God and his boundless love. Behind the realm of immanence lay one of transcendence. Behind the languages of humanity another form of address. Behind the perfection of human knowledge another truth. Weil felt transformed, "touched by God."

NOT RESPONSIBLE FOR HER ACTIONS

It was and never is easy to find a language for the experience of the unconditional. After all, its essence lies in bursting the boundaries of human rationality and demanding the recognition of a realm beyond reasons and causes, beyond communication and method, of space and time as the actual origin of all our lives, which bestows meaning upon it. That Simone Weil, unlike many others, did not immediately go around euphorically telling everybody about the breakthrough she had experienced—to communicate her experience of God to the world with missionary zeal—may be at least partly because of her previous attitude to the practicalities of life, as well as her severely weakened physical state. Nothing in her concrete activities changed, and nothing had to change. Instead, as a left-wing trade union activist, she had already lived according to the imperatives of God's kingdom during all the years leading up to this event.

In her case the transformation that she had experienced concerned not only her own actions, but also the foundation on which they rested, and their valued source. What had changed was the place, the hot spot in her consciousness, where the self-understanding of her mission came from. From now on it was no longer about the interpersonal and the immanent, but the divine and the transcendent. It no longer fed solely on constructed arguments, but fed predominantly on mercifully granted experiences. Hence it no longer followed universal calculations and considerations, but followed unconditional professions of faith.

In November 1938, Simone Weil—to put it in terms of her own words and anxieties—both as human being and philosopher, had definitively become "unaccountable." Because in line with the Pauline hymn of Philippians 2, her reason now no longer counted in the here and now, but loved in the name of something higher, something transcendental.

THE BLIND LIGHT

But what had *really* happened? In Weil's specific case, is the obvious thing not to describe this experience first and foremost as a psychological or psychiatric phenomenon? A hallucination on the brink of pain-induced unconsciousness, a soothing trick of the subconscious, an ordinary delusion caused by strong medication . . . the possibilities of placing Weil's experience in a distinctly more mundane context are plentiful. Who believes in ghosts, after all? Or even more so, the loving real presence of the Son of God through the medium of a tortured body?

That other ways of framing the event are possible is beyond question. Because the essence of the aforementioned experiences means that rationalizations of this kind have no limiting relevance, or even plausibility, for the consciousness in question. In the end, nothing in the world is more real than concrete experience. And for the consciousness doing the experiencing, no experience is clearer and more certain in its content than the kind described.

In other words, the one thing that limits any attempts to examine and investigate such mystical experiences of transformation or breakthrough, not least from an epistemological viewpoint, is the fact that from now on, for the person who had the experiences, those experiences represent the ultimate standard for what evidence, clarity, certainty, and even reason may mean. The urge to confirm their content scientifically appears, from the point of view of the "illuminated" person, just as meaningful (or indeed meaningless) as the attempt to use the latest available methods to check whether the so-called "standard meter" in Paris is really a meter long. Anyone who, like Weil in November 1938, has "seen the light" does not need a physicist to confirm that it is real and has a warming power. Instead, such individuals go on living, as they say, "in their own world," which also claims, in a way that is troubling for other people, to be the only real and pioneering one.

The normal Christian term for this way of life is "sainthood." But of course, the philosophical tradition in the narrow sense also gives accounts of the reality-opening power of experiences of this kind. In the form of the bright light at the end of the emergence from the Platonic cave, the lightning-like meditative insights of René Descartes, or the climbing of Ludwig Wittgenstein's metaphorical ladder of knowledge in the *Tractatus Logico-Philosophicus*. You need to jump from its last rung—without a net or anything like an argument—so that the world can be "correctly understood" for the first time. Yes, hadn't Sartre, or rather Roquentin, given the indisputable impression of penetrating the essence of things in a state of extremely ambivalent self-dissolution, in the contingent "paste of things"?

Simone Pétrement, Weil's close friend and future biographer, maintains that the only imaginable outward guarantee of such a mystical evidential experience consists of the life that follows on from it.[15] In that light, there are no identifiable reasons to doubt the authenticity of Simone Weil's experience of God.

Not that her behavior from then on appeared different in any way. However, it does assume a different coloring, and understands itself entirely in terms of Christian love and a passionate willingness to accept suffering. Thereafter the headaches were accepted and valued both as possible portals into transcendence, and as the culminating darkness of the political situation. Weil recorded in her notebooks: "You could not have wished to be born in a better time than this, when everything has been lost."[16] That could have been written only by someone who had, in a new way, ascertained what it was that was actually unlosable; and by someone who, in their own way, henceforth assumed the task of saving it.

BACK TO THE SOURCES

In November 1938, however, there was no denying that humanity in Europe was going through a deep and severe crisis: "The great expectations inherited from the three preceding centuries and above all from the last century, the hope of a progressive spread of knowledge, the hope of general well-being, the hope of democracy, the hope of peace are all in the process of disintegrating rapidly."[17]

As a philosopher and journalist, Weil could see only one genuine way out of this crisis that would heal civilization: rather than return to the "things themselves," in her view humanity had to return to the "sources themselves." She understood committed readings and rereadings of the great source texts of humanity, like an archaeologist, revealing layer by layer those values and primal impulses that had been so plainly scattered and repressed.

After her own experience of transcendence, for Simone Weil the unequal battle against the political realities of her own time could be fought only by regaining the divinely inspired fundamental values set out in the most ancient testimonies and epics of classical high cultures. These were in particular the works of Plato and Homer, the Upanishads and the Bhagavad Gita, as well as the texts of the Stoics and the Evangelists. They were all, in Weil's view, ultimately inspired by the same light, which fanned out only spectrally in different ways according to the era and culture that had shaped the consciousness in question. Like Martin Heidegger, whom she consistently ignored, or Walter Benjamin, of whom she had never heard, Weil interprets the Western tradition as a process of long, continuous darkening and progressive remoteness from the essential.

In her work, human beings draw their actual dignity and sanctity from openness to the light of love itself, and hence of a source that is ultimately not of only human origin and cannot be granted solely a human guarantee. The true sources of our sense of being are transcendent, and as such remain safe from purely human intervention—and more particularly from the intervention of universal understanding or pure reason (or rather what might be politically defined as such within a particular era).

Conclusively, then, the love of one's neighbor takes the place of solidarity, the love of one's enemy the place of class struggle, the completely debased form of existence of the "slave" the place of the "proletarian." After all, Weil had already written in the conclusion of her factory diary, in the end it is always about "the class of those who *do not count*—in any situation—in anyone's eyes . . . and who will not count, ever, no matter what happens (notwithstanding the last line of the first verse of the *Internationale**). . . . One always needs to have some *external* signs of one's own worth for oneself."[18]

But what if these outward signs are completely absent in times of the greatest darkness? Who then saves, what then secures human rights? One's own value? Was it really other human beings? Were they dependable? And if they were, from what sources and in what way? These are precisely the questions that were to make Ayn Rand, in another part of the world, almost lose her mind.

BLOCKED

"Permission refused."[19] In May 1937, Ayn Rand learned of the ultimate failure of her attempt to bring her parents from Leningrad to join her in New York. Even though all the documents were present, and Rand had even paid in advance for her parents' crossing, the authorities refused to allow them to emigrate without giving reasons. This was hardly surprising. Certainly not at a time when the tyranny of the Stalin regime was reaching yet another climax. Following on from the

* "The earth shall rise on new foundations, / We have been naught, we shall be all."

show trials of the previous year, from the spring of 1937 both party and people were cleansed of "hostile elements." Practically, this meant that week after week, in the early hours of the morning, thousands of people were rounded up from their homes by the secret police and dragged to the basements of the NKVD, to be interrogated, and, in many cases, tortured, forced into confessions or denunciations, and then either executed on the spot or sentenced to years of forced labor in the gulag. According to a decree passed in 1937, spouses and children could be found guilty at the same time as "wife of an enemy of the people" or as "family member of an enemy of the Revolution."[20] The Revolution was literally devouring its own children twenty years on.

Even today the years 1937–1938 in Russia are remembered as the time of the "Great Terror." Everyday life was defined by a climate in which, as an eyewitness put it, "no one knew what the next day would bring. People were afraid to talk to each other or meet, above all families in which the father or the mother had already been 'isolated.'"[21] This must have applied in a particularly pronounced degree to a family whose daughter, having emigrated to the United States, as a writer and journalist frequently railed against the "Russian experiment." Ayn's very existence, as she was well aware, represented a genuine risk to the lives of her relatives. With her typical unwillingness to compromise, she cut off all further contact after the news arrived. She would not even confirm that she had received the telegram.

The family crisis led to a creative one. For the first time in her life, Rand experienced writer's block.[22] For months the hours spent at her desk had produced nothing but a swirl of thoughts leading nowhere, interrupted experiments and rejected sketches. Admittedly the theme, the main characters, and the essential lines of development of the new novel were clearly fixed. If Rand didn't know which event would tie the different strands together dramatically in the end, however, she was unable to go on working, or indeed even to start. In her own words, she was "going crazy."[23]

The problem was no doubt Rand herself, her own creative source and power. Everything depended on one compelling idea. But merely wanting something, as Rand would have been the first to admit, achieves nothing in this field. Quite the contrary.

HYMN

By the summer of 1937, her husband Frank had once again been cast as the gangster Guts Regan for a run of *Night of January 16th* in Connecticut. The couple rented a cottage on the coast. While Frank rehearsed and acted, Rand searched for new thoughts and, more important, new ideas on the beach.

At first more as a way of distracting herself and giving free rein to her imagination, she put into action a plan from her early student days. Stretched out on her lounger with a view of the water, she tried her hand at a dystopian science fiction story.[24] The starting point was a society in a final state of total collectivization. The people here are not allowed even a residual feeling of their individual uniqueness. Indoctrinated from earliest childhood ("We are nothing. Mankind is all. By the grace of our brothers we are allowed our lives. We exist through, by and for our brothers who are the state. Amen"[25]), the inhabitants always speak and think in the first person plural, even when addressing their own feelings, wishes, or fears. Because "all men are one, and . . . there is no will save the will of all men together"[26]—at least this is what is decreed by the "World Council," which speaks for all and is therefore necessarily right.

Down to the last details, Rand's sketch is based on the science fiction novel *We*, secretly passed around during her Leningrad student days, written by her compatriot Yevgeny Zamyatin in 1920–1921. Instead of just names, in Rand's version people also have robotlike numbers; the collective in the form of the state is omnipotent and godlike, and any individual deviation is severely punished.

It was as if a valve had been opened. In less than three weeks she captured her 100-page novella on paper on the beach. First Rand's hero Equality 7-2521 happens upon a tunnel from the far-off time before the "Great Revolution," where he begins to record thoughts on stolen parchment ("It's a sin so think words no others think and put them down upon a paper"[27]). Soon he, too, is carrying out experiments on frogs and other animals that allow him to make a new discovery of the miracle of electricity and even reinvent the lightbulb.

During his daily job as a streetsweeper his eyes often meet those of the fieldworker Liberty 5-3000. The liberating light of recognition is soon joined by that of love ("We looked into each other's eyes and knew that the breath of a miracle had touched us"[28]). The two manage to escape into the forbidden forest of their forefathers. United there, they begin a new life in an Edenic wilderness, the journey into their shared freedom finding its actual climax and conclusion in the rediscovery of the first, most important, and actually liberating word in human language: "My hands . . . My spirit . . . My sky . . . My forest . . . This earth of mine . . . Many words have been granted me, and some are wise, and some are false, but only three are holy: 'I will it.'"[29]

The revolutionary rebirth of the self-determining rational human being under the conditions of total collectivism ends, like the novella itself, with "the word that can never die on this earth, for it is the heart of it and the meaning and the glory. The sacred word 'EGO.'"[30]

WORKING ON THE MYTH

Human self-empowerment on the basis of the "ego" becomes the actual healing event that allows one to enter the earthly paradise... as Rand's entire tale is imbued with Old Testament themes and those from Greek mythology: the light of the other world is reached by climbing through the tunnel in the cave; the blasphemous theft of divine fire occurs in the form of the discovery of electricity; Equality 7-2521 first sees the liberating reflection of his face in the surface of a pond. It is only logical that the saved individuals should end up baptizing themselves with the names Prometheus and Gaia.

True to the leitmotif of unconditional self-affirmation, Rand weaves motifs from her very own escape story into her novella: like the hero Equality 7-2521, at the time of her escape from the Soviet Union, Rand was in her early twenties; and in her case her first act after her successful flight was a regenerating renaming of herself. On the ship from Estonia to England, Alisa Rosenbaum gave herself the name "Ayn Rand."

The choice of her first name may have been motivated by her admiration for the popular Estonian-Finnish author Aino Kallas,[31] who connected politically charged tales of freedom with mythical motifs from the world of the Nordic sagas. Asked by a fan about the background of her curious first name, Rand replied in January 1937: "I must say that 'Ayn' is both a real name and an invention. The original of it is a Finnish feminine name which is spelled in Russian thus: 'Айна.' Its pronunciation, spelled phonetically, would be: 'I-na.' I do not know what its correct spelling should be in English, but I chose to make it 'Ayn,' eliminating the final 'a.' I pronounce it as the letter 'I' with an 'n' added to it."[32]

Hannah Arendt while she was working on her doctorate in Heidelberg, 1927.

The Russian American philosopher and author Ayn Rand.

Simone Weil in the combat uniform of the International Brigades, 1936.

Simone de Beauvoir in her hotel room, Paris, 1945.

I to the power of *n*: self-baptism as a statement of faith. Rand's work on her own freedom myth began on day one after her flight and found in the novella *Anthem* only one way of expressing the "motive and purpose of my writing."[33]

In line with the multiple biographical layers of *Anthem* is the fact that Frank O'Connor and Ayn Rand married in 1931, just as her frequently extended visa for the United States threatened to expire once and for all. A classic green-card decision out of love that allowed Rand to go on living in the Garden of Paradise of the Free.

SKYSCRAPERS

Once the novella was completed, it was back to Manhattan, where the pair, along with their two cats, had by now moved into a three-room apartment on the Upper East Side, lovingly decorated by Frank. To Rand's great disappointment, however, she did not manage to find a taker for *Anthem*. Further theater projects and a planned dramatization of *We the Living* came to nothing. She also learned that Macmillan, the publisher, had inadvertently destroyed the plates of her first novel after the first edition, and was now unable to supply any more, even though sales miraculously continued a good year and a half after the first publication. Rand could hardly help sensing yet another conspiracy on the part of the "pink" New York publishing scene. Still, the sale of the film rights for *Night of January 16th* lightened the financial burden ($5,000, or approximately $85,000 in today's money).[34]

She had still not advanced a step further in the direction of finding a plot. Meanwhile, despite their affection, Rand's relationship with Frank—her "Cubby-Hole," as she called him—was moving further and further away from her ideal. In purely practical terms, Frank's New

York life was a huge relief to her, but in aesthetic terms it was a crushing disappointment. It was as if the orchestra of his dreams had simply ceased to play. Without any open contradiction or even grudgingness, he fit fully into the role of the caring homebody but was entirely lacking in initiative and, what was more, seemed not remotely inclined to provide spontaneous service to Rand's increasingly elaborate fantasies of seizing possession of the world "like an animal."[35] Instead, they found that they were now increasingly reliant on each other for entirely mundane reasons.

Whoever or whatever was going to release her from her deep autumnal gloom, the intervention was clearly not to be expected from her husband. What Frank plainly lacked was a leading impulse, a unifying theme for his life, one last, foundational, and entirely autonomous "I will it" at the heart of his existence. For Rand this was an essentially unacceptable situation. Indeed, it was the epitome of human shortcoming.

From her earliest youth she had known exactly why she was in the world: to forge her own happiness in life and to create stories that showed the world as it should be—and not as it unfortunately was. Something similar applied to her superhero Howard Roark, except that as an architect he found his happiness in erecting buildings in which people would really live and feel at home in the world in the truest sense of the phrase. Like gods dwelling at great heights, form and function were to become one: human beings seen as skyscrapers.

A COMPELLING IDEA

So back to the drawing board. Still, Rand had a clear notion of the fundamental conflict determining the novel. She would use the fall and rise of Howard Roark as an exemplary depiction of the struggle between individualism and collectivism in a human soul.[36] The invention of a suitable plot in 1937–1938 was further complicated by developments in global politics. It was simply no longer possible to restrict the theme to its psychological aspects. If the superman Roark was really to stand for everyone, the struggle surrounding his creation would have to be more than purely aesthetically and privately motivated.

Rand continued to brood. For research purposes, in the late autumn of 1937 she started working as a secretary in the architectural office of Ely Jacques Kahn, which specialized in building skyscrapers. Only Ely Kahn, to whom Rand had been introduced through acquaintances from the conservative milieu, knew about her true mission. In March 1938, just before lunchtime, Rand asked her boss in passing what commissions presented the greatest challenge, to which Kahn replied without hesitation: housing. "The moment he said 'housing,' something clicked in my mind, because I thought, well now, there is a political issue and an architectural issue; that fits my purpose."[37] Roark in public housing, that was it!

During her lunch break, Rand put the whole plot in place: at the end of the novel her hero would be brought before the court for personally destroying a model project of social housing built from his own designs, just before it was completed—to protest against planning changes that had been imposed during the final phase by a public committee.

The project, Cortlandt Homes, was to exist entirely according to his will—or not at all! He had conceived it! He had designed it—no one else! Which was why it was for him and no one else to decide on the existence or otherwise of the housing project. No form of expropriation could be tolerated, particularly not when it concerned interventions in the creative integrity of the work. Here the brilliant egomaniac was fighting back against the committees of the "far too many." Perfectionism versus the logic of compromise. Prime mover versus second-hander. Roark against the people. Whose rights needed to be preserved? In whose name? And in what way?

ECCE HOMO

Rand pursued the metaphorical trail laid by Nietzsche, deep into the heart of her plot: the exemplary revaluation of the altruistic canon of values that really bound Christianity and communism very closely together. As Nietzsche wrote in *Ecce Homo*, under the heading "Why I Am a Destiny":

> I know my lot. Some day my name will be linked to the memory of something monstrous, of a crisis as yet unprecedented on earth, the most profound collision of consciences, a decision conjured up *against* everything hitherto believed, demanded, hallowed. I am not a man, I am dynamite—And for all that, there is nothing in me of a founder of religions—religions are for the rabble; I need to wash my hands after contact with religious people . . . I don't *want* any "disciples"; I think I am too malicious to believe in myself; I never address crowds . . . I have a terrible fear of being declared *holy* one day: you can guess why I am publishing this book *beforehand*—it should prevent any mischief-making with me . . . I don't want to be a saint, and would rather be a buffoon . . . Perhaps I am a buffoon . . . And nevertheless—or rather *not* nevertheless, for till now there has never been anyone more hypocritical than saints—the truth speaks from me.—But my truth is *terrifying*, for

> *lies* were called truth so far.—Revaluation of all values: that is my formula for the highest act of self-reflection on the part of humanity, which has become flesh and genius in me. My lot wills it that I must be the first *decent* human being, that I know I stand in opposition to the hypocrisy of millennia . . . I was the first to *discover* the truth, by being the first to sense—*smell*—the lie as a lie . . . My genius is in my nostrils . . . I contradict as no one has ever contradicted before and yet am the opposite of a no-saying spirit. I am an *evangelist* the like of which there has never been; I know tasks so lofty that there has not yet been a concept for them; I am the first to give rise to new hopes. Bearing all this in mind, I am necessarily also the man of impending disaster. For when the truth squares up to the lie of millennia, we will have upheavals, a spasm of earthquakes, a removal of mountain and valley such as have never been dreamed of. The notion of politics will then completely dissolve into a spiritual war, and all configurations of power from the old society will be exploded—they are all based on a lie: there will be wars such as there have never yet been on earth. Only since I came on the scene has there been great *politics* on earth.[38]

Nietzsche was Rand's dynamite, Roark her American demolition expert. But what would it all be worth if there was no way of establishing great politics in a psychology of true individual greatness? A psychology that would also do justice from within to the ideal description of autonomy for which she was striving? To carry out the requisite research Rand did not even need to leave the apartment. In fact, she had the one absolutely exemplary study object that she needed: herself. "The model for Roark's psyche was my own."[39]

THE POISON OF RECOGNITION

Rand conceived Roark's heroic single-mindedness on the basis of the image of her own mind. And for that reason, it was also very clear where the true condition for the success of self-determination lay. As she wrote in her diary:

> 10 November 1938. It's terribly bad to be conscious of yourself as others see you. [Whether they see you as] good or bad. Take yourself for granted. The consciousness that feels alone—without the weight of other eyes watching—is the only healthy consciousness.[40]

What might appear to common sense as a severe mental distortion, if not actual narcissistic personality disorder, in Rand's world represents the ideal state of every ego. To be truly free means first and foremost to be free of the always normatively charged presence of others, which is not perceived more clearly anywhere than through their eyes, through their gaze. Rand is speaking in these terms, using the words of her favorite writer, Victor Hugo, when she refers to the "beast of other people."[41]

An image with incredibly broad, not least social, and philosophical consequences. If we agree with Rand, a person who seeks to achieve his autonomy or even only his self-image through the battle for recognition has already lost it by taking it up in the first place. In other words, there is no happy consciousness in and through the view of others—not even in terms of friendship or love. Because:

> Friendship: Roark is the only one capable of real friendship—because he is able to look at people in themselves, unselfishly—

> because he is too selfish, because they are not a part of him in any way. He does not need them basically, does not need their opinion of him, and [therefore he] can value them for their own sake, a relationship of two equals. Roark does not want to impress himself upon others, because he does not need it.[42]

In other words, only a person like Roark can really unconditionally honor other people—and himself—as "ends in themselves," since only a person of his kind feels no need to use or instrumentalize other people for his own purposes. He does not psychically need them. Either for his self-worth or for his position in the world. If there is a psychological original sin, it is falling into the hell of others and hence of inevitable self-misrecognition; it lies for Rand in the question: What do you think of me?

BRAND-NEW DAWN

Like Simone Weil, Ayn Rand was troubled by the question of what human dignity threatened to become in such times, if it depended completely upon the granting or withdrawal of social recognition. Weil's experience had led her to locate the foundation of dignity in a sphere of divine and loving transcendence that liberates, or rather heals, the consciousness from the illusion of the ego in the name of a loving God: before you, I am, like everyone else, ideally nothing but an eternally open vessel of active brotherly love. Rand's experiences, on the other hand, inclined toward securing unconditional dignity by bestowing upon the desiring ego a practically godlike sovereignty and inviolability: like every other free-born person, I am ideally a whole world and an eternally bubbling source of rational self-love. But for both, and with equal clarity, the truly infernal scenario is handing over responsibility for the origins and guarantees wholesale to other people, even to all other people.

Hence a consciousness that truly loves the world lies in something other than the gaze of other people. For Weil, this is God's love, while for Rand it is godlike self-love. In the Roarkian ideal, as Rand sees it, this consciousness is always completely focused upon the achievement of concrete active goals set by individuals themselves. So, in fact, it thinks as little about itself as it does about other people, and only about what it reasonably seeks to achieve at any given moment. In the best case it advances serene and undisturbed in pure action. It is a consciousness of purely enjoyed delight in existence—and thus describes a state the attainment and stabilization of which is the explicit goal of any of humanity's doctrines of wisdom. The usual depictions of this state show people with a gentle, oblivious smile on their lips.

It is only logical that Rand, a Nietzschean, goes a step further by transforming this smile into a complete and confident laugh and puts it right at the start of her novel—in connection with a completely clarified state of consciousness, inspired by a lake. *The Fountainhead* opens as follows:

> HOWARD ROARK LAUGHED.
>
> He stood naked at the edge of a cliff. The lake lay far below him. A frozen explosion of granite burst in flight to the sky over motionless water. The water seemed immovable, the stone—flowing. The stone had the stillness of one brief moment in battle when thrust meets thrust and the currents are held in a pause more dynamic than motion. The stone glowed, wet with sunrays.
>
> The lake below was only a thin steel ring that cut the rocks in

> half. The rocks went on into the depth, unchanged. They began and ended in the sky. So that the world seemed suspended in space, an island floating on nothing, anchored to the feet of the man on the cliff.[43]

The world as an ego-island—held by nothing but a human being standing on the cliff, ready to leap into a new life. Once it was in place, even with the beginning of 1939, there was no task that Ayn Rand didn't feel up to.

ONE-WAY STREET

Take yourself for granted . . . at least Walter Benjamin hated this (to him) new language from the very first day. But it was no use. In his tiny apartment at 10 rue Dombasle, the unofficial headquarters of the Paris "tribe," they sat together evening after evening, drank tea, played chess, and, yes, taught themselves English. As if adapting the Berlin script from 1932 and 1933 as faithfully as possible, conditions in the French capital were worsening by the month. With the crucial difference that now there was not a single country on the European continent that could be considered safe for fleeing Jews.

Above all, Hitler's Reich had received a further boost in March 1938 with the Anschluss of Austria. The Warsaw government tried to prevent 20,000 Jews from returning to Poland by denying them citizenship in their absence. In France, too, the tightening of residency requirements in May of that year plainly applied to the new movements of refugees. In 1938, a tenth of the four million inhabitants of Paris were foreigners—including around 40,000 fleeing Jews. Echoing the defamations spread by German journalists, the French media held this group responsible for growing tensions in both domestic and foreign policy in their own country. The first waves of arrests and expulsions of refugees began during the spring of the year, leading many to take their own lives in despair. At the same time, in the capital of now-annexed Austria, Adolf Eichmann set up the Central Agency for Jewish Emigration, whose goals and practices would subsequently be extended to other territories in line with the will of the Nazis.[44]

When Hannah Arendt, in a newly written chapter of her Varnhagen book, quoted her heroine as saying, "How horrible it is, always having to legitimize oneself," she was also describing the dark core of her own situation, both psychologically and administratively. Nothing could have been more absurd than the idea of taking oneself simply "for granted" as a German Jew in Paris in 1938.

Encouraged by Benjamin to go back to her unfinished book, Arendt turned her thoughts about Rahel in the two concluding Paris-set chapters of the book to the issue of finding a viable identity under the conditions of a non-Jewish and structurally extremely anti-Semitic majority society. And compared with the early Berlin passages the tone turns caustic, even combative.

THE MOST BASIC LIES

Here Arendt applies the distinction between "pariah" and "parvenu," established by the French sociologist Bernard Lazare (1865–1903), to the analysis of the Varnhagen case. Having been born into a proscribed group, the pariah adopts the position of a social outsider, while parvenus, as social climbers, distinguish themselves by overcoming during their lives the limits and exclusions imposed upon them in the cradle. This was true of Rahel, the daughter of a Jewish banker in the age of German Romanticism, who rose into court circles through a late marriage to the diplomat Karl August Varnhagen von Ense, who had been elevated to the Prussian aristocracy. Finally, by converting to Christianity, she completely shed her Jewish roots.

In Arendt's view this was in the end an impossible obliteration of one's own pariah origins, which could be achieved only at the cost of lasting dissimulation and emotional numbness. The psychological cost of such a total "assimilation to the German host culture" lay in adapting "one's taste, one's life, one's desires completely [to those of others] in a kind of all-denying choice prior to any choice." This represented, in Arendt's words, a "much more generalized lie than simply hypocrisy."[45]

As with the phenomenon of the "second-hander"—which Ayn Rand used with reference to her neighbor Marcella Bannett as the key to her Nietzsche-inspired critique of alienation—the type of the outwardly successful (Jewish) assimilationist became for Arendt the prime example of a thoroughly heteronomous heteronomy (the state of being governed by external forces), which in extremis could penetrate so far into people that they no longer perceived it as such. The more fixed the mask, the greater the blindness to the true sources of the self. For that reason, with reference to the parvenu existence Arendt also spoke of the "great poisoning of all insight and outlook."[46]

If, however, there is even a spark of alertness to one's own "sense of life," in Rand's words, the parvenu will sense or be shocked into awareness because of individual key experiences that "what he has become he never wanted to become, for he could not have wished it."[47]

SALVAGED ASSETS

What in the end saved Rahel from the complete darkening, typical of the parvenu, of her vision of herself and the world was a particular sensitivity that she herself described as her "unspeakable faults."[48] One of these was what she called "too much consideration for the human face."[49]

For Arendt, sensitivity to the demands of the person directly in front of her—instinctive, perhaps, but certainly uncalculatingly—does not only identify the true center of the pariah; in fact the pariah "instinctively discovers human dignity long before Reason has made it the foundation of morality."[50]

As if in an open dialogue with the moral philosophy of Immanuel Kant, Arendt is here laying the foundation of her own ethics of true self-determination in the face of the Other. It is, however, no longer the Kantian "respect for the law within me," but the salvaged spontaneous capacity to be touched by the suffering face of one's immediate neighbor in the orientation of one's own will. *Gratitude,* for the existence of other people in the world, and active *concern,* for their always given vulnerability, are for Arendt the two true sources of our moral life. And it is no coincidence in the concrete context, just as it is no coincidence in terms of philosophical and systematic orientation, that these two predispositions are the very ones that are essentially alien to Ayn Rand's superhuman ideal figure, Howard Roark.

In Arendt's world, a being like Roark perfectly embodies the values of the parvenu. In a passage from the Paris Varnhagen chapters: "He [the parvenu] dares not be grateful because he owes everything to his own powers; he must not be considerate to others because he must esteem himself a kind of superman of efficiency, an especially good and strong and intelligent specimen of humanity, a model for his pariah brethren to follow."[51]

For Arendt's heroine Rahel, on the other hand, nothing is really unified; in the course of her biographical development everything becomes increasingly disunited, misaligned, "in-between," apparently inconsistent and in the most salutary sense hopeless ("I can swear to almighty God that never in my life have I overcome a weakness!"[52]). It is here that her salvation as a "human being" lies, in the darkest situation and the darkest time, her lasting openness to the route of self-knowledge and love of the world. A philosophical way that is especially open to the pariah. Because Rahel's loophole is "the same loophole through which the pariah, precisely because he is an outcast, can see life as a whole, and the very road upon which the pariah can attain to his '*great* love of free existence.' It is offered to the pariah if, though unable to revolt as an individual against the whole of society, he disdains the alternative of becoming a parvenu, and is recompensed for his 'wretched situations' by a 'view of the whole.' That is his sole dignified hope: 'that everything is related; and in truth, everything is good enough. This is the salvage from the *great* bankruptcy of life.'"[53]

TRIBAL ETHICS

The ideas Arendt set out in the Rahel chapters that she wrote in Paris go far beyond "trivialities,"[54] in the sense that outsiders provide a particularly interesting perspective on the dynamics at work in what is supposed to be the center. In fact, she was surreptitiously setting out an ideal of existence, and also an ideal of research, one which was highly political in nature and served as a guide to the whole "Paris tribe": it was her position of complete marginalization and exclusion (psychological, social, professional) that granted her a unique ability to be touched and affected by the external world. In terms of her writing practice, this led to her acting like what Benjamin termed "rag-and-bone men" and "moles." It meant collecting pariah testimonies that offered a way out of the tunnel, testimonies that would allow people in the present day to see how humanity could previously have been led into such darkness. Since, as Benjamin put it in a 1938 letter to his intellectual friend Gershom Scholem, who was in New York for research purposes at the time, "the current epoch, which makes so many things impossible, most certainly does not preclude this: that the right light should fall on precisely those things in the course of the historical rotation of the sun."[55]

Many traces, almost all of them, lead initially to the nineteenth century; these origins needed to be found and brought to light.[56] And not in terms of an academic research interest, but rather those of a shared mission. During these dark months, Benjamin went on working intensively on essays about Kafka and Baudelaire, and on his big project devoted to the emergence of the Paris shopping arcades; Blücher, the string-puller, was talking to his people about ways of rescuing Marx and Engels, who had been kidnapped by the parvenus; Arendt worked on her Rahel and the multiply distorted history of Jewish assimilation—and hence not least a kind of prehistory of Zionism as a political movement.

This shared tribal ethos yielded a good number of precise maxims for everyday practice; for example: Take sides unconditionally, but don't belong entirely to any side, whether communist or Zionist. It was imperative that the acknowledged impossibility of "rebelling against death as an individual" must not lead to a willingness to submit one's own independence of thought to the diktat of a subjugating "party logic."

No end justifies a means where that means will inevitably, when put into practice, defeat the end. And what ultimately was the goal of political action if not the preservation of the mature and independent spontaneity of one's own thought? So instead of identifying as a party or a special group, the "Paris tribe" presented itself as a close circle of friends, whose members cultivated their increasing marginalization rather than lamenting it. A circle, what was more, whose sustaining binding forces were based not so much on innate affinities as on promises delivered, and primarily the promise—the only way in times of greatest darkness—of shaping one's own future.

There was no shortage of purely external existential constraints. Just as there was no cause to romanticize the increasing fragmentation of their own existence. "Ultimately, the much-vaunted freedom of the excluded towards society is seldom more than the entirely free right to despair."[57] No human being can live or even think freely without some kind of environment to provide security. And in 1938, even in France, that environment was being dismantled piece by piece. Since the Youth Aliyah had moved its headquarters from Paris to London, Arendt had been threatened with the loss of her job. The triangle of work, residency, and identification papers necessary for survival was tightening with each new law. Anyone who showed up for work with expired papers risked expulsion from the country. The same was true of those who refused to show their papers, and who were apprehended. Above all for volatile existences such as those of Blücher and Benjamin, with their special legitimation papers of "*réfugiés provenants d'Allemagne*" (refugees from Germany), this was an almost daily worry.

And it was hardly as if they could dare to leave the country. But Benjamin did so in the summer of 1938, in response to an invitation from Bertolt Brecht to come and delight him in his Danish exile with his chess-playing skills, honed in the company of Hannah Arendt.

Arendt occasionally risked traveling to Geneva to see her old family friend Martha Mundt, not least with a view to bringing her mother, who by now felt very ill at ease in Königsberg, to Paris.

With the failure of a two-state solution proposed by the British (with Jerusalem remaining part of the British protectorate), the situation in Palestine had distinctly worsened, and was heading straight for a kind of civil war between Jews and Arabs. "Concerning the Jews," Arendt wrote from Geneva to her Stups in Paris on October 22, 1938, "I am extremely worried about Jerusalem and in general. It can get one *so* down that one could almost become happy again."[58] Rahel's voice, Arendt's personality. Its fundamentally life-affirming quality could not be brought down by anything or anyone. A happy accident of natural spontaneity.

ABNORMAL DEPENDENCY

Meanwhile, different constitutions—like that of housemate "Benji," for example—struggled to maintain an even keel. On February 4, 1939, he wrote to his friend Scholem in Jerusalem: "A period of severe depression accompanied the onset of winter, and all I can say about the depression is *je ne l'ai pas volé* [I didn't steal it]. A number of things coincided. First of all, I was confronted by the fact that my room is practically useless for working in winter. In summer, I have the option of opening the windows and countering the racket the elevator makes with the din of Paris street noises; not so on cold winter days."[59]

There were also annoyances in far-off New York with Adorno and Horkheimer of the Institute of Social Research, his last paying employers. Still, work had to go on, which wasn't easy, "since the isolation in which I live and especially work here creates an abnormal dependency on the reception my work encounters."[60]

Finally, in June 1939, Scholem was left with no option but to tell his friend of a "boundless gloom and paralysis" in his emotional state: "It is impossible *not* to reflect on our situation, and by 'our' I am not only referring to us Palestinians. The horrifying catastrophe that Jewry has gone through these last six months, and whose dimensions nobody is really able to grasp, this utter hopelessness in a situation in which hopes are invented only to mock us (like the shameful 'project' of sending the Jews to 'colonize' British Guiana), all of these things descend on you sooner or later and brush away any brightness of spirit. . . . To me, the debasement of Palestine to the arena of a civil war is in the end no more than one lost opportunity among many. . . . The chance of salvaging a viable Palestinian settlement[61] over the course of the next world war is being endangered just as much by us as by the Arabs and the English. Abominable things occur from among our ranks as well, and I shudder when I try to consider what the sole consequence might be. We are living in terror: the capitulation of the English in the face of this terror leads the fools among us to believe that terror is the only weapon with which we, too, can achieve something, notwithstanding our special conditions."[62]

For Scholem, the only ray of light during those months was the book that Hannah Arendt had sent him "on Rahel." He was "*very* pleased" with it, and it struck him as "a superb analysis of what took place then and shows that a relationship based on fraud, such as the German Jews had with Germanness, could not end without misfortune. . . . Pity, I don't see how the book will ever find a publisher."[63]

If they could not know that their own lives were safe, at least they could know that their writings were. Following Benjamin's example over many years, Arendt had also sent her Rahel manuscript[64] to Scholem the archivist—probably with the unspoken hope that he might manage to see it through to publication from Palestine. Not a chance. There, too, pure questions of survival dominated everyday life and thought.

In what Benjamin complained was also a "particularly cold spring" in meteorological terms, the hope for a future "free life" could mean only putting as much salt water as possible between oneself and old Europe. But there, too, all hope of solutions for the foreseeable future appeared to be blocked. If one was not invited specially to America by a university or a similar institution, the waiting time for a U.S. visa was "four to five years." An unimaginably long time for people who could not, in fact, predict what the coming four months or even four weeks held for them.

Still, that spring Blücher and Arendt had finally found an apartment to share—one to which Arendt's mother, Martha Beerwald, who had fled Königsberg in April 1939, moved as well—probably not to Blücher's, or even to Arendt's, total delight. What was left? There are moral duties that go far beyond promises freely given. And the duties to her mother, at least for Arendt, were unquestionably among them.

NO FUTURE

"All that year," Simone de Beauvoir recalled, "I had gone on trying to live exclusively in the present, to grasp each flying minute."[65] But with the spring of 1939, this attitude had reached its limit. Particularly since Sartre and Beauvoir's emotional life was at this point assuming a form that rivaled the geopolitical situation in complexity. After three shared years in Paris, the triangular arrangement of Sartre–

Beauvoir–Olga had turned into a series of overlapping polygons. According to her delicately balanced timetables, Beauvoir was cultivating, alongside her relationship with Sartre, liaisons with Olga (who was at this time engaged to "Little Bost"), Little Bost (although Olga was under no circumstances to know about that), and a pupil from her previous year's *baccalauréat* class, eighteen-year-old Bianca Bienenfeld (with whom Sartre had also been in a relationship since early 1939). Sartre was also in a serious relationship with Olga's younger sister Wanda (which Sartre consistently denied in the face of all the other relationships). Beauvoir (and Sartre) were also beginning another relationship with a former pupil named Natalie Sorokin. And those were only their serious liaisons.

Entirely in line with the pact they had made ten years before, in their letters Beauvoir and Sartre spared each other no details, however humiliating, about their love affairs. Beauvoir's life-defining urge "to enjoy every moment" in the face of a gloomy future, without ever putting herself at risk in any true sense as a human being, had in other words produced an everyday network of asymmetrical relationships and dependencies that eluded any kind of benevolent description.[66]

Perhaps this situation contains what elevates truly literary people above the great mass of scribblers: the will, purged of all ethical dimensions, to place all experiences, all relationships, all adventures at the service of a possible fictionalization. To instrumentalize them into pure devices for one's actual purpose in life.

Sartre had never been one to moralize about his own existence. Beauvoir saw things a little differently. She was increasingly troubled, above all, by the triangle of lies that she was maintaining with Olga and Little Bost.[67] At first that had less to do with purely ethical concerns about Olga than it did with Beauvoir's deep and particularly sexual passion for Little Bost, whom she reassured at this time in letter after letter: "I have only *one* sensual life, and that is with you."[68] With Sartre, she went on, she still had physical relations, "but very little, and it is mostly out of tenderness and—I'm not sure how to say this—I don't feel that engaged because he is not that engaged in it himself."[69]

In the spring of 1939, Bost had been called up for military service. At the outbreak of war, Sartre was also mobilized. If Beauvoir thought about this now apparently inevitable war, it was because it threatened to rob her life of both its intellectual and its sensual core. Who would she be then? Who or what would keep her in the world?

When she boarded the train for Amiens on July 6, 1939, to visit Bost, who was stationed there, she wrote Sartre a series of letters that give a representative picture of her life at the time:

> 6 July 1939
>
> My dear little creature,
>
> At the Flore I met a very nervy Kos. [Olga], who'd just seen off Wanda. We went for a stroll and . . . talked about our relationship, with which she declared she was absolutely delighted. . . .
>
> I'm in the dumps. I haven't had enough sleep these last few days and I'm worn out. Also, I've received a first tax demand—without allowances—and the amount really is 2,400 F. And yesterday Kos. asked me unexpectedly for 300 F—for debts and rent . . . Kos. talked to me at length about Bost, and though I don't feel any remorse so far as she's concerned, I do have a sense of superficiality and guile, that will melt away when I see Bost, but that deprives me of all pleasure in leaving.[70]

And two days later, from Amiens:

> 8 July 1939
>
> . . . At 11 o'clock Bost had to put his uniform back on, I walked him to the barracks and went home. He was very nice, but deeply dejected, and I was a bit too; it just feels very abrupt, you can't really talk or be with the person, and at the same time it's the last few hours of the visit, it goes nowhere, and that leaves you gloomily apathetic.[71]

PREPARED FOR BATTLE

A fragmented life, last hours, gloomy indifference—the mood of an entire nation. Meanwhile, for Beauvoir—and her letters show this very clearly—the gaze into the abyss that summer was also in some respects a salutary one. She had never worked so hard, never moved so closely to the ideal of her own writing. For months she had been working, as if possessed, on a novel that was to amount to the sum of her intellectual journey so far. At Sartre's instigation, it stayed close to her own lived experiences. At the philosophical core of the work, however, lay the tension that Beauvoir had confided to her diary at the age of nineteen as the key question that preoccupied her: "the opposition of self and other."[72]

Everything in the situation of their lives refers to this. Not only that she and Sartre were experimenting with the tension between perfect acceptance and cold rejection. According to Beauvoir, the two central illnesses of any evolving consciousness were concentrated, in a uniquely clear way, in the amorphous figure of a looming war: on the one hand, knowledge of one's own finitude, and on the other, knowledge of the existence of other consciousnesses: "Like death, which we discuss without ever having actually faced it," Beauvoir would recall, "so rational awareness in other people [*la conscience d'autrui*] remained for me a mere hypothesis; when I came to realize its actuality, I felt that I was at grips with as shocking and unacceptable a fact as death. Absurdly enough, this one could complement the other; by depriving the other of life, he lost all power over the world and me."[73]

The extermination of the Other to preserve what was supposedly one's own. Politically, this meant the will to war. In a private context, however, it meant the will to murder. And herein lay the main plot of a philosophical bildungsroman of a very particular kind. Beauvoir had been working on it since 1938 with an unfamiliar inner fire: "At last I was embarked on a book with the firm conviction not only that I would finish it, but also that it would find a publisher."[74]

EQUALS

Originally, the victim of the perfect murder was supposed be a fictional version of Simone Weil—in Beauvoir's intellectual world so far Weil had been the "great Other." "Because of the awed admiration she inspired in me at a distance, I had thought of using Simone Weil as a model for the protagonist I set up against me."[75] But here, too, Sartre provided a crucial cue. Olga, he argued, was much better suited as the intolerably other consciousness within the context of the plot; indeed, she was almost typologically perfect: younger, more closed, moodier, more stubborn, more egocentric.[76]

Following the triangular arrangement around Olga, which she had enjoyed and endured with equal intensity, Beauvoir would depict the struggle of her consciousness for authenticity and hence pour the subject of her philosophical life's work into the form of a novel. And just as Ayn Rand could proudly state that she herself had been the object of her psychological research for her hero Howard Roark, Beauvoir's heroine, the dramaturge and rising author Françoise, was based on her own psychic image. In the novel Olga becomes the student actress Xavière, and Sartre the brilliant theatrical director Pierre, while the scene is finally moved from Rouen to the artistic milieu of Paris bars in 1938. The guiding plan was completely theoretical, while its concrete decor was entirely realistic. Excellent premises in themselves. In particular, the philosophical aspects of the arrangement of tensions were clearly present in Beauvoir's mind. It would be a typology of three different ways in which a consciousness faced up to the obvious reality of other consciousnesses.

According to this plan, the heroine Françoise (Beauvoir) embodied the type of immaculate consciousness: "Françoise . . . regarded herself as conscious mind *et praeterea nihil* [without substance], the only such in existence; she had allowed Pierre to share her sovereign position, and now they both stood together at the centre of a world which it was her compelling mission in life to explore and reveal."[77]

This consciousness sees itself as absolutely pure in three respects. First, it is not sullied, transfigured, or otherwise unsettled by the influence of other consciousnesses. Second, it is pure in its effort to reveal the world as it presents and displays itself. Third, it is also pure in the sense that this consciousness proceeds not primarily by evaluation, but rather by description—above all while deliberately eschewing anything that is normally called subjectivity: "She was an utterly transparent creature, without features of individuality."[78] Against the background of her many years of studying Husserl, Beauvoir presents her Françoise in other words as the exemplary embodiment of a consciousness that is purely phenomenological and hence in the best sense open to experience, which seeks and finds its actual center of meaning not in itself, but in the world. Here phenomenology becomes psychology, abstract epistemology secretly a concrete character study.

Xavière's (Olga's) consciousness is conceived as the exact opposite of Françoise. Rather than being open to the world and neutral, it remains closed in on itself and egocentric. Rather than being constantly joyful and enjoying life, it is decidedly moody and hesitant. Rather than being focused and loving truth, it is butterfly-like and prejudiced. "In Xavière I wanted to portray the opacity of a human mind turned in upon itself."[79] At the same time, this stubborn closure in Xavière's case goes hand in hand with an unconquerably resistant person whose outline is clearly defined. In philosophical terms her consciousness embodies the attitude of an anxiety-driven skepticism that refuses to know and above all to acknowledge any access to the world apart from its own.

The third figure in the tableau, Elisabeth occupies the position of a consciousness deeply determined by others—in the book she is introduced as Pierre's sister and a dilettante painter.[80] Not unlike Hannah Arendt's presentation of Rahel Varnhagen as a parvenue yearning for recognition, Elisabeth, although, in the words of her creator, "ultimately she went hunting after emotions and beliefs, . . . felt she could hold none of them permanently: she reproached herself for this disability of hers, and her self-contempt spread devastatingly outward till it embraced the whole world. . . . That universal truth—indeed, the very essence of the universe as we know it—belonged to *other people*—in this case to Pierre and Françoise."[81] Elisabeth knows that she herself is really too strange ever to be able to fully recognize and acknowledge herself. Only others can perform that feat for her. Her actual misfortune consists of precisely that knowledge.

Like three balls on a billiard table without holes, Beauvoir sends these three characters bouncing off against each other in turn—with Pierre (Sartre) effectively the untouchable black eight ball in the game, the actual trigger and prize of the collisions.

WAR OF THE WORLDS

Over its 450 pages, the novel *She Came to Stay* unfolds as a continuing dialogue variation on a single theme: the question of the conditions for the possibility of true self-discovery in the face of the Other. A representative extract:

> "May I read your book some day?" Xavière asked with a coquettish pout.
>
> "Of course," said Françoise. "I'll show you the first chapters whenever you like."
>
> "What's it about?" . . .
>
> "It's about my youth," said Françoise. "I want to explain in my story why people are so often misfits when they're young."
>
> "Do you think young people are misfits?"
>
> "Not you," said Françoise. "You're a superior soul." She thought a moment.
>
> "You see, when you're a child, you very easily resign yourself to being regarded as of little account, but at seventeen things change. You begin to want to have a definite existence, and since you still feel the same inside yourself, you foolishly have recourse to external guarantees."
>
> "How do you do that?" asked Xavière.
>
> "You seek the approbation of others, you write down your

thoughts, you compare yourself with accepted models. Now, take Elisabeth," said Françoise, "in a sense, she has never passed that stage. She's a perennial adolescent. . . . Elisabeth annoys us because she listens slavishly to Pierre and me, because she's constantly remodelling herself. But if you study her with a little sympathy you'll perceive in all that a clumsy attempt to give a definite value to her life and to herself as a person. Even her respect for the social formulas—marriage, fame—is still a form of this anxiety."

Xavière's face clouded slightly. "Elisabeth is a vain, pathetic jellyfish," she said. "That's all."

"No, that isn't precisely all," said Françoise. "You still have to understand the cause of it."

Xavière shrugged her shoulders.

"What's the good of trying to understand people who aren't worth it?"

Françoise repressed a movement of impatience. Xavière was affronted as soon as anyone but herself was spoken of indulgently or even fairly.

"In a way, no one is worth it," she said to Xavière.[82]

Françoise is the consciousness of pure, benevolent understanding, Xavière a narcissistically encapsulated consciousness based on proactive self-assertion, and Elisabeth a consciousness of knowing inauthenticity, impelled by false desires for the approbation of others. Each observes and keeps watch on the others, each becomes an open question and a painful annoyance to the others. An infernal triangle of dramatic density that makes an amicable outcome impossible, particularly from Françoise's point of view.[83]

Deeply unsettled by Xavière's desires, rivalry, and fundamental difference, Françoise loses her state of pure consciousness over the course of the plot, and is forced to acknowledge the actual emptiness in herself. Soon she sees herself facing a situation that Beauvoir, as the author, describes as follows: "Now another danger threatened her, one which I myself had been endeavouring to exorcize ever since my adolescence. Other people [*autrui*] could not only steal the world from her, but also invade her personality and bewitch it. Xavière, with her outbursts of temper and spitefulness, was disfiguring Françoise's inner self."[84]

As examples of every different consciousness on the way to becoming itself, the heroes of the novel on the eve of the great conflagration play out their very own "war of the worlds."[85] This, too, is a war that, in its own way, may reach an end only with the total extermination of the Other.

THE NEW SITUATION

The fact that Simone de Beauvoir, in her thirtieth year, did not see herself as having adequate intellectual moorings does not mean, however, that her personal struggles for recognition had reached their conclusion. On the contrary. With the publication of *Nausea* (previously *Melancholia*) in the spring of 1938, Sartre had become the new shooting star of French literature, whose work and style enthusiastic critics placed on a par with Kafka. At the same time, Beauvoir's novel was definitively rejected by editors at both Gallimard and Grasset. Deeply insulted, Sartre forbade her to go on sending out the manuscript.

While he now had what might be called a name, she remained a literary nobody, and risked being reduced to the "woman by the author's side" on the literary scene—the template was ready and waiting. By this point, the struggle between self and Other, examined in microscopic detail by Beauvoir, would have been obvious as a defining tension between the two gender roles. Was the starting point with which a man engaged in the dialogical play of self-discovery not already fundamentally different from that of a woman? Does the woman not see herself as a pariah from the outset in this struggle for recognition?

Just as Hannah Arendt, in her ongoing research into Rahel at the same time, maintains that a Jewish woman can really assimilate only under the conditions of an all-too-real social anti-Semitism—if she also assimilates to its anti-Semitism—Beauvoir saw that any conscious assimilation of a female consciousness to social roles that devalue women a priori necessarily meant also internalizing their misogyny.

Rather than "woman" and "man" meeting as equals in the diagram of "I" and "Other," an openly subordinate Otherness was already established. This was the role of the *deuxième sexe*, the second or indeed "other" sex. It would take Beauvoir another ten years as well as the experience of another world war to develop this idea, which had the potential to decipher society itself. Then she would emerge once and for all from Sartre's shadow as a thinker.[86]

She already had the intellectual tools required to decipher the specifically feminine situation in 1938–1939. But her guiding question at that time was quite clearly not yet what it might and could mean to be "a woman," but what it meant to be only this woman, the woman she was herself.

IN THE FACE OF FEAR

Still, over the previous ten years of her adult life, in the face of all resistance from her family, Beauvoir had been able to escape the predominant role of the caring wife/mother. Without submitting to the prevailing logics of desire, she had deliberately pursued the strategy of someone in between, someone always ready for pleasure. Here the "only necessary relationship" with Sartre, characterized by a life of polyamorous bisexuality, was proof of the possibility of a radically different way of living. At the same time, Beauvoir's attitude toward her female lovers during this period can be seen as sharing the attitude and approach that Sartre had toward his countless affairs. Beauvoir's approach seems to be dominance that is free of both enjoyment and empathy: venial little games for the satisfaction of her own ego—without a deeper concern for the consequences of her own actions in the consciousness of others.

While Sartre in his letters to Beauvoir praises himself as a "consummate fumbler," and in this role speaks of "droplet-shaped buttocks" or the astonishing willingness of his latest conquests to engage in "intimate kissing," Beauvoir likes to stress how indifferent, pleasureless, and even disturbing her dalliances with former pupils are—all the way to specific complaints about the unpleasant smell of feces she noticed during intercourse with her conquests. Beauvoir spoke about her lovers to Sartre from "man to man," as subject about objects. She had at least internally accomplished that form of assimilation.

The crucial ethical step from care for the self to care for the Other was plainly more difficult temperamentally for Beauvoir than it was for others.

However, the concrete threat of war empowered her in this respect. Particularly since at this time Beauvoir's continuing project of "integrating philosophical ideas into her own life" was given crucial new motivation. During the spring of 1939, she and Sartre engaged in an intensive study of the writings of Husserl's student Martin Heidegger, particularly his work *Being and Time*.

Following the methodical instincts of his teacher, in this work Heidegger engaged in a comprehensive analysis of human existence.

Thrown into the world without ground or support, in Heidegger's view, human existence must apply itself to the task of grasping itself as resolutely as possible in the ever-present foreknowledge of the looming nothingness of death. A philosophical call to courageously lived authenticity, then, that found particularly fertile ground in Sartre and Beauvoir. Against the constantly inauthentic diktat of the great anonymous "*man*" (the pronoun "one"), Heidegger introduces the vague mood of anxiety—particularly the anxiety of death—as a foundation of true resolve. According to Heidegger, the tense calm before the storm, the almost unbearable boredom of an almost total lack of event, are the triggers of existential determination.

Another letter from Beauvoir to Sartre, written during the days of her visit to Bost, stuck in his barracks in Amiens, clearly reveals Heidegger's influence on her sense of the world.

> 7 July 1939
>
> . . . I spent the whole day in a dreary café waiting for Little Bost, who never showed up. . . . It turned out that wait of several hours yesterday constituted excellent circumstances for reading Heidegger, whom I've almost finished and managed to understand—at least superficially. In other words, I know what he means but can't check out the difficulties, though I'm aware of heaps of them. What's more, I'm so ruthless at present that I don't regret a day like yesterday, extremely disagreeable as it was in every respect, for it provides me with a standard day highly suitable for use in a novel.[87]

The fear of boredom, the fear of death, the fear of the distorting power of others, as well as the courage to find and cultivate one's own voice that springs from it. All these things came together that summer and, in Beauvoir's hands, after many years of fumbling experimentation, were shaped into a work.

Sartre and Beauvoir spent August with friends at a beach house on the Côte d'Azur. Time itself seemed to hold its breath. Sartre taught Beauvoir how to swim. By the end of August, they were back together in an almost deserted capital. Sartre summed up his impressions thus: "Paris was strange. Everything was shut. Restaurants, theaters, shops . . . and the districts had lost their individual faces. All that was left was a totality, which was Paris. A totality that was already *the past* for me and also, as Heidegger says, held together by nothingness."[88]

With nothingness right in front of his eyes, Sartre, too, found new resolution. Over dinner he suggested to Beauvoir that they should definitively consolidate "forever" the pact they had tentatively agreed on ten years previously. They would never part, they would stay together forever—a philosophical marriage in the face of death.

On September 1, 1939, the Wehrmacht attacked Poland. Two days later France, too, was at war.

VI

VIOLENCE: 1939–1940

Weil without enemies, Beauvoir without Sartre, Arendt on the run, and Rand in the resistance.

A RELENTLESS SPECTACLE

The conflict between two enormous armies, each numbering in the millions, was initially combat-free—and free of victims. Entrenched behind the lines, the French waited for the charge of the Wehrmacht. Days of tension turned into weeks, soon into months. Simone Weil lived through that "*drôle de guerre*" (phony war) in her parents' Paris apartment. In November 1939, an article in a medical journal gave her father Biri the idea that his daughter's years of suffering might be the result of a displaced case of sinusitis. All the symptoms agreed with that diagnosis. As therapy it was recommended that the chronically inflamed frontal sinus be treated with a cocaine rinse. Without entirely relieving the pain, the measure appeared to have some effect.[1] A positive development at least.

Waiting for the expected excess of violence, Weil wanted to establish the nature of its consequences for her country: Wherein lies the essence of a war? On what dynamics is it based? And not least: Under which conditions might it be justly fought? To this end, she consulted what she took to be both the greatest and the most generous testimony of war in Western history. In the winter months of 1939–1940, she produced, under the title "The Iliad, or the Poem of Force," a meditation on the nature of the violence of war that is one of the most profound philosophical documents of the era.[2]

First of all, according to Weil, the particular aspect of the situation of war consists in its limitless relationship with violence, which leads to an objectification of human beings, because: "To define force—it is that *x* that turns anybody who is subjected to it into a *thing*. Exercised to the limit, it turns man into a thing in the most literal sense: it makes a corpse out of him. Somebody was here, and the next minute there is nobody here at all; this is a spectacle the *Iliad* never wearies of showing us."[3]

In fact, however, as the *Iliad* insistently tells us, the logic of this objectification has much greater and more devastating effects. Like a philosophical daily commentary on the phony war between France and Germany, Weil's essay emphasizes the overlooked effects of the war situation in the consciousness of all those involved:

> Here we see force in its grossest and most summary form—the force that kills. How much more varied in its processes, how much more surprising in its effects is the other force, the force that does *not* kill, i.e., that does not kill just yet. It will surely kill, it will possibly kill, or perhaps it merely hangs, poised and ready, over the head of the creature that it *can* kill, at any moment, which is to say at every moment. In whatever aspect, its effect is the same: it turns a man into a stone. From its first property (the ability to turn a human being into a thing by the simple method of killing him) flows another, quite prodigious too in its own way, the ability to turn a human being into a thing while he is still alive. He is alive; he has a soul, and yet—he is a thing. An extraordinary entity this—a thing that has a soul.[4]

War thus creates an entirely new state of existence, robbing human beings of what it is that actually makes them human and guides them: openness, plasticity, the living quality of their souls in the face of the Other. With a view of the Greek world of war, Weil also grasps this "curious state" in which an animate Other is perceived and treated only as a thing, as a state of "slavery." If the usual consequence of a lost war was enslavement by the victors—particularly those who had not actually taken part in the events of the conflict, such as women and children—the state of enslavement is like "death but death strung out over a whole lifetime; here, surely is life, but life that death congeals before abolishing."[5] War as a shared situation effectively "enslaves" everyone, since in every individual it represents a fundamental shift with regard to the "Other" as a declared "enemy."

KNOW THYSELF!

As a convinced patriot, Weil stressed her country's obligation, precisely in a situation of defensive war, not to blind itself to the oppressive and slave-like relationships that it had created and that it still maintained as a colonial power around the world. On November 25, 1939, the writer Jean Giraudoux, recently appointed commissioner general of information, published an article in *Le temps* in which he spoke of the "110 million men" throughout the world "attached to [France's] metropolitan center by ties that are not those of subordination and exploitation." Weil could contain herself no longer. The same day she wrote a furious letter of protest: "There is a passage . . . that caused me acute pain. I wish with all my heart that I could persuade you to ask yourself if it is so when you assert that France's colonial dominions are not bound to her by ties of subordination and exploitation."[6]

Particularly in time of war, the philosophical imperative of "Know thyself!" had to be observed. Because what inevitably goes hand in hand with the "petrification of souls" is an increasing blindness to the consequences of one's own violent actions. In this context, Weil recognized the potentially world-healing value of the *Iliad*. Its entire representational intention was designed to heal those who had fallen in war from that specific blindness.

> Force is as pitiless to the man who possesses it, or thinks he does, as it is to its victims; the second it crushes, the first it intoxicates. The truth is, nobody really possesses it. The human race is not divided up, in the *Iliad*, into conquered persons, slaves, suppliants, on the one hand, and conquerors and chiefs on the other. In this poem there is not a single man who does not at one time or another have to bow his neck to force. The common soldier in the *Iliad* is free and has the right to bear arms; nevertheless he is subject to the indignity of orders and abuse.[7]

> Perhaps all men, by the very act of being born, are destined to suffer violence; yet this is a truth to which circumstance shuts men's eyes.[8]

The actual goal of an "enlightenment" thus cannot lie in removing force from the world. Not even as warlike violence. Because an absolutely nonviolent coexistence could succeed only if there were no longer any differences in power in the social relations between people. And that state in turn would be one that could be created and maintained, if at all, only with extreme, indeed total, social force. No, if it happened, it would have to be based on liberation from blindness to the conditions and consequences of one's own actions in war. But also, it would require liberation from historical coincidences, in which one finds oneself as either an inflictor or a victim of violence. Only when one's eyes are opened to it can there be a measure and a sense of fellow feeling that points the way out of the spiral of death and killing, because "only he who has measured the dominion of force, and knows how not to respect it, is capable of love and justice."[9]

GEOMETRY OF CHANCE

As the state of war became a reality, a suspicion appeared in which the slightest irritation, however small, could trigger a murderous response. Precisely because in a life-and-death situation nothing and nobody wants to be subject to the power of chance, an extreme excess of power unfolds and becomes the actual ruler of events. While she refined her text, Weil was soon able to report on this paradoxical distortion from her own experience.

When the Soviet Union invaded Finland on November 30, 1939, Weil's brother, André, a professor of mathematics at the University of Strasbourg, was on a research year in Helsinki with his wife. Strolling through the city, he walked past a building that housed Finnish artillery, and was arrested and interrogated. Because of his origins, he was held on suspicion of espionage. When a search of his apartment uncovered extensive correspondence with Russian colleagues, the Finnish security services became further convinced of their assumptions. It didn't help that they also found documents that appeared to be written in a strange code. In fact, these were his wife's shorthand exercises: in the evening André read passages from Balzac's novel *La cousine Bette* to her for transcription practice. To the Finns this was hardly a credible story. He was lucky not to be executed on the spot. Instead, after further investigations, André was put on a boat to Sweden accompanied by two police officers; there he was arrested again and interned. It was the start of a lengthy extradition process in which Simone supported him the best she could from Paris, writing numerous letters in a secret code the two of them devised.[10]

At the same time, the German army was gradually changing its plans for an attack on France (code name Fall Gelb, or Case Yellow). The chief reason for this was a misfortune that occurred on January 10, 1940, when a German courier aircraft on its way from Münster to Cologne got lost in the fog and was forced to make an emergency landing in Maasmechelen, Belgium. A chance passenger, one Helmuth Reinberger, did not have time to destroy the documents on board. As a result, the plans for the German attack were in enemy hands and the army was forced to come up with a completely new strategy. Hitler opted for Operation Sichelschnitt, or "Sickle Cut," the brainchild of Erich von Manstein.

Born purely out of chance, the operation would help boost the propaganda that Hitler was "the greatest field marshal in history" as the war progressed, not least in the eyes of his closest advisers.[11] Had the notion of "clairvoyance," so frequently cited by the Führer himself, not been involved here? As had happened in earlier times to the mythical "blind seer" Homer, the presumed author of the *Iliad*, early in 1940, Simone Weil's gaze became prophetically keen. She saw that chance would eventually catch up with the "greatest" leaders, the ones who saw themselves as absolutely in control:

> The man who is the possessor of force seems to walk through a non-resistant element; in the human substance that surrounds him nothing has the power to interpose, between the impulse and the act, the tiny interval that is reflection. Where there is no room

> for reflection, there is none either for justice or prudence. . . . Since other people do not impose on their movements that halt, that interval of hesitation, wherein lies all our consideration for our brothers in humanity, they conclude that destiny has given complete license to them, and none at all to their inferiors. . . . This retribution, which has a geometrical rigor, which operates automatically to penalize the abuse of force, was the main subject of Greek thought. It is the soul of the epic.[12]

Once gripped by the fire of warlike violence, without anyone to contradict them, the victorious powers lost all circumspection, and finally any understanding of their vulnerability and the fallibility of their own actions. It is under the banner of chance, on which all things depend, that a total leader paves the way for his own downfall. This course of events is not due to divine intervention, but derives from the nature of violence itself, even in Homer. More than anything else it requires moderation, and more than anything else, precisely in wartime, it leads to its opposite. The more fundamentally a warlord misunderstands himself because of the huge amount of power and control at his disposal, the more certain it is that he himself will be consumed by the essence of violence and ultimately toppled.

For that reason, the question that Weil needed to answer even before any fighting had taken place was whether and if so how her own nation could escape feeling soulless and, hence, in a crucial sense defeated during the war. Anyone who read the *Iliad* properly understood it would take nothing less than an actual miracle, or at least a superhuman effort. "A moderate use of force, which alone would enable man to escape being enmeshed in its machinery, would require superhuman virtue, which is as rare as dignity in weakness. Moreover, moderation itself is not without its perils, since prestige, from which force derives at least three quarters of its strength, rests principally upon that marvelous indifference that the strong feel toward the weak, an indifference so contagious that it infects the very people who are the objects of it. Yet ordinarily excess is not arrived at through prudence or politic considerations. On the contrary, man dashes to it as an irresistible temptation."[13]

DEATH AND TIME

In the face of death, remaining moderate is superhuman. In a direct inversion of Heidegger's ideas in *Being and Time,* which had simultaneously granted Simone de Beauvoir and Jean-Paul Sartre a new understanding of freedom and authenticity, Weil saw the greatest seduction of war, and the fear of death that it entailed, as releasing a kind of existentialism of ruthlessness in the soul of every individual. With the tangible prospect of one's own death, one loses any perspective for the shape of a future beyond the war. While Heidegger elevated the fearful "Dasein's running ahead into its being bygone" ("Vorlaufen des Daseins zu seinem Vorbei"[14]) to a condition of true self-understanding, Weil sees that as the sure path toward an all-extinguishing self-misapprehension. This is given exemplary form in the relationship between the consciousness of a soldier and the phenomenon of time as future:

> Once you acknowledge death to be a practical possibility, the thought of it becomes unendurable, except in flashes. True enough, all men are fated to die; true enough also, a soldier may grow old in battles, yet for those whose spirits have bent under the yoke of war, the relation between death and the future is different. . . . For

> other men death appears as a limit set in advance on the future; for the soldier death is the future, the future his profession assigns him. Yet the idea of man's having death for a future is abhorrent to nature. . . . The mind is then strung up to a pitch it can stand for only a short time; but each new dawn reintroduces the same necessity, and days piled on days make years. On each one of these days the soul suffers violence. Regularly, every morning, the soul castrates itself of aspiration, for thought cannot journey through time without meeting death on the way. Thus war effaces all conceptions of purpose or goal, including even its own "war aims."[15]

Trapped in the eternal present of the constant imminence of death, the consciousness is numbed to the idea of a future "beyond" war. And so the consciousness helps make the experience of war more spectrally unreal, leading to an ever greater dehumanization of those who are killed day after day in pursuit of war's so-called goals, to the point where the act of killing ceases to be a means to an end and instead becomes an end in itself. Nothing can stop that spiral apart from death itself. "If the existence of an enemy has made a soul destroy in itself the thing nature put there, then the only remedy the soul can imagine is the destruction of the enemy. . . . The man possessed by this twofold need for death belongs, so long as he has not become something still different, to a different race from the race of the living."[16]

UNIQUE SENSITIVITY

It is thus the dehumanization produced by the essence of violence that gives war its actual terror, as well as its soon apparently inescapable pointlessness. This process is mutually reinforcing. None of the parties involved can be spared this dynamic—neither victors nor losers, perpetrators nor victims, heroes nor the innocently subjugated.

> And both, at the touch of force, experience its inevitable effects: they become deaf and dumb. Such is the nature of force. Its power of converting a man into a thing is a double one, and in its application double-edged. To the same degree, though in different fashions, those who use it and those who endure it are turned to stone. . . .
>
> But however caused, this petrifactive quality of force, twofold always, is essential to its nature; and a soul which has entered the province of force will not escape this except by a miracle. Such miracles are rare and of brief duration.[17]

And yet, in Weil's view, humanity's history has multiple testimonies of this miracle, the leap to a higher level, breaking out of darkness into light. Be it in the form of concrete individuals and the founders or objects of religions—like the Buddha, Krishna, Socrates, or Jesus—or in the form of culture-bearing texts and epics such as the Bhagavad Gita or the Gospels or, above all, the *Iliad.* Weil sees their overall view of warlike events as inspired by a light of mercy for all beings in war. A love for each individual; the desire for justice and peace for their tormented souls; the revenge-free willingness to be friends with the enemy as well as a shared grief over the dark state of the world into which they have been thrown.

> It is in this that the *Iliad* is absolutely unique, in this bitterness that proceeds from tenderness and that spreads over the whole human race, impartial as sunlight. . . . Justice and love, which have

> hardly any place in this study of extremes and of unjust acts of violence, nevertheless bathe the work in their light without ever becoming noticeable themselves, except as a kind of accent.[18]

> Whoever, within his own soul and in human relations, escapes the dominion of force is loved but loved sorrowfully because of the threat of destruction that constantly hangs over him.[19]

Referring to the oldest epic of that cultural complex that had within a few decades returned for a second time to the dynamic of war, Weil set out the conditions for a future peace that could be more than just the prelude, impelled by blindness and revenge, to yet another war.

Around the time when she was finishing work on the essay, a good five million soldiers, ready for combat, were facing each other at the front lines. They had no doubt about the resolution and the universally dehumanizing end goals of the army. But a victory fought and possibly won in the same spirit, Weil warned her compatriots, would be almost even more humiliating than defeat.

In the end, her country could guard against such a defeat—the only one that would be truly forgivable—solely by bathing in the very light that inspired the *Iliad* itself. For Weil this was synonymous with the light of the Gospels, and with the light with which she herself was filled—as she knew from her own deep experience. Which is why her language at the end of the essay changes, setting the tone for her thought in the coming war years: from sober analysis to prophetic admonition, from this world to another, from pure argument to a call to awakening: "But nothing the peoples of Europe have produced is worth the first known poem that appeared among them. Perhaps they will yet rediscover the epic genius, when they learn that there is no refuge from fate, learn not to admire force, not to hate the enemy, nor to scorn the unfortunate. How soon this will happen is another question."[20]

PARACHUTISTS

Simone Weil's seriousness about her existentialism of mercy is proven by an everyday episode from May 1940. The *drôle de guerre* was in its ninth month. It couldn't go on much longer. When, back home over dinner, she asked what should be done with a young German parachute jumper if he landed right that moment on the balcony of their apartment, her father replied that he should immediately be handed over to the military police. Furious, Simone said that she could no longer sit at the same table as someone who could express such an attitude.

Simone Pétrement, Weil's good friend, who was a guest that evening, at first thought it was a joke.[21] But Weil now actually refused to eat another bite. It was certainly not the first time that she had dramatically used the refusal to eat as a threat—and thus violently exploited her parents' constant concern for her physical well-being. As might have been expected, her father corrected himself, for the sake of the peace of his soul, while still at the table and promised hand on heart not to turn the soldier over to the authorities should such a situation ever arise.

On May 10, 1940, Hitler launched Case Yellow, and set the Wehrmacht in motion in the direction of France. On June 13, Paris was officially abandoned by the French government and declared a "free city" by the victors. A day later the first German troops reached the city. By that point parachutists were no longer needed.

EXODUS

On June 9, 1940, Simone de Beauvoir suffered her first nervous breakdown. The father of Bianca Bienenfeld had learned from senior military circles of the imminent invasion by the Wehrmacht. The next day the family would flee to the west. Summoning the last of her strength, Beauvoir packed a suitcase. Only the barest necessities—including her correspondence with Sartre, which had lasted for ten years. When she got into the car on the evening of June 10, she and the Bienenfelds were in the vanguard of what French people still call "the Exodus." Within a few days, more than three million inhabitants fled the Germans advancing on the center of Paris from the north.

The chaos was inevitable: crammed trains, blocked roads. In provincial towns overwhelmed by the onslaught, gasoline ran out first, followed shortly afterward by food. Once out of the direct line of fire, Beauvoir wanted to carry on westward to La Pouëze, to the country house of an old friend and patron, Madame Morel. Beauvoir got there two days later, "in an extremely sombre state." Those were, she wrote, "among the worst days of my life."[22]

The Maginot Line hadn't survived the assault of Hitler's Wehrmacht for even a week. How was it possible? Betrayal? Sabotage? Or were the Nazis as overwhelming as their propaganda claimed?

Jacques-Laurent Bost, as far as Beauvoir knew, was fighting for his life in a military hospital with an abdominal wound. Sartre's last letter to her was dated June 8: "I no longer hope positively that we will win the war (neither do I think that we will lose it: I don't think anything, the future is closed)."[23]

Was Bost still at the front, or had he already been brought home? "For three days," Beauvoir wrote, "I did nothing but read thrillers and wallow in despair. The village was full of relatives and friends. We listened to every bulletin with feverish intensity. . . . One evening the doorbell rang about nine o'clock: someone had seen parachutists about. . . . The next day we learned that these supposed parachutists had been ordinary weather balloons."[24]

BORDERLINE SITUATION

But what if the Germans did actually arrive? There was no shortage of hideous fantasies in the village. On June 22, with a mixture of disbelief, despair, and hope, Beauvoir heard a report on the radio to the effect that the elderly Marshal Pétain had signed an armistice at Compiègne. "I felt as though I were a character in some futuristic novel: it was still the same familiar village, but time had gone haywire. I had been projected into a moment of time which had no connection with my own life. This was no longer France, not yet Germany, but betwixt and between, a no man's land."[25]

Beauvoir thought she was in a waking nightmare. Six weeks earlier her novel project had been accepted for publication.[26] Just as she and Sartre were sharing the certainty of decisive breakthroughs that spring. Like the work on an infinitely complex jigsaw puzzle that they had been working on together for ten years, the pieces now finally seemed to be coming together: How could the relationship between consciousness and reality be grasped? What were the consequences for one's own freedom? And for a life that was lived authentically? And not least: What part did the existence of other people play?

Not only had Sartre's 400-page treatise *L'imaginaire* (*The Imaginary: A Phenomenological Psychology of the Imagination*) been published as a book in February 1940: since the beginning of the year he had been working like mad—interrupted only by daily balloon measurements at the front—on a new big work about "nothingness." He reported this almost euphorically to Beauvoir, whom he addressed with her nickname, in a letter from the front of January 15, 1940:

> My charming Castor
>
> Another hard-working day . . . philosophy . . . it had to be. This morning I reread Heidegger's lecture *Was ist Metaphysik?* and spent the day "taking a position with regard to him" on the question of nothingness. I had a theory of nothingness. It was not yet very well formulated, and now it is . . . the philosophy that I am doing is selfish. In my life it plays the role of protecting me against melancholy, disillusion and sadness of war, and I am also trying once again to protect my life, and I am now also trying neither to protect my life retrospectively through my philosophy, which is obscene behaviour, nor to adapt my life to my philosophy, which is pedantic; instead, life and philosophy are really one. I read a beautiful sentence in Heidegger about this, which could be applied to me: "The metaphysics of Dasein is not only metaphysics about Dasein; it is the metaphysics that creates itself as Dasein."[27]

These were the same days in which Beauvoir was able to tell her "dear little creature" how the novel was going: "I really think you'll heap me with praise when you read my 250 pages (for there'll be at least 250, o little so-tardy one)."[28] Beauvoir's communication two days later clearly reveals not least how profoundly Heidegger's impulses to authenticity had also shaped her own thinking; Bienenfeld, she complained to Sartre, was getting terribly on her nerves, since she "didn't understand at all, when I told her morality was above all an existential stance. Indeed, in the whole world she's being the most devoid of any existential feeling. . . . She doesn't in the least live her situation in the world . . . she's the *'das Man'* [the They] and nothing else."[29]

NOTHING BUT FREEDOM

Just as Beauvoir and Sartre read Heidegger as a theorist of nothingness, the problem of freedom was not one that could be approached, let alone solved, purely in terms of the intellect. Rather, an objectively ascertainable fact, freedom was something that had to be grasped through action in a situation. Precisely because it was based on nothing but that decision, it was unconditional. Heidegger himself had said in 1929 that "freedom is and can only be in the setting-free. The sole adequate relation to freedom in man is the self-freeing of freedom in man."[30] So under the banner of nothingness humanity was irrevocably exposed to the situation of freedom—indeed, was practically condemned to it. In the end the renunciation of this self-liberation deriving from the need for security of "das Man" was itself a kind of decision.

During Sartre's final leave from the front, in April 1940, he and Beauvoir addressed these subjects on long walks beside the Seine. "During the days that followed we discussed certain specific problems, in particular the relationship between 'situation' and freedom. I maintained that from the angle of freedom as Sartre defined it—that is, an active transcendence of some given context rather than mere stoic resignation—not every situation was equally valid: what sort of transcendence could a woman shut up in a harem achieve? Sartre replied that even such a cloistered existence could be lived in several quite different ways. I stuck to my point, and in the end made only a token submission."[31]

Was freedom that sprang from the source of nothingness always unconditional, as Sartre claimed? Or, as Beauvoir argued, did freedom not always have to be understood as freedom in a situation—and hence as essentially conditioned by that situation? Those were open questions and attitudes that applied more clearly than ever to Beauvoir's own unusual situation in La Pouëze. She only had to look in the mirror or out of the window, isolated from those most important to her, as if petrified with fear, in a country house in the far west of a beaten nation. What did "grasping oneself" mean in a France that was occupied by the Nazis? What chance was there of *overcoming* the situation?

"Then something exploded under our windows, the plate glass in the restaurant across the way flew into slivers, a guttural voice barked out some words in an incomprehensible language, and they were upon us—all very tall and blond, with pink complexions. They marched in step and looked straight ahead; it took a long time for the column to pass. Behind them came horses, tanks, trucks, artillery, and field kitchens.... The Germans did not cut off children's hands; they paid for their drinks and the eggs they bought on the farms, and spoke politely; all the shopkeepers smiled at them invitingly. They started in on their propaganda straight away."[32]

ON THE MARCH

Of course, Nazi propaganda, like propaganda everywhere, was aimed first and foremost at manipulating the relationship between a situation and people's decisions, according to their own purposes. However, there was a crucial difference, and this was openly declared by the Nazis. Ultimately, their goal was the forced creation of people who would no longer consider or even sense freedom as an option. For these people, the alternatives of quiet resignation or active overcoming would be permanently out of reach. In the totalitarian dream, a collective of Dasein would be based on the blind obedience of those who were absolutely identical and absolutely conformist.

The "politeness" and "correctness" of the German occupying forces in France—which Beauvoir had initially noted with relief—in no way contradicted this interpretation. On the contrary, it confirmed it in the strangest way. Because the rules that kept the Wehrmacht soldiers in step as they marched into the village were also designed to apply to their treatment of the subjugated population: "Look neither right nor left, but adhere strictly to the commanded rules." This was the regulation.

According to the deranged racial categories of the Nazis that lay behind such rules, "the French" were not so-called *Untermenschen*. Consequently, the goal on the part of the occupiers did not involve physical extinction or bodily enslavement, but first and foremost a spiritual and existential subjugation. In other regions conquered by the Nazis, "one" behaved entirely differently. Thus, above all far into the war zones it would be difficult to find comparable eyewitness accounts by Ukrainians or Poles of the Wehrmacht marching into their villages or cities[33]—accounts from people who were classified as *Untermenschen* in the racial worldview of the Nazis. Not to mention the treatment of the Jews, not least in France.

HOMECOMING

Toward the end of June 1940, something like everyday life had returned at least to La Pouëze. The farmers were back at work, the shops and cafés newly reopened. This was when rumors reached Beauvoir that the first prisoners of war were already on the way back to their families. She decided to hitchhike her way to Paris.

But the only sign of life that she found in her hotel after an eventful odyssey was a short letter from Sartre dating from June 9—the same day on which Beauvoir had fled Paris. He had "worked well" and was "full of little experiences."[34] That could have meant anything. Or nothing, as Beauvoir wrote in her diary: "I recovered a kind of gaiety this morning after feeling more miserable last night than I ever had in my entire life. The weather was lovely. I took my usual place at the Dôme.... Suddenly, with all the strength I could muster I believed in an 'afterward' . . . where we would live together. . . . It was the first day that I came out of my shell and stopped living like a crushed bug and tried to become a person again."[35]

To the neutral observer, her situation could have been worse. Her parents were wealthy, the Kosakiewicz sisters were also safe in the countryside near Rouen, and Natalie Sorokin was already on the way back to Paris by bicycle. Even Beauvoir's school teaching was due to resume shortly. "A kind of life was again taking shape around me—it was interesting to see how one lived a separation like this one. At first there was a kind of suspension; the world and the entire present were put between parentheses . . . almost no living image of Sartre; a vague, stereotypical image and the very word 'Sartre' reappeared without being called forth whenever I stopped being active or thinking precisely. . . . All in all, what I'm waiting for most precisely, when despite everything I grasp an orientation in time, is a letter."[36] A textbook example of self-analysis trained in phenomenology. Who needs an unconscious if they have a consciousness? The latter was quite complex enough.

PROJECT HEGEL

As a result of her analysis, "the Beaver" ("Castor" in French), as Beauvoir was known to Sartre throughout their life together, imposed new projects and strict routines upon herself. Anything but standing still. Because with stillness comes emptiness, with emptiness fear. These new projects also included cycling. During these days Natalie Sorokin patiently taught her how to do it: "Two hours of classes, then by bicycle to the Dôme, where I did some reading, then lunch with Sorokin—I rode the bicycle to the Bibliothèque Nationale to work on Hegel for three hours—then went for a long ride from the library to place de l'Étoile, to the Pont de Neuilly and all along the quays down to Auteuil; the weather was lovely; I rolled along and was enchanted to be able to go on a real outing."[37]

Whether the letters reached him or not, from now on she would give Sartre a regular daily detailed account of her life. And even if the movie houses and theaters were closed, the libraries weren't. From July 6, Beauvoir spent the hours between two and five in the afternoon in the reading rooms of the Bibliothèque Nationale—studying the writings of Georg Wilhelm Friedrich Hegel. Hegel of all people. What could his *Phenomenology of Spirit* have had to do with Husserl's or Heidegger's "phenomenology"?

Apart from the name, apparently nothing at all. Instead of the courage of authenticity born of the situation, Hegel's thought revolved around the courage to abstract entirely from one's own situation to comprehend it. Rather than concentrating on one's own consciousness, the focus lay upon an anonymous world spirit. Rather than a freedom born out of the experience of nothingness, his was a logic of absolute consequentiality born out of the concept of nothingness. Freedom: for

Hegel that meant an insight into the necessity of dynamics that were in the end far removed from the action and inaction of concrete historic agents. Beauvoir wrote: "In Hegel I found a tranquillizing influence. Just as at the age of twenty, my heart bleeding because of my cousin Jacques, I read Homer 'to set all humanity between myself and my private grief,' so now I endeavoured to sink this present experience of mine in the 'trend of world-development.'"[38]

In that first summer of the occupation, Beauvoir read Hegel's epic *Phenomenology of Spirit* as a poem of a redeeming self-incapacitation in the name of a higher logic. "I went on reading Hegel, and was now beginning to understand him rather better. His amplitude of detail dazzled me, and his system as a whole made me feel giddy. It was, indeed, tempting to abolish one's individual self and merge with Universal Being, to observe one's own life in the perspective of Historical Necessity, with a detachment that also carried implications concerning one's attitude to death. How ludicrous did this brief instant of time then appear, viewed against the world's long history, and how small a speck was this individual, myself! Why should I concern myself with my present surroundings, with what was happening to me *now*, at this precise moment?"[39]

While Beauvoir clearly felt the seduction of a thought that, in her words, saw every individual "as an ant in an anthill,"[40] her inner resistance to it remained equally deep. If a self truly sensed itself, it could not be indifferent to the place and role that it held in the world. Its own spontaneous feeling and sensation spoke out vividly against it.

Then, on July 11, news finally came from Sartre! From a camp near Nancy, hastily scribbled in pencil two weeks before: "My charming Castor, I am a prisoner and am being treated well again, I can work a little and am not too bored."[41] Emotion, even joy, but not a hint of the hoped-for emotional liberation. Sartre was alive, and imprisoned, or at least that was what she thought she knew. The crucial question was how long he would still be kept prisoner. It could be years: "You know, Hegel's horribly difficult, but also extremely interesting. You must know him—it's akin to your own philosophy of nothingness."[42] How, exactly, they would have to explore together one day. Until then they had to keep trying to insulate themselves against their inner emptiness.

FIRMLY RESOLVED

The Beaver's therapy—"letters, bicycle, Hegel, letters"—was becoming increasingly effective. On July 14, the anniversary of the storming of the Bastille, Beauvoir told Sartre about a series of events that would prove to be crucial for the coming months: "On Boulevard Raspail I passed some armoured cars laden with Germans, all in black. They were tank crews, I think, with their black uniforms, big berets and death's-head insignia. I sat down at the Dôme and read some selected passages from Hegel; I found one sentence that would do marvellously as an epigraph for my novel. . . . I suddenly experienced a brief moment of intellectual ardour. I felt like doing some philosophy, talking to you, taking up my novel again. But I'm too undecided to get back to the novel—I shan't be able to touch it before seeing you again."[43]

Beauvoir's genius had returned. The novel had come back to her consciousness. The essential people of reference had come back to Paris: Olga, her sister Wanda, and soon also Little Bost, who had by now recovered. That autumn the "family" returned to its previous life the best it could. Sartre's letters now came extremely irregularly from a German punishment camp (Stalag XII-D) near Trier. Work on Beauvoir's novel progressed swiftly. The motto she had found in Hegel's *Phenomenology of Spirit* guided her through the last third. It comes from the chapter on "the master-and-slave dialectic," and in Beauvoir's transcription reads: "Every self-consciousness must pursue the death of the other."[44]

Between the world spirit and that of one's own existence there was, even in Hegel's work, a third category of consciousness: the consciousness of the Other or Others. To this very personal problem, she would respond with unconditional resolve in the form of Françoise and Xavière. By December 1940, a version of the work was already complete. Its closing passage reads:

> [Françoise] put her hand on the lever of the gas meter. . . . It was only necessary to pull down this lever to annihilate her. "Annihilate a conscience! How can I?" Françoise thought. But how was a conscience not her own capable of existing? If it were so, then it was she who was not existing. She repeated: "She or I." She pulled down the lever. . . . They would think it was an accident or suicide. "In any case there will be no proof," she thought. . . . Her act was her very own. "It is I who will it." It was her own will which was being accomplished, now nothing at all separated her from herself. She had at last made a choice. She had chosen herself.[45]

The ending of a novel that is, in fact, only the beginning. Because Beauvoir, too, felt that winter that she herself had finally made a choice. To reject silent resignation and to embrace actively overcoming her situation.

SCUM OF THE EARTH

At least they had escaped the camps. More could simply not be expected from this world in the summer of 1940. Just like Heinrich Blücher, Hannah Arendt had used the chaos that had arrived with the capitulation to flee from her internment. Along with a total of two hundred so-called *prisonnières volontaires* (voluntary prisoners) she had stormed out of the women's camp at Gurs near the Pyrenees, with nothing but her toothbrush. From Gurs, Arendt walked for days at a time, first east toward Lourdes, where she met Walter Benjamin, who had just fled Paris. "This was the time of defeat, and after a few days the trains stopped running. No one knew what had happened to families, husbands, children, and friends. Benji and I played chess from morning to evening, and between games we read newspapers, to the extent we could get our hands on them. Everything was as fine as could be—until the ceasefire terms were published, along with the infamous extradition clause."[46] This was on June 22, 1940.

Along with the abolition of the right to asylum, this treaty contained an obligation to hand former German citizens over to the Nazis "upon demand."[47] The Jewish refugees understood what this step actually entailed. It was thus just a matter of time before the Gestapo would start working through the lists that they had drawn up long before, even in France, and begin the deportations to the East.

It was only with the greatest reluctance that Arendt left Benjamin, who was clearly suicidal, behind in Lourdes and set off in search of Blücher. The most plausible meeting point was Montauban, a good 180 kilometers to the northeast. As the town had a socialist mayor who welcomed refugees, by early July it had developed into a kind of nexus for the ex-internees who were wandering through the country. In fact, on her arrival there Arendt found numerous Paris friends and members of the "tribe," most important Lotte Sempell Klenbort and the Cohn-Bendits.[48] And a few days after that, more by chance than anything, also her "Monsieur." Like Arendt, he had been crossing the country on long marches with former fellow prisoners. The pair, officially engaged since January 1940, moved into an abandoned photographer's studio.

Arendt and her companions understood that they had, in comparative terms, fallen on their feet in Montauban. In his book *Scum of the Earth*, the war reporter and author Arthur Koestler, who was also escaping across the country and was Benjamin's friend and neighbor on rue Dombasle, gave an account of the situation of other "Gursiennes."[49] Guided by the hope of being found there most quickly by their relatives or husbands, many of them stayed near the camp for weeks. While some worked in the fields for farmers in return for bread and lodging, others were forced to prostitute themselves in the provincial bars and cafés. In his notes Koestler reports on a "moderate orgy" that an adjutant had organized in the back room of the Sus bistro with three Gursiennes, "two Polish women and one German Jewess. Made them drink Pernod plus rum ... Met in the lavatory the Jewish girl, sick and crying; said: 'Do you think he'll give me a *sauf-conduit*?' When back, Lefèbre asked me whether I slept with the girl. Said I was an idiot; yesterday he had had a Jewess for 20 francs, and her husband had known about it—'nice old chappy, looked like a doctor or something.'"[50]

LIVING CORPSES

News of suicides came in more and more often. If people were still capable of anything like the freedom to make decisions—and Arendt believed this too—there were situations they should avoid. The subject had already arisen several times in Lourdes with Benjamin, who repeatedly warned that one could not know when it was too late for oneself. There had also been suicides in Gurs, indeed, a collective suicide had even at one point been discussed among the internees as a form of protest. But in response to the observation that they were there "*pour crever*" anyway, Arendt remembered, the mood had suddenly lifted. After all, the view prevailing in the camps was that "one had to be abnormally asocial and unconcerned about general events if one was still able to interpret the whole accident as personal and individual bad luck."[51]

To understand the unfolding disaster in its course and its goals, Arendt believed one had to draw abstract conclusions from individual notes. The universe didn't mean it personally. Not even the Nazis did that. That was precisely where, if one understood it correctly, their actual bestiality lay. They were not concerned with the persecution or extermination of any individual, not even with the extermination of the Jews in their entirety. In fact, their actions followed the insane vision of the extinction of all spontaneity of behavior or even feeling, the plan to turn "every individual human being into a thing that would always behave the same way under identical conditions."[52]

In her later analyses of the logic of the concentration camps, Arendt speaks of this totalitarian goal of total objectification—almost exactly as Simone Weil does—as the "preparation of living corpses."[53] The first thing that needed to be understood in the analysis of the nature of the camps, in fact, was that "the psyche *can* be destroyed even without the physical destruction of the physical man."[54] "The first essential step on the road to total domination is to kill the juridical person in man. This was done, on the one hand, by putting certain categories of people outside the protection of the law and forcing at the same time, through the instrument of denationalization, the nontotalitarian world into recognition of lawlessness."[55]

That goal had been reached by 1940. As Arendt maintains in her 1943 essay "We Refugees," the German Jews in France had even created "a new kind of human beings—the kind that are put in concentration camps by their foes and internment camps by their friends."[56] Having been first jailed "because we were Germans, we were not freed because we were Jews."[57] Their crime lay not in any individual deed or action, but rather in their mere existence, which was why the majority of camp inmates were recruited among people "who had done nothing whatsoever that, either in their own consciousness or the consciousness of their tormenters, had any rational connection with their arrest."[58] They were thus, in terms of their recognition as individuals, placed among rapists, murderers, and other criminals.

Any people who, in the chaotic days of June, had not found the courage to flee on their own initiative, were soon back in the heavily guarded camps, and could ponder for themselves how long it might take for the French guards to be replaced by German forces.

TRANSIT

Was it more illegal to go or to stay? More dangerous to apply for a passport or just to leave? Plans were hampered by the regulatory confusion that prevailed in Montauban. The chaos on the French side was too great—it was not quite clear what the rules were or who was passing them on behalf of whom.

Once Pétain was installed in office as chief of state of Vichy France, his first official duty on July 11, 1940, was to abolish the constitution by presidential decree. Rather than follow the motto "Liberty, Equality, Fraternity," the new *état français* would now obey the principles of "Work, Family, Homeland." For the refugees, this was a particularly bitter form of derision. After all, they had now been robbed of these fundamental principles for the second time in barely ten years: they had abandoned their professions; they had lost their families, either left behind or interned; they had left their homes. For all her innate temperamental serenity, and despite the solidarity and friendship she had found on the ground, during those days and weeks Arendt, too, was fighting her very own battle against inner petrification.

Enfeebled by weeks of flu, on August 2, Walter Benjamin, still staying in Lourdes for now, wrote a letter to Theodor Adorno in New York, which impressively documents the situation of almost all German Jews in the new France:

> The complete uncertainty about what the next day, even the next hour, may bring has dominated my existence for many weeks. . . . I hope I have thus far given you the impression of maintaining my composure even in difficult moments. Do not think that this has changed. But I cannot close my eyes to the dangerous nature of the situation. I fear that those who have been able to extricate themselves from it will have to be reckoned with one day.[59]

A week later he revealed more about his situation in a letter to Arendt in Montauban:

> All I know at the moment is that people in New York believe that . . . there should be a visa for New York waiting for me in Marseille. You might imagine that I would happily have gone there immediately. But it seems impossible to receive the document without confirmation from Marseille. Several days ago I sent a telegram there (with RP [return postage]) in

> order to receive the confirmation required. I have still not received a reply. So my uncertainty continues, all the more so in that I don't know whether my attempt to immigrate may not be defeated by an attempt to pay a "visit." A violent heat-wave encourages my inclination to keep my life, both physical and mental, on the back burner. . . . The great fear that I feel when I think of the fate of my manuscripts, is a twofold pain. Little contact with friends; little news.[60]

This is the writing of an isolated person whose flame is about to be extinguished. He is no longer primarily concerned with himself, but rather with the potential loss of his life's work. Weeks before, Benjamin learned that the Gestapo had searched his Paris apartment and confiscated all the manuscripts there.

For Arendt and Blücher the road to freedom also led to Marseille, the last free port of unoccupied France, the only city through which visas and/or a passage across the sea to North Africa could be organized. From Montauban it was two or three days by bicycle. The number of visas being issued was considerably lower than in the previous year, but Arendt could depend on the help of her ex-husband, Günther Stern, who now lived in California, and on contacts and support from the Youth Aliyah network. Monsieur Heinrich, as her spouse, would also be allowed to travel. The situation of Arendt's mother, who had also arrived in Montauban from Paris, was more complicated.

Countless thousands of refugees in Marseille wanted only one thing: to get out of France as quickly as possible. But nobody knew exactly how that was to be done. At least not legally. Because apart from a visa from the host country, a transit permit through Spain and Portugal was required, and above all a valid document to travel out of France (*visa de sortie*). The last was impossible. The black market flourished with all kinds of documents, some of them even genuine. For example, Simone Weil, also stranded in Marseille with her parents, received a tip-off that if someone wanted to go to Casablanca first, their final destination was irrelevant. In August 1940, she acquired three visas from the Consulate of Siam, only to establish afterward that these were valid just for ships traveling directly from Marseille to Siam. But no such ships existed, and they never had.[61]

ANGEL OF HISTORY

On September 20, 1940, when Arendt and her husband Heinrich Blücher met again in Marseille, Benjamin was already in possession of all the documents he needed for a passage from Lisbon to New York—as well as a dose of morphine that, as he told his former neighbor Arthur Koestler a few days earlier, would be enough to kill a horse.

Arendt remembered meeting Benjamin very clearly: "When I saw him, the Spanish visa was valid for another eight to ten days. Getting that sort of visa in those days was completely impossible. He asked me, in a fit of despair, which he should do. . . . I said . . . it was highly uncertain how long such [Spanish] visas would be available. Of course, we would prefer to go together, all three of us, I said. In that case he could come with us to Montauban. But no one could take the responsibility for this. Rather on the spur of the moment, he decided to leave."[62]

Meanwhile, Arendt and Blücher went back to Montauban, their luggage now containing not only two visas for the United States but also a manuscript by Benjamin that he had entrusted to them by way of farewell. It was the essay "The Concept of History," which he had probably written in Lourdes.[63] In this loosely arranged tableau of twelve philosophical sketches, he poetically condenses the whole of his thinking about the relationship between time, historicity, and the role of the individual. Sketch VII contains the figure of an "angel of history":

> His eyes are wide, his mouth is open and his wings are spread. This is how the angel of history must look. His face is turned toward the past. Where a chain of events appears before us, he sees one single catastrophe, which keeps piling wreckage upon wreckage and hurls it at his feet. The angel would like to stay, awaken the dead and make whole what has been smashed. But a storm is blowing from Paradise and has got caught in his wings; it is so strong that the angel can no longer close them. This storm drives him irresistibly into the future to which his back is turned, while the pile of debris before him grows toward the sky. What we call progress is this storm.[64]

In 1940, with his back to the future, Benjamin's angel was able to see in the history of so-called progress nothing but an accumulating pile of rubble and also a mountain of corpses; without the possibility of pausing, of remembering, of assembling in memory. Not even an angel's wings could resist the power of the storm. However, the essay ends with a curiously redemptive vision, in which Benjamin places himself within a tradition that, despite Scholem's lifelong coaxing, Benjamin would never quite grasp as his own.

> This does not imply, however, that for the Jews the future turned into homogeneous, empty time. For every second of time was the strait gate through which the Messiah might enter.[65]

Read, and read out loud, time and again—these lines came to accompany Arendt's daily persistence and contemplation in Montauban.

Hitler's planes were flying their first bombing raids on England, and the military situation was once again looking darker. Meanwhile, new transports of prisoners were arriving in Gurs: hundreds of Jewish women and children from North Baden and Karlsruhe, initially deported by the Gestapo to France, where there was still capacity.[66] The gates to freedom were beginning to close. Nothing was learned for a long time about Benjamin's passage over the Pyrenees, then rumors that Arendt refused to believe for a long time. On October 21, 1940, she, too, had certainty. She picked up her pen to inform Scholem in Palestine of the fate of their mutual friend:

> Dear Scholem,
>
> Walter Benjamin took his own life on September 29 in Portbou on the Spanish frontier. He had an American visa, but on the twenty-third the only people the Spanish allowed to pass the border were those with "national" passports. I don't know if this letter will reach you. In the past weeks and months I had seen Walter several times, the last time being on September 20 in Marseille. The report of his death took nearly four weeks to reach both his sister and us.
>
> Jews are dying in Europe and are being buried like dogs.[67]

It was time to get going. For Blücher and Arendt too, the moment had to be right. The two set off toward the Pyrenees in early January. Benjamin had taken the route over the mountains, a climb of several hours along hidden paths, and the refugee helpers from the Emergency Rescue Committee who had helped him were the same who helped Arendt on her flight. Among them was a former fellow prisoner from Gurs, Lisa Fittko. But this time they managed the passage. With a valid visa for the

United States, Hannah and Heinrich finally reached Lisbon later in January. Now only a ship separated them from the "land of the free." "When we arrived in Portbou," Arendt would write to Scholem, "we searched in vain for his grave. It was nowhere to be found. His name was nowhere."[68]

MISHAPS

If world history were not so awful, it would be a joy to live"—a maxim of Arendt's with which Ayn Rand would have been able to identify throughout her life.[69] Above all in the winter of 1940–1941. On November 5 of that year the American electorate helped the Democrat Franklin Delano Roosevelt to his third term. For Rand this was not only a political catastrophe but also a very personal defeat. Throughout a long autumn, as a campaign worker, she had knocked on doors, distributed pamphlets and stickers ("Wendell Willkie: America's Hope"), delivered speeches in praise of her candidate in halls and movie theaters, and even argued with hecklers: "Who are you to talk about America? You're a foreigner!"—"I chose to be an American. What did you do, besides having been born?"[70]

In the end, Wendell Willkie, a self-made millionaire from Indiana, hadn't a ghost of a chance. He was put on the podium as a surprise candidate by the Republicans at the last minute, and his campaign suffered from the fact, soon brought to light, that he had been a member of the Democratic Party until 1939. This was a serious blow to his credibility, particularly in the influential circles of what was known at the time as the "Old Right."

Rand's enthusiasm soon waned as well. Eight years after the launch of the New Deal, unemployment was still at more than 15 percent. Rather than put his pro-business agenda consistently center stage, Willkie preferred to address the electors long-windedly from his "roots in rural Indiana." He had not even managed to make a clear declaration against the United States' entering the war along the lines of a conservative "America First" policy. Rand's judgment after his defeat was as might be expected: "Willkie was the guiltiest man of any for destroying America, more guilty than Roosevelt, who was only a creature of his time."[71]

Thus 1940 ended for Rand just as it had begun: with a fiasco. Hoping for another theatrical success, earlier in the year she had interrupted work on her new novel, *The Fountainhead,* to produce a stage version of her first work, *We the Living.* The reworking of the novel for the theater proved, predictably, to be pure torture. But the play was commissioned by several renowned Broadway producers, which meant that it was potentially very lucrative. It premiered in New York with great fanfare on February 13, 1940, under the title *The Unconquered*—and the same night critics described it as one of "the season's mishaps."[72]

Rand locked herself in her room for two days. Not even Frank was allowed to come in. When she left it again, the first thing she did was write a donation letter for the Fighting Funds for Finland, addressed to Major General John F. O'Ryan: "Dear Sir, Enclosed please find my contribution to your fund for the purchase of armaments for Finland. Allow me to express my admiration for your work in behalf of this great cause."[73] Facing an overwhelming Soviet enemy, the Finnish army, only 300,000 strong, had managed to hold its position throughout three months of the "winter war." A shining example of the will to resist.

THE TOOHEY PRINCIPLE

The next morning Rand was sitting at her desk again. Time was marching on. The previous year she had missed the first deadline for the novel. According to her contract, the manuscript had to be ready by October. In fact, this was impossible, since not even a third of it had been written. The cul-de-sac was closing in by the day. But Ayn was encouraged by the precedent of the Finns: giving up was not an option.

Above all since the enemy was revealing itself ever more clearly. Culturally, the military conflagration with which Hitler and Stalin were now threatening the world had been preceded by another form of warfare in countries including the United States. Rand's mission was to take these forms of cultural infiltration based on wrongly understood guiding concepts and bring them clearly to light—embodying them as impressively as possible as characters in a novel.

One crucial Damascene experience in this context goes back to 1937, when Rand attended an event by the British political scientist and journalist Harold Laski at the left-oriented New School for Social Research in New York.[74] For years Laski, a genuine star intellectual in the United States who often boasted of having Roosevelt's ear, gave lectures on contemporary social questions—particularly often, in line with the spirit of the age, about the tense relationship between democracy and capitalism.

Rand could hardly grasp her luck. There he was—the anti-Roark par excellence! In return for their applause, the rhetorically skillful Laski, with the obvious arrogance of his performance always slightly muted by a hint of irony, and using all the right words and all the right theories, gave an enthusiastic New York cultural set exactly what they had decided they thought was correct, as the result of long years of quiet subversive propaganda. All she had to do was observe him, listen to what he said, and write it down.

A suitable name for Laski was also quickly found. As always in Rand's novelistic universe, it was a suggestive one: Ellsworth M. Toohey. A great and diabolically devious adversary of Roark's, Toohey was the subject of the whole of the second of four parts of the novel. In spring 1940, Rand definitively captured him as a fictional character. As the most influential art critic of the most influential newspaper in the country, Toohey would pursue his leveling mischief from New York.

> Toohey's [purpose is] to ruin the strong, the single, the original, the healthy, the joyous—with the weapon of "other people," of humanitarianism.[75]

> Toohey has risen to a position of great power in society. He is the undeclared dictator of the intellectual and cultural life of the country. He has "collectivized" all the arts with his various "organizations," and he allows no prominence to anyone save to mediocrities of his choice, such as Keating, Lois Cook, and others of the same quality.[76]

> Toohey destroys all independence in people and all great achievement. . . . To discredit great achievement, he sets up standards which are easy for the phonies.[77]

As far as Rand understood, the actual cultural precondition for the totalitarian advance lay in the complete and deliberate fogging by the media of the judgment of each individual. And this was nowhere more apparent than in the sphere of aesthetic judgment: in the judgment of works of art.

In his role as master of the leveling process, the art critic Toohey, for Rand, therefore embodies a banality of the supposedly "good" (as the "humanitarian," the "social" . . .). In fact, however, this is directed at the very ability that marks an individual as an individual and enables the individual to act as such—a sense of what is truly beautiful, and of how human existence should and could actually be. In Rand's vision, the hero Roark pursues consistently and with an almost superhuman refusal to compromise that "sense of life." The target of Toohey's journalism in the novel is the courage embodied by Roark as well as the ability to make independent judgments and create new things. Or in other words: to think, invent, and act without relying on the support of others.

In the summer of 1940, in a new outline of the novel, Rand developed the social and political aspects of the "Toohey Principle" in a narrower sense, and aligned them with the threatening global triumph of European totalitarianism:

> [Toohey] is basically sterile; he has no great passion for anything and no great interest in anything save other men. Thus he decides not to attempt to seek superiority, but to do better: to destroy its very conception. He cannot rise. He can pull others down. He cannot reach the heights. He can raze them. Equality becomes his greatest passion.[78]

> He understands fully the basic antithesis, the two principles fighting within human consciousness—the individual and the collective, the one and the many, the "I" and the "They." . . . He knows that the source of all evil and all sorrow, of all frustration and all lies is the collective sense, the intrusion of others into the basic motives of a man. And since he is dedicated to the destruction of greatness, he becomes the enemy of the individual and the great champion of collectivism.[79]

> His life program is simple: to destroy men by tying them to one another; to preach self-sacrifice, self-denial, self-abasement; to

> preach the spiritual slavery of each man to all other men; to fight the great creator and liberator—Man's Ego. Toohey is famous as "The Humanitarian." . . . Universal—without even the dignity of a master. Slavery to slavery. A great circle and an utter equality. Such is Ellsworth M. Toohey.[80]

FALSE EQUALITY

In 1940, Rand also saw the world as being on the brink of totalitarianism. And in that situation she developed a theory of radical evil, the ultimate political goal of which was total enslavement and the destruction of the individual. Initially she saw this as manifested by a leveling mass high culture, celebrated by self-confessed cynics such as Toohey, in the name of undifferentiated equality—and of nothingness. In Toohey's world indifferent pleasure makes way for pleasurable indifference; the courage to use one's own intelligence for a blithe willingness always to make judgments on behalf of everyone, and in line with them all; the capacity for discernment, previously a cultural guarantor, for the will to absolute indifference.

In a central passage of the novel, Ellsworth M. Toohey expresses this credo—in dialogue with the star architect Peter Keating, whom Toohey celebrates, but who is in fact completely talent-free: "I don't believe in individualism. . . . I don't believe any one man is one thing that everyone else can't be. I believe we're all equal and interchangeable."[81]

To Rand's ears this is the totalitarian guiding principle writ large. If one only knew how to listen properly, it was by now the universally prevailing view, indeed even in America it formed the actual light in which every public statement was judged to be reasonable, morally explicable, and/or pertinent.

This vision of complete equality as total interchangeability and thus of individual nothingness began with judgment of works of art and sought its inhuman end point in the complete loss of basic consciousness—namely the undeniable uniqueness of each individual self.

MANHATTAN TRANSFER

In both military and cultural terms, it was clear that this process was fully under way—precisely and not least in the public life of the United States. Hence, as would have been obvious, Rand based the central figures of her novel, which is set in the late 1930s in New York, on real people of the time. Roark was psychically a twin of Rand herself, and his professional work as an architect clearly followed the career of Frank Lloyd Wright—whom Rand deeply revered, and with whom she repeatedly (and unsuccessfully) attempted to make personal contact. Toohey was Harold Laski, a prototype of the left-wing New York intellectual. Finally, the figure of the media mogul Gail Wynand, in whose publications Toohey performs a leading role, drew in his essential features from the most influential and also the trickiest newspaper publisher in the United States, William Randolph Hearst.

According to Rand's basic idea, now revised, the work would become more than a timeless allegory of the struggle between the individual and the collective in our spiritual life, and instead a key novel about America's self-abandonment under the banner of the totalitarianism that was triumphing all over the globe. A terrifying scenario represented, at least in Rand's world, by one person above all: President Roosevelt, a man who in fact possessed almost dictatorial levels of power.

In this light, Rand's decision to abandon everything, regardless of financial straits and menacing deadlines, and commit herself with her characteristic determination to volunteering for the Republican electoral campaign, was the purest self-interest; she had already experienced firsthand what the Toohey Principle was capable of. As far as possible, she wanted to prevent the worst political developments from taking place in her new home. There was also no doubt that Rand felt very personally oppressed and traduced by the dynamics she described, by all the Tooheys of New York's cultural life.

For the moment, in November 1940, she had to acknowledge herself as having been defeated on all fronts, both professionally and politically. Her play had been pulled after only five performances, the contract for her novel had been definitively canceled by the publishers, and her relationship with her agent Jean Wick had been profoundly shaken.[82] Furthermore, in Europe, Hitler and Stalin were inexorably advancing, and the bulk of the American electorate was clearly unable to put two and two together. She hadn't even been able to keep the spacious apartment on Park Avenue in Manhattan. By now she and Frank were living not far away, in a two-room basement apartment near Lexington Avenue.

RAND'S CONSTITUTIONAL PATRIOTISM

There were, however, some encouraging signs of the times. During her many public appearances, and above all during conversations with ordinary voters, she had familiarized herself with a clear-sightedness and a political rationality that transformed her formerly elitist attitude toward the "far too many." What was missing, in fact, was not the sense of freedom in the electorate, but only the correct language to mobilize it effectively. However serious the situation might have been, it was not by any means hopeless. Particularly if she managed simply to turn the tables; in other words, to counter all the obviously totalitarian opinion-formers in culture and journalism with, in true Leninist fashion, a pro-freedom elite. To revive "from above," and with the support of the mass media, the truly American longing for "life, liberty, and the pursuit of happiness" that made the country unique.

At the end of 1940 and the beginning of 1941, what Rand imagined ever more clearly was a political counterrevolution based on the clearest and most profound political documents: the American Declaration of Independence and Constitution. These promised to protect each individual's freedom to make decisions. Rather than relying on an ethnically defined people or even just a nation, this movement would mobilize entirely under the banner of a document, which made it pure constitutional patriotism.

And that patriotism was also something she had discovered during her months campaigning in the streets, newspaper offices, and political clubs of New York. Rand was by no means as alone and isolated in her political beliefs and intellectual preferences as she had felt all those years before, sitting at her walnut writing desk. During the autumn she sounded out writers including Albert Jay Nock, author of the 1935 bestseller *Our Enemy, the State*; the journalist and Nietzsche translator H. L. Mencken, whose columns, as brilliant as they were controversial, revealed him as one of the biggest critics of Franklin Delano Roosevelt; and the writer and literary critic Isabel Paterson, an author of columns for the New York *Herald Tribune* with whose positions Rand broadly identified.[83]

Because throughout the 1930s Roosevelt had been able to claim the adjective "liberal" for his form of politics, such writers identified themselves as "libertarians" as a deliberate way of distancing themselves from Roosevelt's approach. Of course, it would not be easy for such radical individualists to become enthusiastic members of a political organization, let alone a party, even if it consisted of nothing but what might be termed an organization against organizations. Nonetheless, this was precisely the group that Rand had in mind when she set about drawing up a first foundational document in January 1941. In Russian Revolutionary style, she chose the format of an "open letter" to the American electorate.

I WANT YOU!

To illustrate the drama of the situation, Rand began her letter—perhaps not very cleverly, from a psychological point of view—by hurling invective at that very electorate.

> You who read this represent the greatest danger to America. No matter what the outcome of the war in Europe may be, Totalitarianism has already won a complete victory in many American minds and conquered all of our intellectual life. You have helped it to win. . . . Don't delude yourself by minimizing the danger. You see what is going on in Europe. . . . What other proof do you need? Don't say smugly that it can't happen here. . . . Could it happen in France? People would have laughed at you had you asked such a question a year ago. Well, it has happened in France—France, the mother of freedom and of democracy, France, the most independent-minded nation on earth.[84]

Meanwhile, Rand was still strictly opposed to America's entering the war. The only thing she was concerned with was the ideological struggle on the home front. But that was precisely the area in which resolute resistance was required, because: “The Totalitarians do not want your active support. They do not need it. . . . All they want from you is your indifference.”[85] Above all because, contrary to what other analyses suggested, totalitarianism was not something new in the history of the world, but an ancient phenomenon. Here Rand fell back into her old Nietzschean elitist language—totalitarianism, in her view, “is the attempt of the worthless and the criminal to seize control of society. That element is always there, in any country. But a healthy society gives it no chance.”[86] Closely enmeshed with this striving was the second element common to all totalitarian movements—clearly apparent in Nazi Germany and Stalin’s Soviet Union:

> The State is superior to the individual. That the Collective holds all rights and the individual has none . . . this is the crucial point. . . . These horrors are made possible only by men who have lost all respect for single, individual human beings, who accept the idea that classes, races and nations matter, but single persons do not, that a majority is sacred, but a minority is dirt, that herds count, but Man is nothing. Where do you stand on this? There is no middle ground.[87]

To channel this decision for each individual, Rand defined the core of an open society, which needed to be defended uncompromisingly, as “the principle of Individual Rights, Individual Freedom, Individual Value. That is the principle against which the present great world conspiracy is directed. That is the heart of the whole world question. That is the only opposite of Totalitarianism and our only defense against it.”[88]

This battle needed to be waged right now, and with the same methods, both hidden and explicit, that the opposite side had long been using for its own purposes—propaganda and journalism—and that, Rand maintained, it had in most cases completely underestimated—the great arts designed for a wide public: literature and film.

It was in novels and films, she argued, that subjectivity was actually created and shaped. Truly deep and popular works shaped the consciousness of a person much more extensively and lastingly than superficial phenomena such as journalism or advertising. The battle had to be fought not least on that terrain; indeed, in the American context it had to be recognized and accepted as a battle in the first place. After all, as Rand said in the conclusion of her letter to the nation, one thing was absolutely certain, at least to her: "The world is a beautiful place and worth fighting for. But not without Freedom."[89]

Without a book contract, without any income or any concrete notion of what might happen in 1941, Rand first sent her letter to the writer and dramatist Channing Pollock, another potential member of the libertarian group she hoped to set up. In her defense of the United States, Rand had decided to go all the way to the end. And she was not a woman to change her convictions once she had made them. She would confront the coming storm with all the powers at her disposal. And not with her back to the future, but facing into it.

VII

FREEDOM: 1941–1942

Beauvoir liberates herself, Arendt isolates herself, Weil writes her will, and Rand her birth certificate.

AS IF LIBERATED

A year after the occupation of Paris, Simone de Beauvoir felt a new sense of existence. Rigidity made way for resolve, depression for an active will to confront life, and mortal fear for a feeling of contentment "but quite differently from before. Events had changed me. . . . I was at last prepared to admit that my life was not a story of my own telling, but a compromise between myself and the world at large. By the same token, setbacks and adversities no longer struck me as instances of injustice. There was no point in rebelling against them; you had either to find a way to get around them, or else put up with your lot. I knew the future might hold some exceedingly dark hours for me, and that I might even become engulfed in that darkness forever. . . . Throughout the spring and summer I took advantage of every spare moment: I finished my novel."[1]

Sartre's return from the prisoner-of-war camp was a major factor in her change of mood. However, where Beauvoir's newly found attitude of carefree flexibility was concerned, his presence was at first rather unsettling: "What did [disorient] me rather was the stringency of his moral standards. Did I buy things on the black market? A little tea occasionally, I told him. Even this was too much. I had been wrong to sign the paper stating I was neither a Freemason nor a Jew. . . . He had not come back to Paris to enjoy the sweets of freedom, he told me, but to *act*. How? I inquired, taken aback."[2]

Through political commitment and *résistance*! By the end of March 1941, a few weeks after his return, he called an initial meeting in the Hôtel Mistral. It took place in Beauvoir's room. Former pupils of Sartre, friends of Bost, and students of Merleau-Ponty, who was by then teaching at the university. They were all thoroughly determined. Although none of them knew what they were determined to do.

The hotheads in the group argued in favor of isolated attacks. But where would they get the bombs, and the skills required? Above all because Sartre saw the need for action as lying primarily in thought. "If the democracies won," he wrote, setting out his agenda, "it would be essential for the Left to have a new programme. It was our job, by pooling our ideas and discussions and research, to bring such a programme into being. Its basic aims could be summed up in two words—though their reconciliation caused vast problems—which also served as a watchword for our movement: 'Socialism and Liberty.'" But if Germany were to win the war, "our task would be to see that she lost the peace."[3] Which seemed much more likely early in the spring of 1941.

In Egypt and Norway, Greece and Yugoslavia, the Wehrmacht was enjoying huge successes. Intoxicated by its own forces, on June 22, 1941, it attacked the Soviet Union, in contravention of the pact between the countries, without the declaration of war and to Stalin's absolute surprise. As in the Balkan campaign, Operation Barbarossa was also planned as a blitzkrieg. The army leadership allowed a maximum of four to six weeks for the advance. The main struggle declared by Hitler, the "battle of the Teutons against the Slavs,"[4] would be waged relentlessly. The declared goal was not only victory, but extinction in the sense of a "merciless, total annihilation of the enemy." Further steps were already fixed: "Afghanistan, India, Iran, the Turks, Syria, Iraq, North Africa, Gibraltar, Malta and the Atlantic Islands."[5]

The outbreak of total war coincided with the beginning of the genocide of Europe's Jews. On June 22, 1941, some 3,000 German soldiers in a special unit began shooting Jews. Initially men, then women and children. (By April 1942, the total number of Jews killed in that way would be in the region of 560,000, or an average of more than 10,000 executions per week.[6]) From now on there would be no going back.

The consequences of the escalation were also immediately apparent in France. "In the Occupied Zone, the most extreme measures yet known were taken against [the Jews]. With effect from February 2, a decree forbade them to change their place of residence or go out after eight o'clock in the evening. . . . Jews of French nationality were shut up in the camp at Pithiviers, and others, very many others, deported to Germany."[7] Not least, pressure mounted against the many active Resistance cells in Paris, which made it difficult for Sartre to establish the contacts he needed. His reputation in these circles was not the best in any case. In part this was because of his celebrated transformation into a bourgeois café libertine, but also because of the story he circulated about the reasons for his liberation. He had been allowed to leave on the grounds of faked health problems (difficulties with balance) as well as his squint. Or, to keen Resistance ears, to establish the contacts that he was really seeking, while being shadowed by the Gestapo. Either the man was a well-intentioned dilettante or a spy in disguise. Perhaps both at once. But at any rate he was not a trustworthy comrade. In the words of Samuel Beckett, with whose "Gloria" Resistance group Sartre also attempted to make contact: "There were always those whom no one took seriously, neither the *résistants* nor the Gestapo. Sartre seemed to many people to be among these."[8]

Just as a person can become completely absorbed in the role of a waiter when customers issue their orders, Sartre finally felt reliant on the benevolence of others in his role as Resistance activist.

Even Beauvoir had doubts about his new project. He was, however, indispensable to her neither as an erotic nor as a political hero, but only as a conversation partner and an intimate source of inspiration: "It was impossible to be depressed for long in his company. . . . His inquisitiveness and enthusiasm would animate every last corner . . . such a lot still to see and understand and love."[9] At last he was there again, the person with whom she could really talk and argue about everything: whether it was the latest refugee chic of the *parisiennes* (fabric turbans), the bizarre mini sculptures of Alberto Giacometti (a café conquest of Sorokin's), or the concept of sympathy in the phenomenology of Max Scheler. How could one, if one read his writings, ever imagine that one could feel and think exactly as one's partner did? No matter how loved and admired one might have been? What sort of urge was that?

EMANCIPATED AT LAST

Another good question. For Beauvoir, however, it was not the central one. Throughout the whole of the previous year, when she had been completing her first novel, the tension between Hegel and Heidegger was working away within her. More precisely, the problem of how the universal can have a meaning if the individual does not.

Hegel's system represented an anonymous universality of the world spirit, which threatened to disable the actual individual even more thoroughly than the conformist pressure of a faceless "they." Heidegger, on the other hand, stood for the radical resoluteness of the individualized Dasein, which remains primarily and above all concerned with the acquisition of his (and no one else's) authenticity. The crucial philosophical breakthrough for Beauvoir can be dated precisely to January 9, 1941—two months before Sartre's return to Paris. The entry in her war diary reads:

> One idea that struck me so strongly in Hegel is the exigency of mutual *recognition* of consciousnesses—it can serve as a foundation for a social view of the world—the only absolute being this human consciousness, exigency of *freedom* of each consciousness in order for the recognition to be valid and free: recognition in love, artistic expression, action, etc. At the same time, the existential idea that human reality *is* nothing other than what it *makes itself* be, that towards which it transcends itself.[10]

Far from striving for a simple synthesis of Hegel and Heidegger, Beauvoir appropriated certain motifs from their thought and, against the background of her years of reading and discussions (with Sartre), created a new philosophy of freedom based on mutual existential recognition. Rather than modeling the relationship between "self" and "Others" as a battle, which can know only mutually dependent masters and slaves, Beauvoir declared it to be a situation that could be won solely by each together and at the same level. No man is an island. Instead, the true precondition of my freedom lies in the freedom of the other consciousness—indeed, if the idea is consistently thought through, in the free acknowledgment of all other consciousnesses. Politically, this leads to the demand for a liberation struggle for all under the banner of mutual existential emancipation—each for the sake of their own freedom: freedom *and* socialism.

In this new philosophy of Beauvoir's, the proposition that "human reality *is* nothing but what it *makes* itself" was essentially inspired by

Heidegger. At a minimum this meant the explicit rejection of any form of any invisible guiding hand, cunning, or law ruling the world of human beings. Be it Hegelian, Marxist, or religious in nature, no faceless dialectic behind all being, no determining evolutionary laws on a purely economic basis, no destiny, no day of judgment, no fate. The true creator and the sole standard lay in the acting human being, thrown into the freedom of their Dasein—as one among others. The fire of individual freedom and the fire of political freedom were thus in fact one and the same. And it blazed in each of us—for everyone.

Nothing testifies more clearly to Beauvoir's consciousness of a breakthrough autonomously achieved than her feeling of committing something like a betrayal of the one who remained the only necessary Other in her life:

> I am far from the Hegelian point of view that was so helpful to me in August. I have become conscious again of my individuality and of the metaphysical being that is opposed to this historical infinity where Hegel optimistically dilutes all things. Anguish. I have finally realized the state that I nostalgically longed for last year: solitude, as complete as when facing death. Last year I was still with Sartre—now I live in a world from which Sartre is absent, gagged. Psychologically I was at times stupidly proud to feel so solid and to get on so well. But today, those superficial defences are no longer of any help to me. I have vertigo. The hope of maintaining one's very *being* is the only reason for which I think it is worth accepting death. It's not a matter of having "reasons for living"—it's not a matter of life, but of something more than that. To make oneself an ant among ants, or a free consciousness facing other consciousnesses. *Metaphysical* solidarity that I newly discovered, I, who was a solipsist, I understand what was wanting in

> our antihumanism. . . . There is no other reality than human reality—all values are founded on it. And that "towards which it transcends itself" is what has always moved us and orients the destiny of each one of us.
>
> Since November 21 I have sought only to flee—because this solitary return to work seemed almost a betrayal to me. Now it has come about on its own. And yet, I seem to work in his name as much as in mine. More than ever I feel (while being inconsistent) that I would kill myself if I were never to see him again.[11]

In January 1940, after more than a decade of philosophical ascent, Beauvoir felt that she had finally escaped the cave of her consciousness. Solipsism had become metaphysical solidarity, hedonistic narcissism the anxiety-free declaration that one is one thrown being, and hence one mortal being, among many others. There were no deeper reasons or final proofs to be delivered here. Instead, however, there was something much more fundamental: clear consciousness of being able to grasp this newfound freedom. Not as an ant or as a master, but as an authentically liberated individual.

POSITIVELY CHARGED

Almost every couple must go through a phase of readjustment after a lengthy separation. Above all if the experiences they have had during that time are so formative. In the case of Beauvoir and Sartre and their mutual estrangement in the spring of 1941, however, there were also, as we have seen, profound philosophical divergences.

On his return to Paris, Sartre plunged into work on his magnum opus *Being and Nothingness*—or more precisely, the chapters on

"Temporality."[12] When this thousand-page book was published in July 1943, it contained, right at the end of the treatise, exactly five pages on matters of ethics. Under the heading "Ethical Implications," Sartre declared that in terms of his philosophy it "amounts to the same thing whether one gets drunk alone or is a leader of nations. If one of these activities precedes over the other, this will not be because of its real goal but because of the degree of consciousness which it possesses of its ideal goal; and in this case it will be the quietism of the solitary drunkard which will take precedence over the vain agitation of the leader of nations."[13]

This position, in its content-free nihilism, utterly contradicts the position reached by Beauvoir. Was that really what Hitler and Stalin lacked from a moral perspective, and where they fell down as human beings? An inadequate degree of consciousness of their ideals? A lack of self-transparency, of authenticity?

As a human being and as the woman by his side, Beauvoir would spend her whole life devoting the greatest care to managing her intellectual relationship with Sartre, above all with regard to his genius. But also with regard to his philosophical originality. This, however, did not fit with the internal dynamic of the trend that would, under Sartre's egocentric patronage, go on to conquer the Western world under the name of "existentialism" from 1943 onward. In reality, the crucial breakthrough in the question, identified by Sartre as early as 1945, of whether "existentialism [was] a humanism,"[14] and hence of where its ethical core might be found, was made by Beauvoir.[15] Sartre, it might be added, did not adequately note this fact.

For Beauvoir, however, this was not a cause for any particular grief, either during or after the war. By the summer of 1941, their everyday life as a couple had reestablished itself. The main factor that contributed to their harmony was the reconquest of their beloved shared routines. Chief among them was their six-week teachers' holidays. Once they had illegally crossed the border, from mid-August until the end of September they cycled together through the "free" south and enjoyed each other's company as they had done in their earliest years. "Beaver" Beauvoir explored the landscape and the sights of the Côte d'Azur, while her "best-loved little one"—less naturally athletic—used his free hours to write under beach umbrellas.

The idea that Comrade Sartre, on behalf of the group, was actually traveling as part of an underground mission was soon quietly forgotten. Particularly since he was being showered with gifts, even out of Paris. André Gide politely referred him to André Malraux. The welcome in Malraux's summer villa was as warm as it was nourishing ("chicken Maryland, exquisitely prepared"[16]) but was also without consequence. Not even Colette Audry revealed herself to him as a communist comrade. That summer, Sartre's dream of becoming a Resistance leader burst as predictably as a used bicycle tire on a dirt road. In her memoirs, Beauvoir describes the fiasco in the tone of a relieved mother: "Sartre had brooded over this plan of his for months . . . so it hit him hard to abandon it; but abandon it he did, though his heart told him otherwise."[17]

And in fact, back in Paris the family situation seemed much calmer, in the best sense, not least where sexual matters were concerned. Sartre now concentrated almost monastically on Wanda, while Beauvoir stuck to the nightly timetable that she had drawn up the previous autumn (twice a week Sorokin, twice Olga, twice Bost . . .).[18] Flings, like that between Sorokin and Sartre, barely came into it. Not that they were all aware of it, but the family members now took care to respect the "individual quirks" of their relationships. "Twosomes were the general rule. When I was chatting in the Flore with Olga or Lise, when Sartre and Wanda went out together, when Lise and Wanda were having a tête-à-tête, none of us would have dreamed of joining their table. People found this behaviour preposterous, but to us it seemed both natural and obvious."[19]

While questions of lodging, food, and clothing in that cold and snowbound winter of 1941–1942 meant that it was a "considerable effort to keep up a decent minimum of appearances,"[20] the family managed to treat forced confinement as a series of new creative opportunities. This marked the beginning of the time about which Sartre would later say, "We were never freer than under the German occupation."[21]

For Beauvoir as an author and philosopher this new freedom had already begun in January 1941. The transformation in her relationship with the world played a central part in her new novel. While the first had concerned primarily the *psychological* aspects of the struggle between the "self" and the "Other," the second was to do the same for *social* and *political* factors. "I would like my next novel to illustrate this relation to the other in its existentiel [*sic*] complexity. It's a beautiful subject. To *suppress* the other's consciousness is a bit puerile. The problem gets back to the social, etc."[22]

This turned out to be a particular kind of challenge. "(But how unrewarding it is to write about social matters, and how can I avoid sounding edifying and moralising?) I should be able to handle social subjects (strikes, riots, the actions of a leader) in order to mark the relation to the other (freedom, facticity)."[23]

To stage a strike—a revolt—in such a way that it stressed the true connection with the Other, without sounding flatly edifying or moralistic: that was among the hardest things anyone could achieve. And it was something Simone Weil would experience for herself at the same time.

THANKSGIVING

If the inhabitants of Saint-Marcel d'Ardèche turned away from her out of fear or even nausea, never before had Simone Weil felt more blessed than she did in the early autumn of 1941: "Admirable landscape, delicious air, rest, leisure, solitude, fresh fruits and vegetables, spring water, wood fires—nothing but sensual pleasures,"[24] she wrote in a letter from her "House of the Four Winds"—in fact, a dilapidated wooden hut on the edge of the forest, where rats darted over the rotten floorboards at night.

A mistress of the farmer? A Jewish refugee? Or merely a mental patient who had been taken in out of kindness on the Thibons' farm? No one in the village really knew what this woman in the navy blue loden coat was doing there. Every morning they saw her gaunt figure sitting on a stone bench near the spring, absently reciting poems in a foreign language. It could be only a matter of time before she started preaching to the animals.

Via Catholic friends from Marseille, Weil had been hired as a harvest worker on the farm of Gustave Thibon, an Ardèche farmer and author. As her letters from the summer reveal, her burning desire was that of "transforming the efforts of my body and soul into potatoes and things of that kind among a people who may go hungry."[25]

So she could hardly have ended up in a better place: "Without the horror of affliction that at this time submerges so many parts of the earthly globe, the present situation, as far as it concerns me personally, would suit me completely. The government of my country could not do me a greater good than forbidding me from being active in the intellectual professions and so making thought for me a gratuitous affair, as it should be. Since my adolescence I dreamed of the marriage of St. Francis with poverty, but I felt that I must not go to the trouble of marrying it, since one day it would come to take me by force and it would be better so."[26]

According to the law, as a Jew, Weil could no longer teach at her country's schools. She repeatedly asked the ministry for the deeper reasons behind the decree that had been passed, since she had not received a Jewish education, had never in her life visited a synagogue, had never witnessed a Jewish ritual, and had never for a day in her life felt like a Jew. On what basis was she now being presented as a Jew?

Weil's letter to the ministry, dripping with sarcasm, was not aimed in any way at her being spared, but was a reductio ad absurdum of the criteria being applied. In any case, she would manage to expel herself. She didn't need anyone to do it for her. Certainly not the government of her occupied homeland. By their fruits shall ye know them!

TENSE EXPECTATION

Weil's original plan to also work on the wine harvest, to the point of complete exhaustion, was unexpectedly thwarted late in October (perhaps by Thibon, with a view to protecting her), and she was obliged to return to Marseille, where her parents had now spent more than a year hoping to be saved by a passage to the United States.

During this time Weil's thoughts revolved almost compulsively around baptism and the question of when it would be suitable, and under what conditions, to take the first and holiest of all the sacraments. Simone Weil felt profoundly religious, even touched by God. But what would be the consequence for a person, a philosopher, like herself? How far could one take one's voluntary submission to present oneself before God? Or would she be committing genuine sacrilege with the explicit *will* to submission? Was salvation even conceivable outside the Catholic

Church? And would the request to be admitted into its bosom not represent a shameful lack of solidarity with all those who were lost and without salvation, who would go on being outside it? Could that be right?

She was tormented as she waited for a solution, a sign. The Dominican priest Joseph-Marie Perrin advised her to seek and desire nothing—in this last and most important question of faith—but the will of God.

In deep turmoil, and condemned by circumstances to inaction, Weil experienced her winter months of waiting as the most productive in her life. Apart from numerous lectures about Greek philosophy and its mystery cults,[27] which she delivered in the crypt of the Marseille Dominican order, and also published in *Cahiers du Sud*, a journal that set the intellectual tone of the era, particularly in non-communist circles, Weil's spiritual energy flowed above all into her notebooks.[28]

On the basis of her experiences of religious awakening, and in direct dialogue with the great ancient sources of wisdom of what Karl Jaspers termed the "Axial Age" (Platonism, Hinduism, Buddhism), Weil sought to find—and she expressed this in loosely arranged sentences and entries—clarity about what she saw as the crucial questions: the value and origin of the self, and its relationship with the Other, with God, with society, and with the historical situation; the nature and origin of love and goodness; the fundamental human tension between finitude and infinitude, immanence and transcendence.

SELFLESS

If we compare Weil's *Notebooks* with Beauvoir's diaries and writings from the same time, we have the extremely strange impression of a telepathic contact between two minds resonating tensely at either end of an infinite piece of string. Because in the *Notebooks* Weil takes the human situation of fearful knowledge about one's own mortality and finitude as the starting point of her philosophical investigations, albeit with a distinctly different thrust from those thinkers who, by 1941–1942, were already known as "existentialists."[29]

> Dasein—a truth in Existentialism, but they have mixed it with a temptation.[30]

With the use of the term "Dasein" in the German original, Weil is clearly referring to Heidegger's work *Being and Time*. Indeed, in the state of anxiety—as a representation of future nonbeing—the essential truths of existence are revealed. However, rather than enduring the void of this abyss and taking it as a purifying opportunity for complete "de-creation" of the self, that void is converted in existentialism, according to Weil's criticism, into the basis of an authentic self-empowerment under the banner of the freely willing "I," the "I want."

With the very first step toward philosophical consciousness, existentialism, according to Weil, branches off in the wrong direction of the preservation and rebellion of the self. And in this way it became the precursor of a purely mundane egoism, the egoism of self-apprehension, whose obstinate lostness surpasses everything that even the dullest conformism of a tradition-hampered "they" was able to achieve. As the entries in her *Notebooks* have it:

> The egoist sacrifices everything, not to himself, but to the comforts of existence; it is not the same thing.[31]

> Man would like to be egoistic and is unable to be. This is the most striking characteristic of his misery and the source of his greatness.[32]

> If one could be an egoist, it would be very pleasant. It would be a proper rest. But one cannot, literally, be one.[33]

In essence this is precisely the thought process Beauvoir was going through in 1941–1942 as she looked back on the shape of her own life. But where Beauvoir connected the freedom of the self in terms of a "metaphysical solidarity" with the existence of others, Weil deems this movement to be merely another flight. The truly liberating goal is not devotion to others in solidarity, but merciful self-renunciation under the banner of divine transcendence. Because:

> We possess nothing in this world—for chance may deprive us of everything—except the power to say "I." It is that which has to be offered up to God, that is to say, destroyed.[34]

From which it follows, for Weil's existentialism, that a Dasein would be capable of doing only good after this last and first act of redeeming self-destruction:

> Whatever the "I" does is bad, without any exception, including good, because the "I" itself is bad.[35]

> To let necessity act within the self. (Renunciation of personal will.)[36]

Thus, good action—and here Weil, in the traditions of both Eastern and Western mystics, walks clairvoyantly toward the limits of language itself—consists of an eminent form of inaction, which even affects the decision to accept divine love. In terms of the problems regarding Catholic baptism, which preoccupied Weil at this time, an autonomous decision is out of the question. Who am I, in the end, to make a choice for or against God—deliberately to opt for or against him? The most arrogant of all thoughts, the most profound of all imaginable heresies: "As fast as I become nothing, God loves himself through me."[37]

WITHOUT "WE"

What Beauvoir's existentialism saw as a worldly treatment for nihilism, Weil saw as the very source of the illness. And this diagnosis applied even more aptly to the attempt to channel the individual "I" into the openness of an ethical existence through the idea of a liberating "we." "One must not be *I*, but still less must one be *We*."[38]

For Weil, the shift from "I" to "We" marked the genuine transition to the realm of evil. Above all when that "We" was addressed in the sense of "society" and politically mobilized. Allowing one's own actions to take their bearings from "society"—from its well-being, use, and continuing existence—would be the most devastating conceivable way for a Dasein to rid itself, in a supposedly moral sense, of its own insignificance: "In society, the individual is something infinitely small."[39]

But in Weil's view the human being is not small enough. Because in comparison with the transcendent infinity with which Dasein faces God, the infinity of the social is only a secondary and derivative substitute, earthbound and hence practically diabolical. Weil joins with Plato in describing this sphere of the social and of social pressure as "the Great Beast": "Obedience to the Great Beast: that is wherein the social virtues lie."[40]

Even Beauvoir could wholeheartedly concur with this. But in the *Notebooks* Weil's critique of "the great We" goes far beyond this commonplace, and quite fundamentally takes aim against the sphere of the social as the ultimate object of moral action (in whichever form). Even Ayn Rand could not have put it in such extreme terms: "Man is a social animal, and the social element represents evil."[41]

But since the human person is a social animal (or, to quote Aristotle, a *zoon politikon*), there is no way for the person out of this evil, as Weil goes on to maintain—and in her description of this paradoxical situation she even reveals herself to be an inspired reader of Kafka:

> There is nothing we can do about it. . . . It follows that life cannot be anything else but a spiritual laceration. This world is uninhabitable. That is why we have to flee to the next. But the door is shut. What a lot of knocking is required before it opens! Really to be able to enter in, and not be left on the doorstep, one has to cease to be a social being.[42]

There is a goal—but no way to get there. At least not one that purely earthbound individuals could find for themselves and travel. Insofar as the portal to another world may be opened during our lifetimes, it certainly won't happen as the result of our knocking. It will happen only as an act of mercy.

For Weil, the actual seduction of the "Great Beast" lies in the entirely chimerical hope of being able to find, via the way of earthly transcendence, something that can be reached only through the divine transcendence of the One.

WITHOUT OPIUM

For Weil's sense of herself as a Christian, deeply immersed in the spirit of Plato, there is simply nothing that springs solely from the earthly sphere or belongs to it alone. There is nothing that feeds only on the finite immanence of human existence that could be called "real," "good," or even justifiable in the true sense of those words. For the same reason, any humanism based on earthly foundations loses sight of the origin of all goodness as surely as the essence of finite existence, which keenly aspires to transcendence.

> We must do away with the very notion of humanism, and at the same time what is opposed to humanism, by recognizing the fact that humanism is the Christian faith.[43]

According to Weil, the humanist fallacy had previously assumed its most socially influential and historically devastating form in vulgar political Marxism with its purely vertically aligned promises of progress.

> The Great Beast is the only object of idolatry, the only ersatz form of God, the only imitation of an object which is infinitely distant from me and is yet me.[44]

> The great mistake on the part of the Marxists and of the whole of the nineteenth century lay in believing that by walking straight in front of one, one necessarily rises up into the air.[45]

Consequently, for Simone Weil:

> Not religion, but revolution is the opium of the people.[46]

At the same time, according to Weil, a yearning for revolution on the part of communism/socialism is marked by a psychological distortion, which in its usual totalitarian form is factually indistinguishable from racially motivated National Socialism:

> Socialism consists of attributing good to the conquered; racialism, of attributing it to the conquerors. But the revolutionary wing of socialism makes use of those who, although of lowly origin, are by nature and by vocation conquerors; so it arrives at the same system of ethics.[47]

Which is also why:

> Totalitarianism is an ersatz form of Christianity.[48]

In the winter of 1941–1942, for Simone Weil, the philosophy of freedom of "metaphysical solidarity" in a world without God lauded by Simone de Beauvoir (freedom *and* socialism) meant the direct path into a permanent hell of the Great Beast. It prepared the way into the eternal idolatry of a mutually blinding search for authenticity. This could not, in fact, be further from what it might mean for human beings truly to seek or find themselves—or rather really to lose themselves.

ETHICS OF ACCEPTANCE

The little whippersnapper of the ego has been extinguished, the Great Beast of the We put out of action, but what is the state of the You of the Other? What becomes of the central Christian commandment to love our neighbor in a conception originating neither in self-determining subjects nor in something like overall social responsibility? How is the relationship with the Other established and determined? Weil's direct answer is through the attentive and unalterable acceptance of their essential vulnerability, their suffering:

> To accept the woes of others while at the same time suffering on account of them. Acceptance is nothing else but the recognition that something is.[49]

> *To contemplate the woes of others without turning away one's gaze; not only that of one's eyes, but also that of one's attention, as a result of revolt, sadism, or some inner consolation of one kind or another—that is beautiful.*[50]

> To manage to love God through and beyond the misery of others is very much more difficult than to love him through and beyond one's own suffering.[51]

The practically meditative immersion in the suffering of others serves no other purpose than to become aware of it. Suffering is. Existence *is* suffering. Recognizing in this sense that another person is suffering, and asking for what reasons and how one might stand by him is therefore, for Weil, not evidence of an (ethically) developed consciousness. Instead it demonstrates that one has not even begun to internalize what a truly ethical existence might consist of. Against this background there is no problem that can be solved by asking the questions: Why be ethical? Why help anyone else? Am I my brother's keeper?

The supposedly philosophical question about finding the foundation of "should be" in "is" is revealed to be the false problem of a worldview that believes it must be able to establish something like a separation between "is" and "should be." But that separation is itself nothing but an effect of the ego to be overcome by the contemplation of suffering. For Weil, in other words, pain and suffering are essentially consequences of action. No problem arises here in the sense of a deeper justification that might be solved by argument. And no such problem truly exists in any case.

What does exist is a lack of attention and, as the result of constant distraction and egoistic considerations, attenuated impulses of concern for others. What does exist for Weil is the all-too-human will to instrumentalize the vulnerability of others for one's own purposes—supposedly "good," "social," or "humanitarian" purposes.

SUPERIOR INDIFFERENCE

Just as a clear vision of the suffering of others does not require norms or even ethical imperatives, it does not need or tolerate explicit encouragements or requirements. The tendency toward the active acceptance of the Other as a suffering being may be different in individual cases, but, in a state of what Weil called "superior indifference,"[52] those individual differences are clearly to be taken as given just as much as the reality of suffering itself.

> We must not augment the inclination to relieve distress—it matters little whether it be strong or weak, for it is natural, and is neither good nor bad—but do away with what prevents it from being exercised.[53]

As regards the existence of Simone Weil, this inclination was clearly quite extreme, indeed almost pathological in the eyes of her fellows. Her ego was weakened and thus made porous to the suffering of others to an unheard-of degree. The supreme good for her would have been to be allowed to pass through the last door with the greatest possible attention and immersion—the ego weakened to an extreme degree—and abolish the boundary between her own being and that of others. It would be the highest good. It would mean becoming very light. It would mean becoming absolutely free at last, even if there was no choice.

> Attention, taken to its highest degree, is the same thing as prayer. It presupposes faith and love. Another form of freedom than that of choice is bound up with it, which is on the level of the will—namely, grace. We should pay attention to the point that we no longer have a choice. We then know our dharma.[54]

> The real aim is not to see God in all things; it is that God through us should see the things that we see.[55]

> I have got to withdraw in order that he may be able to see it.[56]

> To love all facts means nothing else but to read God in them.[57]

Weil's ethic, based on a "superior indifference" and purged of any purpose, approaches positions represented in the Western context by Baruch Spinoza[58] or, in Simone Weil's lifetime, by Ludwig Wittgenstein.[59] But in the Eastern cultural sphere, this also appears in Buddhism and Hinduism—correspondences to which Weil makes explicit reference and explores in her *Notebooks*. What particularly reduces and impedes the inclination among people to act *in the right way* is, she argues, the insistence on the I, or indeed on the We, as the supposed source of all aims and values.

Existentialist commitment is an arrogant crime against the goodness of being—that was Simone Weil's ruthlessly consistent verdict in the winter of 1941–1942. The alternative that she suggested was an ascetic path of salvation free of any form of earthly will. "Certainly, that is not for everyone," Weil stated laconically in her *Notebooks*, "but, then, neither is loving God for everyone."[60] Yet like everything in this world that has weight and value—the beautiful, the good, the just—the origin of his love also lies in another world.

> Supernatural love alone creates reality. In this way we become co-creators. We participate in the creation of the world by decreating ourselves.[61]

CROSSING

Weil's *Notebooks* from the turn of 1941–1942 look like sketches from the world of lonely plains and valleys that a human life must pass through on the way through darkness into light. In it, the same—or almost the same—landmarks are repeatedly approached from different directions, and opened up each time in more and more images,[62] largely because Weil was making those sketches herself along the way.

Rather than a coldly communicable doctrine, let alone a science of first principles, philosophy for her was nothing but a fearless journey along that path. In other words, it is not an objectively defining activity, but rather an existentially transformative one. Hence it is not something that can be delegated or intellectually proclaimed but something that can be conveyed to other people only by means of suggestion. It is a type of guide for those who are already on the same journey. We know from experience that this does not mean everyone or even just many, but always a few scattered individuals. These few, rare people—in this respect, too, Weil reveals herself once more as a pupil of Plato's—are the ones on whom everything ultimately depends in dark times. They carry the light into the world. And the darker the place where they are, the brighter their flame.

Accordingly, these few people cannot—or could not—be precisely characterized or judged in line with purely worldly concepts. And if such an attempt were made, then it would be in terms of profound alienation or madness. That was exactly what happened to Weil during this same period—whether in the Ardèche as a harvest worker or in the spring months in Marseille. Asked by a friend about her other plans, she would give only the unsettling answer that she wanted to "be truly useful. I want to go wherever there is the greatest possible danger . . . where my life will be least protected."[63] She wrote letter after letter to Free French army officers and functionaries, in which she set out detailed plans for missions along those lines. She was clearly under enormous mental pressure. At first sight there was no trace of divinely bestowed tranquility or will-less devotion. Even more so in that she saw her obligation as being to accompany her parents on their crossing to New York. The fear of not being able to return to her suffering homeland once she was in America weighed more heavily upon her than anything else.

The suitcases had been packed since the end of January. The family might have to leave at any moment. Their days were empty but for endless waiting. All other plans were put on hold. During that forced suspension Weil made advances along her journey into liberating "de-creation." With great presence of mind, she filled page after page of her *Notebooks*: "Moments of pause, of contemplation, of pure intuition, of mental void, of acceptance of the moral void. It is through such moments that [man] is able to approach the supernatural. Whoever for an instant bears up against the void, either he receives the supernatural bread, or else he falls."[64]

"I had the impression," Gustave Thibon recalled of their last meeting in the spring of 1942, "of standing in front of an almost transparent creature that was about to return to the primal light. . . . She commented on the Gospel. The words fell from her lips like fruits from a tree. Those words did not translate reality, they placed it, total and naked, within me. I felt myself being elevated above space and time."[65]

Aware that she had set down her spiritual testament—the document of a last will—she handed the *Notebooks* to Perrin and Thibon for safekeeping in April 1942. On May 14, the Weils left Marseille, making first for Casablanca. From the railing Simone called to friends waving on the quayside: "If we are torpedoed, what a beautiful baptismal font!"[66]

THIS MEANS YOU!

At least Hannah Arendt was spared the baptism by fire from German U-boat torpedoes. But even a year after her arrival she had not really warmed to New York. Especially not to the social circles that should really have been most familiar to her—those of the city's Jewish scholars and intellectuals. "You can't imagine," she wrote to Scholem in Jerusalem on April 25, 1942, "how foreign and strange this social life is for us here. (Just to be on the safe side, I left Monsieur at home because of the goy thing.) These people talk about everything that concerns us Jews and about everything that has happened, and they do so with the kind of aloof despair a person can only have if he's not directly involved. This is, pardon me for saying, an awful mistake."[67]

Arendt was convinced that by now pretty much every people on earth was affected, indeed the life of every human being was directly threatened by the Nazis. The fact that neither the Zionists nor the Allies properly understood this was in her view the greatest danger, both for the future of the Jews and for that of all the other people and nations of the world.

"With all that," Arendt continued, "we're doing well. Monsieur works as a sort of expert on all possible book and research projects. I'm writing my things on anti-Semitism and publishing them piecemeal in Jewish publications. . . . On the side, I'm a rather regular contributor to *Aufbau*. I've amicably established myself there as America's most minor columnist."[68]

Almost all of it was true. The couple lived with Arendt's mother in two half-furnished rooms between Central Park and the Hudson River. It was anything but comfortable, particularly since relations between Monsieur and his mother-in-law were increasingly tense. Blücher still blustered his way through the unfamiliar language with the robustness of a New York taxi driver. It wasn't enough for anything more than fragmentary everyday conversation, as Arendt's mother repeatedly observed, and that hardly raised his chances of paid work. The few articles commissioned from him for American military and propaganda purposes he continued to write in German.

A few days after her arrival, Arendt, on the other hand, had thrown herself with all her energy into learning English—in the summer of 1941 she had even spent several weeks living with a family in the country to study the language—and within a few weeks she had written her first pieces. The tone is striking, even in the new language, and by November 1941 she had a column in the German-language weekly *Aufbau*, the essential magazine for circles of Jewish exiles.

The title of the column, "This Means You,"[69] clearly showed the author's intentions, and revealed that Arendt was not greatly in favor of a *peaceful* establishment. Instead, she devoted her first columns enthusiastically to the demand for a special Jewish army recruited from all over the world, which would fight side by side with the Allies for liberation from the yoke of the Nazis:

> A Jewish army is not a utopia if Jews of all nations demand it and are willing to join it. What is utopian, however, is the idea that we might in some way be taking advantage of Hitler's defeat if we are not partly responsible for that defeat.[70]

The following year she would write, in the Buenos Aires–based journal *Provenir*:

> A people whom others will not allow to defend itself against its enemies is not a people but a living corpse. . . . We do not want promises that our sufferings will be "avenged," we want to fight; we do not want mercy, but justice. . . . Freedom is not a reward for sufferings endured and one does not accept justice as if it were crumbs from the table of the rich.[71]

Arendt was firmly convinced that it was only through an armed struggle under their own banner, only through a willingness, visible to the whole world, of those who were being attacked as Jews to defend themselves militarily *as* Jews, that it would ever be possible for her people to escape their role, seemingly fixed by history at least in Europe, as a group of victims. At the same time, a Jewish army from all nations would prevent the risk of splitting the Jews into a people of two worlds as a result of the establishment of Palestine—one people in the homeland of Palestine (Zion) and one of eternal exile and diaspora

(Galuth). One thing was crucial to Arendt, however, both psychologically and politically: such an army would contribute to what she saw as an absolutely necessary normalization of Jewish self-perception and perception of Jews by others as only *one* oppressed people among many other oppressed peoples and ethnic groups in the world. After all, because of Hitler's racially motivated conquests almost "all European nations . . . had become pariah peoples, they were all forced to resume the struggle for freedom and equal rights. For the first time our fate is not a special one, for the first time our struggle is identical with Europe's liberation struggle. As Jews we want to fight for the freedom of the Jewish people, because: 'If I am not for me, who is for me?' As Europeans we want to fight for the freedom of Europe, because 'If I am only for me—who am I?' (Hillel)."[72]

NEW HORROR

Where the fate of Judaism was concerned, even in a new world Arendt argued from a European perspective. And however conclusive her demands might have sounded, by May 1942 she had to acknowledge that her journalistic campaign had failed within Zionist circles. This was even more painful in that the global political situation had crucially changed.

By October 1941, the German advance on Moscow had come to a standstill and with the arrival of the Russian winter hardened into a war of attrition with heavy losses on both sides. Rather than collapsing within a few weeks, Stalin's Red Army was more than holding its own. The fate of Leningrad was a fine example of the new arrangement. Surrounded by the Nazis since September 1941 and subject to a blockade, it was held and defended at any cost by Stalin's troops. In the first winter hundreds of thousands of residents of the future "Hero City" died of starvation, a situation forced on them by the Nazis in violation of international law, and at the same time taken strategically into account by Stalin.

After the attack by Japanese bombers on the U.S. Pacific Fleet at Pearl Harbor on December 7, 1941, the United States had officially declared that it was entering the war. In an alliance with the British, U.S. forces were initially concentrated on the European western front. Their watchword was: "Germany first." By the spring of 1942, Europe saw a two-front scenario that would inevitably overwhelm the fighting power of the Wehrmacht.

In April 1942, again in vain, Hitler's troops made another crucial attempt at a breakthrough in the Soviet Union. It was clear that with the military resources available to them, the defeat of the Nazis was only a matter of time—and it was equally plain that Allied troops were prepared to make enormous sacrifices.

When leading members of the Zionist movement met for an extraordinary conference in New York's Biltmore Hotel on May 9, discussions were under a twofold strain. The information had not yet been confirmed, but by the beginning of 1942 the Nazis had already begun the mass deportations of interned and forcibly ghettoized Jews to special extermination camps in the occupied eastern regions, beginning with Lviv (Lemberg) and Lublin.[73] Clearly the mass murder of Europe's Jews was thus entering a hitherto unimaginable phase. This lent new urgency to the Zionist demand for an easing or even a lifting of immigration restrictions to the British protectorate of Palestine. At the same time, the scenario of an Allied victory was appearing on the horizon, providing the prospect of a politically independent Palestine as a homeland for the Jewish people. Arendt took part in the conference as an observer and was horrified by the decisions made there.

FALSE UNITY

For months Arendt had been concerned that the Zionist movement might harden internally in the face of the terrible situation of the Jews, and above all become nationalistically narrow. To fight against those forces, which were threatening an ideological kidnap of her journalistic campaign on behalf of a Jewish army, in March 1942 she established a political debating circle under the name Young Jewish Group.

With Arendt as the circle's intellectual initiator, the debates revolved around the question of "what kind of . . . political body Palestine Jewry was to form."[74] Arendt approached this question first and foremost as a political theorist, not as a Jew. This may be explained by the fact that the problem of the Jews in Palestine could be seen only as an exemplary concentration of an arrangement that actually affected any people or ethnic group that, as a minority within an existing national state, strove for appropriate representation and self-determination, for the preservation of their identity and language, their religious and cultural properties, their tradition.

In Arendt's analysis it was the idée fixe, born of the spirit of the nineteenth century and obligatory throughout the whole of Europe, of a nation-state as a necessary *unity of people, territory, and state* that had actually led to two world wars as well as modern anti-Semitism (also, as a concept, a child of the nineteenth century). In Arendt's own words:

> At that time antisemitism was still the expression of a typical conflict such as must inevitably occur within the framework of a national state whose fundamental identity between people and

> territory and state cannot but be disturbed by the presence of another nationality which, in whatever forms, wants to preserve its identity.[75]

According to the resolutions made in the Biltmore Hotel under the chairmanship of the social democrat (and future prime minister of Israel) David Ben-Gurion, it was on precisely this model of an ethnically homogeneous nation-state that the Jewish people should seek to create their homeland in Palestine. Aside from the demand for permission for two million European Jews to settle there, this congress resolved on the vision of Palestine as a "Jewish Commonwealth." The actual Arab majority population that also lived there was to be given only minority rights (not including the right to vote).

Arendt was filled with fury and, even more than that, with despair. She saw the Biltmore resolutions in the name of Zionism as a version of the ideal behind the solution to the "Jewish question," which she was convinced had led to political anti-Semitism and also to a "Jewish question" in the modern sense of the term: the idea of a nation-state ideally forming a completely binding unity of people, territory, and state—in which the Jews as a people must inevitably be seen as a deeply disturbing Other.

For Arendt, the Biltmore resolutions were a profound error, in fact a betrayal of the originally emancipating goals of the Zionist movement. In terms of realpolitik, she also considered them both nonsensical and, in the medium term, self-destructive. In her many raging articles over the following weeks and months she described as absurd the idea that a majority (Arabs) within a democratic Jewish Commonwealth should be granted only minority rights. Equally illusory was the idea of a supposedly sovereign nation-state that had to remain permanently dependent on another protective state for its existence and its ability to flourish. This fate, in terms of the map, seemed inevitable for a purely Jewish Palestine:

> Nationalism is bad enough when it trusts in nothing but the rude force of the nation. A nationalism that necessarily and admittedly depends upon the force of a foreign nation is certainly worse. . . . Even a Jewish minority in Palestine—nay even a transfer of all Palestine's Arabs, which is openly demanded by the revisionists—would not substantially change a situation in which Jews must either ask protection from an outside power against their neighbors or come to a working agreement with their neighbors.[76]

Not least, the route they had decided on would make peaceful cohabitation with the Palestinian Arabs impossible in the long term and further inflame the growing pan-Arabic anti-Semitism in the immediate neighboring countries.

The Biltmore Conference marked Arendt's definitive break with institutionalized Zionism. Still, she did not doubt that there might be something like a "Jewish people" that had preserved itself in time and space over the millennia as a politically effective unit and deserved free self-determination as a people. And similarly, as a Jew, she continued to support the ideal expressed by Theodor Herzl of creating a national homeland for the Jewish people. Just not in the form of a classic nation-state in the old European style.

COSMOPOLITAN INTENTIONS

That there were other ways of constituting oneself in a sovereign manner as a political community was demonstrated by her new home, the United States. Since its foundation, it had been created as a "federation," which is to say that it was "constituted of different very recognizable elements, whether of a national or some other political type, which together form the state. National conflicts can only be resolved in such a federation because the insoluble majority-minority problem has ceased to exist. . . . In this union, no individual has dominion over another, and all states together govern the country."[77]

Arendt imagined just such a federal solution—either part of a notional European federation of states or the British Commonwealth—as the ideal solution for a future Palestine. She was thoroughly convinced that "Palestine can only be saved as a national homeland for the Jews (like other small countries and other small nations) if it is integrated within a federation."[78]

Admittedly this form of Jewish patriotism with a cosmopolitan intent made her a lone voice in New York's concrete desert. This was due solely to the fact that her vision in the spring of 1942, in strategic terms, could not have been considered either "philosophical" or benignly well intentioned. There were tangible social and interpersonal reasons for Arendt's increasing isolation within both American and European Zionist circles in New York. It wasn't what she said so much as the way she said it. And as "America's most minor columnist" Arendt always said whatever she said in the sharpest and most strident tone. Even at a time when the Jewish people in Europe were gazing into the abyss of their extinction, she did not spare the sarcasm, the divisive irony, or arguments that amounted to equating Nazi racism with Jewish nationalism.[79] With her eyes wide open, she caused bad blood as a public intellectual. She believed that she owed it to herself and her people. In the name of truth, justice—and the freedom of open and public discourse.

The political demand that she made on the Jews, probably in the darkest moment of their history, was, to borrow a phrase from Simone de Beauvoir, one of "metaphysical solidarity" with all the oppressed peoples of the world—and in the interest of their very own freedom. Even in purely philosophical terms that was a big demand. In practical political terms, however, it was too great a demand, at least in the harsh conditions of the time.

SMALL CRISIS

What Arendt—like Beauvoir, Weil, and Rand—strove to achieve as a philosopher with a real political mission would have been difficult under any circumstances: political effectiveness and at the same time fidelity to one's principles, deep philosophical acuity, and transposition into reality. Around 1941–1942 it was a hopeless undertaking, whether in Paris or New York. Whether in the name of true socialism, Christianity, Zionism, or America; whether in the name of existential solidarity, the Lord Jesus Christ, a Kantian global citizenship, or even radical libertarianism. Precisely because they wanted to think primarily about politics, they were pushed to the edge of politics. For philosophers, if we look back at the history of the guild, that is not really a new experience. And not even one of a necessary loss of freedom. What is the best vantage point to have a clear view of events: from the center, from a distance, or from the outermost edges and abysses?

Thought that merits the name is also a very lonely business. That may be due to the fact that it is essentially an activity in which an absolute focus can be achieved only without reference to others. It cannot generally bear more than one or two intimate confidants. At least that was Arendt's lifelong conviction.

In November 1942, Arendt's column in *Aufbau* was pulled. By this time the Young Jewish Group was already history. We do not need to see it exclusively as a lament when Arendt tells her friend Scholem, months later, more about the lasting effects of her culture shock: "In this country one gets very lonely chiefly because people have so many things to do that, after a certain point, the need for leisure is quite simply no longer there. The result of this is a certain absence (by which I mean absentmindedness) that makes contact between people so difficult."[80]

Remaining attentive in times of absentmindedness. Maintaining the need for leisure and slowness. Being active but not too busy. The classic existential persistence of an ancient European in a new world. The important thing was not to fall into the abyss between "political freedom" and "social oppression" that was in Arendt's view typical of the country.[81] One had to reshape this newly attained freedom according to one's will: to find one's way "in between" it in the best sense—and above all to keep seeking.

At the beginning of the summer another opportunity arose when she was given her first academic job, as an adjunct lecturer at Brooklyn College. The title of the course: Recent European History. Thus a new old model of life was coming into being, as journalist and academic, and with it a one-woman research program: exposing the factors that had led to the current darkness—the European celebrations of death on the part of totalitarianism; its racially motivated desire to oppress; its compulsive idea of the one, single, and united ethnic and state body; its logic of the camp as a place of progressive dehumanization . . . anti-Semitism, imperialism, total domination. All of this could trace its origins back to the nineteenth century. And that trail needed to be pursued.

Arendt already had what she really needed in order to achieve this: the inner freedom to think independently, the people dearest to her as partners in dialogue, and the outer freedom of a country that respected the idea of independence not only in the letter. To express it in one of those idiomatic turns of phrase that Monsieur Heinrich dutifully recorded in his notebook every day, by the end of 1942, Hannah Arendt was not only a "nifty chick" bathed in the waters of the Atlantic, but above all "very much her own woman."[82]

NIETZSCHE'S CURSE

In retrospect it is almost a bit of a shame that Ayn Rand knew nothing about the political projects that Arendt and Beauvoir were bringing alive at almost the same time. She might have been able to draw some inspiration from them in the difficult process of finding a name for her own circle. Something along the lines of: "Metaphysical Egoists," "Young Libertarian Group," or, why not go whole hog, "Freedom without Socialism."

These terms were all better than the names actually discussed in the autumn of 1941, such as "American Neighbors" (Rand: "People's first impression will be that it has something to do with South America"[83]), or the candidate introduced by the founder herself: "Intellectual Aristocrats." Because even that didn't get it exactly right. In fact, it stressed a major problem of the focus of the entire libertarian program: the tension, difficult to resolve, between open elitism and the populism she was striving for. Nietzsche's curse: How was one to convince the majority democratically that the broad mass of the population was essentially inclined to idiocy? That the courage required to make use of one's own intellect had always been, and would always remain, an ideal of the few?

Albert Jay Nock put it like this at one of the group's first meetings: rather than fighting in the name of all for the vision of a political individualism, he advised continuing to cultivate the ideal of liberal self-sufficiency in a very small circle. Where dealings with the masses were concerned, there was only one recipe that ensured autonomy: social distance and everyday independence, not least of an economic kind. The important thing was not to be ordinary. In the light of day more could be neither achieved nor reasonably hoped for, regardless of time or country. Not even in America. Hoping to please the whole world with one's own vision of the good life, presented as having no alternative—was that not the essence of the totalitarian impulse?[84]

The literary critic Isabel Paterson—who had been a columnist with the New York *Herald Tribune* for more than a decade—kindly dismissed the idea, even though she and Rand had become friends over the years, a friendship as deep and intimate as the one Rand had enjoyed during her years in Saint Petersburg with Olga Nabokova, sister of Vladimir Nabokov. It did nothing to alter Paterson's cast-iron principle never to join any group or organization.

AMERICAN DEMOLITIONISTS

Even before the actual launch of the project, the Intellectual Aristocrats were thus reduced to half a dozen well-meaning members of the midwestern middle class and a few old-style right-wingers disappointed by the Republicans. Instead of getting into action with an individualistic functional elite that could be deployed on the ground wherever any kind of training was required, as Rand saw it they would be obliged to retrain themselves. These gentlemen were unwilling even to open their checkbooks enough to provide the starting capital required.

The same applied on a purely private front. Apart from her piecework as a script reader for Paramount Pictures, Rand the full-time libertarian activist had not had any real income. She had also had eight more rejection letters for her novel project. To make matters worse, Frank had lost the half-day job he had struggled to get as a salesclerk in a cigar shop. Well-paid wage work was hard to come by. With the stubbornness of a smoker's cough, the recession carried on, eight years after the start of Roosevelt's New Deal, so that even such a convinced isolationist as Ayn Rand may quietly have welcomed the United States' entry into the war in December 1941.[85]

At least it exonerated her from having to declare the failure of her political ambitions. In the exuberance of warlike patriotism, America First voices would be put on pause for the foreseeable future, and that included libertarian approaches based on a wartime economy in full swing.[86] The community project of the Intellectual Aristocrats was history even before it had begun. The same did not apply to the Howard Roark project.

Quite the reverse. Apparently out of the blue (but in fact engineered by Isabel Paterson), the Indianapolis-based publishing house Bobbs-Merrill showed definite interest, particularly from a newly appointed editor by the name of Archie Ogden. Despite threat of immediate dismissal, he fought for the manuscript, and in the end he had his way.

The contract was signed on December 10, 1941. The advance was a pathetic $1,000, and the proposed delivery date entirely unrealistic (January 1, 1943), but at least there was now a tangible goal. And a direct path into the only freedom that Ayn Rand—like Simone Weil, Simone de Beauvoir, and Hannah Arendt—unconditionally experienced: that of writing as creation. The signing of the contract, three days after Pearl Harbor and one day before the United States officially entered the war, signaled the start of the happiest and most productive year of Rand's life.

SOCIAL DISTANCING

Where the novel was concerned, "I have been [and still am] in an orgy of writing," Rand reported to her new favorite editor on February 19, 1942. "It has been a day and night job, literally. The record, so far, was one day when I started writing at 4 p.m. and stopped at 1 p.m. the next day (with one interruption for dinner). I can not do that often, but that time I did my best writing. I have gone for two or three days at a time without undressing—I'd just fall asleep on the couch for a few hours, then get up and go on."[87] She basically never left her apartment, and apart from Sunday meetings with Isabel Paterson, she suspended all social contacts and reduced both her personal hygiene and her sleep to the bare minimum. As long as her necessary sources of energy were guaranteed: cigarettes and chocolate.

As she had dreamed more than ten years before, in the course of 1942—when she was producing a good twenty-five print-ready manuscript pages per week—she was well on the way from human being to human typewriter. That was the life she wanted: independent, autonomous, self-generating—and in an important sense cost-effective. No thought of any potential readers, society, *critics*. The only thing that mattered in this process was metaphysical solidarity with the work itself. Her focused existence as the personification of superhumanly productive egotism. Who needs an outside world if they can conjure one from within? (And if their husband assumes the daily tasks.)

Not even the year spent as a political activist had been entirely wasted. Long-maintained convictions had clearer outlines, and fresh insights appeared in a more sophisticated form. Particularly with regard to the fundamental question that Rand had already formulated in her philosophical journal for 1934: "Is ethics a necessarily and basically a social conception? Have there been systems of ethics written primarily on the basis of an *individual*?"[88]

If the tension between "individualism" and "collectivism" had still been terminologically defining in the 1930s, Ayn Rand now presented the term "altruism" as the actual enemy of freedom. In this view, altruists were those who, as ethically acting beings, wished to see themselves primarily in relation to others. People, then, who based their thought, action, and creation on the existence of others and their interest: whether with the power-hungry aim of oppression or manipulation or with the sacrificial aim of encouraging or even "saving" them. So in the end everything depended on who was to be seen as the actual recipient of ethical actions: I myself or the Other. Accordingly, Rand noted in her diary in 1942, "when people believe that others are their prime virtue, they have only two alternatives: do what others believe (slavishness) or force their own belief for the good of others."[89] In other words, as the designated recipient of supposedly ethical actions, the Other could be helped only by being oppressed, whether in the form of his own submission or through his oppression. There was no third way.

An ethic in the name of the other—Sartre himself could hardly have put it more strongly—thus became one of mutual affirmation, inevitably requiring a loss of autonomy for both elements of the couple. For that reason the only way out of this situation was to deny, in an act of ethical self-determination, any involvement of the Other in one's own pursuit of the will. Not freedom *for*, *through*, or even solely *with* the Other, but freedom *from the Other*: "Selfishness—not to crush others, but *independent* of others."[90] Precisely because a Randian egotist unconditionally acknowledges the existence of others, precisely because they, too, exist in an eminent sense—with the same presence and value as oneself—it is essential to disengage from them, from their existence and any needs that they might have, when it comes to the definition of one's own will.

Accordingly, the only thing that makes mutual freedom truly possible and guarantees it is a consistently assumed attitude of "metaphysical independence," not something like "metaphysical solidarity." The only truly nonviolent way of making contact with the Other and acknowledging them unreservedly as an equally free human being is in a contract—like a good deal. My word is my bond. Take it or leave it. And live with the consequences. But the most socially flexible way of achieving goals of exchange is clearly economic: through monetary transactions. And the only economic way to make a truly nonviolent exchange between individuals in this sense is absolute laissez-faire capitalism. Finally, the only legitimate system of government in this sense is a democracy that is both as direct as possible and as limited in its interventions as possible.

For Rand, not only was this whole parcel of free coexistence practically tried and tested and, from experience, the lesser evil among human beings, it was actually transcendental. And not only did it work well, it was the only good for mankind. The good par excellence. Because there was no other source of value but human beings (and even if it did exist, the individual would first have to opt freely in its favor).

However, any voluntary deviation from this ideal meant clear-sightedly treading the path into self-induced slavery: ethically as altruism, economically as socialism, politically as totalitarianism. Of course, there were also people who yearned for precisely that. And those who were unable to light the creative fire of freedom within themselves or keep it alight. And who therefore, rather than embarking on the austere adventure of their own "pursuit of happiness" preferred to see everyone else constrained in the name of everyone else. The Toohey Principle in all its aridly civilizing varieties.

If none of this was ultimately based in strict logic, and not every conceptual transition was exactly marble smooth, in 1942 these principles provided Rand with an interpretational matrix that allowed her to structure her novel on three levels at once: as the representation of a timeless struggle of conflicting development goals in the psyche of each individual; as an interpretation of the specific tension of the zeitgeist in America on the eve of World War II; as a doctrine poured into the mold of the novel, which promised to grant an escape route from the hell of the Other in the darkest of times—with the almost religiously elevated Howard Roark as a savior figure.

In December, after twelve months of uninterrupted creative frenzy, Rand reached the actual summit of her work with Roark's speech before the twelve sworn jurors. Like a Socrates of the real America, Roark stands before the jury in the name of the people, to embody in front of and for the whole world precisely those values on which America's widely admired Constitution and Declaration of Independence were actually based.

ROARK'S DEFENSE

The crime of which Roark is accused consists neither of the corruption of youth nor of blasphemy against the gods. It appears at first much more banal, but on closer inspection even more dangerous to the cohesion of the social fabric. He has single-handedly leveled with dynamite a showcase project for which he himself was responsible, just days before it was due to be completed. And only because a public committee (led by Toohey) suggested tiny changes to the original design and implemented them without explicit authorization, hence, strictly speaking, in breach of contract. What the jury has to decide is thus neither the deed nor its circumstances, because Roark does not deny these, but solely the validity and hence the justification of his motive.

In the words of the state prosecutor's office, this motive is quite clearly "beyond the realm of normal human emotions. To the majority of us it will appear monstrous and inconceivable. . . . Even as the dynamite which swept a building away, his motive blasted all sense of humanity out of this man's soul. We are dealing, gentlemen of the jury, with the most vicious explosive on earth—the egotist!"[91]

Now it is Roark's turn to explain himself. He has insisted on doing so without a lawyer. He defends himself. Blind to everything that might indicate any kind of conditionality, at first sight he also appears to the jury as "a man innocent of fear."[92] A remarkable formulation that arises consistently out of Rand's conviction that one's own emotional life is entirely governable by the intellect. Hence there are also unreasonable emotions and affects that a human being may be guilty of—fear, first of all. Also regret. Lack of drive. All openings into the inner void and hence traps for others. They are, of course, alien to Roark. He is nothing but plenitude and will to action, governed by his own imagination and creativity, unleashed by the fire of his genius.

It is only logical that his defense should begin with reference to Prometheus as the first of all creators: "Thousands of years ago the first man discovered how to make fire. He was probably burned at the stake he had taught his brothers to light."[93]

This establishes both the distance Roark has to fall and the guiding theme: the innovative individual as the actual driving force of all progress in civilization—in conflict with the envious horde of the "far too many." The light of creative reason versus the dark thoughtlessness of self-denial. The brave, progressive I versus the fear-driven longing for stagnation of the They.

But what drives the true creator, like the true motives for his actions? According to Roark, it is by no means the desire to be useful or helpful in any way to his fellow men, but only the quest, undertaken with the best will and the best conscience, for a solution to the problem. And hence the will to truth of the work itself.

Insofar as the problem has been newly posed, its solution cannot lie in resorting to rules and methods already established by others. Creativity thus inevitably means the will to confident deviation—not least in the sphere of the social. True creators, the drivers of all human progress, are therefore loners, and need to be. For precisely that reason they are punished and slandered by the masses, and all too often simply lynched. Or else, more rarely, they are celebrated by them, put on a pedestal, and even deified. These two things are equally damaging to the creative individual, the results of both equally dangerous. Not to others, not for them—but *independently* of them. If it's successful, the work is valued.

As Roark sets out the situation to his jury, the source of true creativity and the source of pragmatic reason are one and the same. In the end there is only one form of thought and conclusion. And that is the same for everyone. Even more, as a deliberately controllable ability, it is the unique feature of humanity. Without it, human beings would be incapable of survival. With it, they can potentially do anything.

But each person can think only for himself, particularly in the eminent sense of creation:

> "There is no such thing as a collective brain. There is no such thing as a collective thought.... No man can use his brain to think

> for another. All the functions of body and spirit are private. They cannot be shared or transferred."[94]

Roark's conclusion from this: Copyright is to be preserved and protected. It is an essential part of a person's integrity—as a creative unity of body and mind. Hence anyone who violently attacks those rights takes an ax to the foundations of a civilization based on freedom and progress. Hence a good, fair society unconditionally protects that integrity against violent attack from others.

It protects that integrity particularly against the attack of others who cannot and, more important, do not want to create. Those who as human beings prefer to take refuge in the illusory safety of the "They" and their "good society." Those who deliberately obstruct and oppose the creator—mostly, in line with a perverted kind of propaganda in the name of all—for the lowest of motives. The "second-handers" and their guiding ideology based on the dependency, individual interchangeability, and thus the self-effacement in the name of each individual in the name of all others. Hence altruists: "Altruism is the doctrine which demands that man live for others and place others above self."[95]

What makes this ideology so destructive in Roark's view is not only its profound psychological distortion, but even more fundamentally its factual unassailability. Altruists demand the impossible:

> "No man can live for another. He cannot share his spirit just as he cannot share his body. But the second-hander has used altruism as a weapon of exploitation and reversed the base of mankind's moral principles. Men have been taught every precept that destroys the creator. Men have been taught dependence as a virtue. The man who attempts to live for others is a dependent."[96]

So the actual choice facing any reasonable person in terms of their fellows is not "slavery" or "domination," but "dependence" or "independence." This declared will to independence—and who could that be closer to than the Americans—is not a matter of individual talent or intellectual faculties. No one is too stupid to be themselves. The first important thing is the clear courage to want to use one's own intellect independently; it is the will to be able to say confidently "*I* want," "*I* can and will." But there is nothing at all elitist about this; as an existential option it is as egalitarian, dignified, and democratic as it is possible to imagine:

> "Degrees of ability vary, but the basic principle remains the same: the degree of a man's independence, initiative and personal love for his work determines his talent as a worker and his worth as a man. Independence is the only gauge of human virtue and value. What a man is and makes of himself; not what he has or hasn't done for others. There is no substitute for personal dignity. There is no standard of personal dignity except independence. In all proper relationships there is no sacrifice of anyone to anyone."[97]

For this reason only a community that is based on this courage and protects it unconditionally in line with the Constitution can flourish and prosper as a nation. As the "land of the free," in fact. Far from the mass nationalism of the big collective, Roark reminds the jury of the Constitution like a true American patriot:

> "Now observe the results of a society built on the principle of individualism. This, our country. The noblest country in the history of men. The country of greatest achievement, greatest prosperity, greatest freedom. This country was not based on selfless service,

sacrifice, renunciation or any precept of altruism. It was based on a man's right to the pursuit of happiness. His own happiness. Not anyone else's. A private, personal, selfish motive. Look at the results. Look into your own conscience."[98]

Don't yield an inch to altruism. Not an inch to its presumptions. Not an inch to the undermining of the only rights that demand to be preserved in the name of the independence and integrity of every reasonable human being, man or woman, unconditionally and uncompromisingly: their intellectual and physical property rights.

The high-handed demolition of the showcase Cortlandt Homes was thus not only Roark's full right, but actually his duty as a true American, an act of dignified resistance in a dark time. Certainly, he ultimately did it only for himself for purely—and here the prosecutor was completely right—selfish reasons. But he did it as a surrogate for all rationally gifted people, and thus all those who yearned for freedom, in his country—indeed in the world.

"Now you know why I dynamited Cortlandt. . . .

"I came here to say that I do not recognize anyone's right to one minute of my life. Nor to any part of my energy. Nor to any achievement of mine. No matter who makes the claim, how large their number or how great their need.

"I wished to come here and say that I am a man who does not exist for others. It had to be said. The world is perishing from an orgy of self-sacrificing.

"I wished to come here and say that the integrity of a man's creative work is of greater importance than any charitable endeavor. Those of you who do not understand this are the men who're destroying the world.

"I wished to come here and state my terms. I do not care to exist on any others.

"I recognize no obligations toward men except one: to respect their freedom and to take no part in a slave society. To my country, I wish to give the ten years which I will spend in jail if my country exists no longer. I will spend them in memory and in gratitude for what my country has been. It will be my act of loyalty, my refusal to live or work in what has taken its place."[99]

THE VERDICT

The judgment now depended on the jury, on each single one of them. And of course, in this setup there's a particular appeal in imagining the actual Hannah Arendt, Simone Weil, and Simone de Beauvoir in 1942 as members of this jury. What verdict would they have delivered? How would they have assessed Roark's defense? Dissected his arguments? Responded to his speech?

Was it really only a confident act of "I will" that granted someone value and dignity as a finite being? Or did its source not also lie outside him—perhaps outside this world? Could a flesh-and-blood ego really make free decisions only independently of others, or, quite the contrary, only through and with them?

What about the spontaneity and autonomy of the emotional life? Could it really be unconditionally subjected to the intellect—and if so, with what consequences for the individual growth of the subject? Was Roark really the creative pariah he presented himself as being—or the prototype of a narcissistically deluded parvenu? As a human being, did he really stand beyond the classical cult of genius—or did he want to be elevated precisely to that pedestal?

What about the identity of strictly logical thought and creativity that he asserted? Was there really only a logic of research, only a logical form of knowledge and judgment? What about the origins of creative processes? To what extent could an idea be claimed as private property, when it was quite obviously nothing that a creative individual could produce and conjure simply by an act of will?

Was the world, as Roark argued, actually being destroyed by an orgy of selflessness and self-sacrifice? Or rather by the will to unconditional self-empowerment by manic individuals? Was it really the Atlas-like shoulders of the few on which the whole weight of progress through civilization rested? And not the permanently bent backs of those they systematically exploited?

And not least: What about the nature of the language with and in which Roark addressed the jury? Was that language too, in origin, the work of an egotistical genius from a distant past? And if so, was it definitely that of a human being? Could language be understood as a medium of communication and thought when one imagined it as something that had been called to life independent of the existence of other human beings?

The discussions on the subject among Beauvoir, Arendt, and Weil would have taken several days, possibly even years (or centuries), without ever converging on a unanimous judgment. What else—among independent-minded philosophers—could have been expected? Only fools or ideologues see consensus as a goal of thought.

In Ayn Rand's actually existing fiction, the jury, consisting primarily of reality-hardened representatives of American common sense, took just a few minutes to deliver their verdict.

"Mr. Foreman, have you reached a verdict?"

"We have."

"What is your verdict?"

"Not guilty."

When Ayn Rand set these lines down on paper, she had months of social isolation and uninterrupted creative ecstasy behind her. On December 31, 1942, she personally handed Archibald Ogden the completed manuscript. Her part of the contract was fulfilled. She owed nothing to anyone, particularly not to herself. From now on, the work was in the hands of others. And whatever their judgment might be, at that moment she knew exactly what she had done and created. It was a divine feeling.

VIII

FIRE: 1943

Rand and Beauvoir are in heaven,
Arendt stares into the abyss,
and Weil crosses the final threshold.

ON STRIKE

"I've presented my case in *The Fountainhead*. . . . If [readers] don't respond, why should I wish to enlighten or help them further? I'm not an altruist!"[1] Six weeks after publication, the fate of Rand's second novel also appeared to be sealed. No advertising. No sales. Not even any more disputes. It didn't help that Isabel Paterson, at the other end of the telephone line, started talking about her own disasters. Eight novels so far, all flops. A few weeks before Rand's *Fountainhead* was published, Paterson had published her most ambitious nonfiction book so far, *The God of the Machine*, a cultural-historical hymn to free enterprise and the creativity of the individual. This, too, failed to find any great resonance. What had her friend expected? A hundred thousand copies sold?[2] For a philosophical novel? In Roosevelt's America?

Rand had slogged away at it uninterruptedly for sixteen months. She had spent whole days correcting proofs until well into April. Toward the end she'd been relying on uppers.[3] She was too exhausted to be able to calm herself. A culture that was deaf even to a book like this one deserved its downfall: "What if I went on strike?" she asked her friend. "What if all the creative minds in the world went on strike?"[4] If we just pulled the plug on the "machine"? A coordinated revolt of creative minds until even the most stubborn collectivist would publicly have to admit whose shoulders the whole burden rested on. That, Rand added, after a brief pause in the conversation, could even be a good novel. But no one was going to write it, or at least it wouldn't be her. Tomorrow she would go out and look for some kind of pointless work. Like Frank, she would go into internal exile, and write only at night, if at all. Not for the present day, but for posterity, if at all. That was enough.

In the course of the conversation, Paterson was able to persuade her exhausted friend of the necessity of a different kind of time-out. She invited Rand and her husband to her country house in Connecticut for two weeks. Sleep. Walk. Eat.

NOT A FICTION

While Rand, in July 1943, was doing nothing since arriving in America, *The Fountainhead* started taking off. Purely by word of mouth the first printing (8,000 copies) had almost sold out. Time for a second. To go on feeding the delicate flame. In mid-August, having recovered from her ordeal, Rand told her editor about her new project.

> August 16, 1943
>
> Dear Mr. Ogden:
>
> I am now working on a short non-fiction book. . . . Its provisional title is "THE MORAL BASES [*sic*] OF INDIVIDUALISM." . . .
>
> The book will present, in simple, concrete terms, the the-

> sis of "The Fountainhead"—the statement of man's essential integrity and self-sufficiency, the exposition of altruism as a fallacy and a moral evil, the definition of a proper moral law which is to be found neither in self-sacrifice for others nor in domination over others but in spiritual independence. And (which is not in "The Fountainhead" except by implication) an outline of the proper social, political and economic system deduced from and based on man's moral nature—the capitalist system, its meaning, principles and actual working as the only *moral* system of society.
>
> *Capitalism has never found the moral principle on which it must stand.* We have stood on it in fact, we have built our entire civilization upon it. . . .
>
> [People] have been taught to consider it as a practical, realistic system, but not an ethical one.[5]

No human being, particularly not one who longs for freedom, truly lives on bread alone. Ideas are essential nourishment. If a person wants to live well, those ideas need to be true and have a sound foundation. So the task had been clearly set out: to establish capitalism as the only true expression of a moral coexistence, the only true form of a striving for freedom and self-determination. Its promise was primarily not material but intellectual in nature. Its guiding ideal not affluence but autonomy. Its goal not wealth but self-realization. Its ideal not exploitation but independence. Far from being merely "the lesser evil," it was instead the consistent expression of goodness itself:

> We must define, understand and accept Individualism as a *moral* law, and Capitalism as its practical and proper expression. If we don't—capitalism cannot be saved. If it is not

> saved—we're finished, all of us, America and the world and every man, woman and child in it. Then nothing will be left but the cave and the club.
>
> Look at the tempo of destruction around us. An idea is responsible for that—a fatally erroneous idea. An idea can stop it—a true one.[6]

DEAL!

The book was never written. A month later, the forces of the free market—and particularly those that were in tune with the Randian spirit—had other ideas. Ogden unexpectedly left the company in September. At the same time, *The Fountainhead* appeared on the bestseller lists on both the East and West Coasts for the first time. There was already a fourth printing by October. The marketing department announced a revised nationwide advertising campaign for Christmas. Rand could hardly contain her joy. That was exactly how she had imagined things! Not a trace remained of the weariness of June. Now she was bursting with fresh energy. Isabel Paterson was the first to learn of it:

> October 10, 1943
>
> Darling, thank you immensely for everything you said. Particularly, for saying that I am your sister. Why did you add: "That is, if you also find it so"? I hope you don't have to doubt how I find it.
>
> I know that I will now have to write "The Strike"[7]—you'll push me into it. . . . I find myself dropping everything and

> thinking about that story—which I shouldn't do right now. But by all the signs, I know I'm hooked. . . . That's how I usually start. So may God help me—also you and Frank.[8]

By now even Hollywood had become aware of the *Fountainhead* phenomenon. In mid-November, Rand received a call from the Warner Bros. studio, which she immediately passed on to her agent, Alan Collins. He wanted to ask $25,000 for the film rights and settle for $20,000. That would have put his client in a league with Dashiell Hammett and John Steinbeck. But above all, her livelihood would be secured for years to come. As Rand understood it, this meant that *The Fountainhead* was really taking off. She knew the business and its margins, and instructed Collins to go for $50,000. No concessions. Not a penny less. Or no deal.[9]

It was Frank who took the crucial call. Rand was to write the screenplay herself, at least in a first version. And for that she would move back to Hollywood, all expenses paid—$500 a month. And yes, $50,000 for the rights.

The pair went to celebrate at their regular diner around the corner (this time with the more expensive items on the cheap menus) and stayed awake all night—dreaming and planning. Her mother had been right after all: "Hollywood with its caprices at last used common sense and is forced to admit that white is white."[10] Rand hadn't had a sign of life from her family for years. The siege of Leningrad was going into its third winter.

On the day when the contract was due to be signed, Rand's husband surprised her with a visit to a fur salon on Fifth Avenue: "You can choose any kind of coat you want—as long as it's a mink." Rand chose one that cost $2,400, paid for it immediately, and then swiftly headed down to Paterson's editorial office to show it off.[11]

Modesty is for little people! Especially now that, as a dyed-in-the-wool New Yorker, she had no way of knowing when she would be able to wear it again, because of the "disgusting California sunshine." They would set off to Hollywood in December. Frank in particular could hardly wait. The couple first took the luxury train to Chicago, with real steak in the restaurant car, at a time of rationing.[12] So very close to the ideal, at least for this one moment.

As soon as they arrived in Hollywood, Rand started working on her screenplay. Her first journal entry about it is dated December 13, 1943. It reads: "General theme: Man's integrity."[13]

NEW TRAIN

"I finished my move yesterday evening, then ate some fried potatoes before going off to catch my train. My dear little one, do at all costs reserve your seat, since those corridors are quite frightful!"[14] Sartre had received a princely advance to work on a screenplay in his new rooms at the Hôtel La Louisiane, so in early July 1943, Beauvoir traveled north to Roanne for her summer holidays. It was to be a time to regroup and consider new projects. Whatever she might have expected of Paris in the autumn, returning to her old life was now out of the question. Since July 17, Beauvoir had been suspended from her teaching duties. Admittedly it had been difficult to prove Natalie Sorokin's mother's accusation of corruption of a minor even after a six-month investigation, but the state of the inquiry was grave enough to lead to the withdrawal of Beauvoir's teaching permit. And in that summer of 1943 Beauvoir was officially able to call herself what she had always wanted to be since her earliest youth: a freelance writer and philosopher.

By the end of August, her first novel had finally been published by

Gallimard. In intellectual terms the book was years behind, but that applied less to the relationship figurations around which the plot was based. Without a doubt, these aspects were particularly prominent in the reception of the work. Not least because of Sartre's fame.

As if to illustrate what it meant to be a public author, on the train journey a critical dispute broke out in Beauvoir's compartment, reflecting the preoccupations of the whole country: "I was very much diverted. . . . They drew a parallel between *The Stranger* and *Nausea*—to Camus's advantage—because they found *Nausea* boring in spite of fine passages. But then the moving spirit declared that there'd been good things in *The Flies* all the same, that it was odd it hadn't been a hit."[15]

It was true: Sartre's latest play had been a flop in June. Why exactly was a mystery even to Beauvoir. Reworking political subjects using ancient material was very much of the moment; in fact, it was the only possible way of getting them past the censors. Either that or people had begun to dislike Sartre for putting the play on at all. And in the Théâtre de la Cité, the former Théâtre Sarah-Bernhardt? There were certainly enough people who wanted to see him brought down a peg or two. Not least those who openly suspected him of being a collaborator.

CREATIVE TRANSGRESSION

Nonetheless, Camus had generously praised the work. Immediately after the dress rehearsal he and Sartre had gone for a drink and talked until deep into the night, and joked: *The Stranger, Nausea*, and *The Guest*—the new trio of the new existentialism! And why not?

For all the spontaneous sympathy between the two men, the philosophical differences between Sartre and Camus were unmistakable that evening. But what did that tension mean for Beauvoir's own thought?

Above all for the question of how "metaphysical solidarity" might be defined in the context of an existentialist understanding of freedom?

What was it exactly that established the relationship with the Other? What kind of responsibility did the existence of others entail? To what extent was it a threat, to what extent a condition of my freedom?

As if electrified by the new impulses, Beauvoir promised to Jean Grenier, an editor at Gallimard, an essay, which had flowed from her pen in only a few weeks. One hundred pages in total, and even its title followed the fashion of the return to classical subjects: "Pyrrhus and Cineas."[16] She was quite pleased with it. Its central idea seemed to carry some weight: for the sake of the freedom of one's own intentions, it was important to desire and promote the freedom of others. "The other's freedom can do something for me only if my own goals can, in turn, serve as its point of departure. In using the tool that I have fabricated, the other prolongs its existence."[17]

The forthcoming publication of a book was an excellent example of this. After all, one did not write a book for other people. Any more than one wrote it for an already existing self. One wrote it, in fact, to renew one's own self in the process of writing, and creatively go beyond its previous limits. Or in other words: to transcend oneself.

> Thus it is not for others that each person transcends himself; one writes books and invents machines that were demanded nowhere. It is not for oneself either, because "self" exists only through the very project that throws it into the world. The fact of transcendence precedes all ends and all justification.[18]

Where the fundamental human impulse to the creative project is concerned, two false interpretations should be avoided: just as it should not be undertaken in order to satisfy or fulfill already existing needs of others (whatever form they may assume), it is put into effect in the name of an I or self whose essence could be defined or grasped even more before the act of creation. In fact, the existence of a human being—as someone constantly creating themselves—always precedes their essence, without ever being overtaken by it.

The importance of other people for this permanent self-dynamization lies primarily in testifying to that movement and assigning to its results a place that grants it significance in a world shared by all human beings. And which thus grants one's own existence a point of departure for some kind of new project.

> So here is my situation facing others: men are free, and I am thrown into the world among these foreign freedoms. I need them because once I have surpassed my own goals, my actions will fall back upon themselves, inert and useless, if they have not been carried off toward a new future by new projects.[19]

In this way human existence appeared to Beauvoir as an endless movement toward freedom, constantly finding and inventing itself in the face of others. Without the actual acceptance of her work by others, this dynamic would soon be exhausted. Without its reviving breath, the fire of freedom would soon be extinguished.

In this essay, shortly after the publication of her first novel, Beauvoir defines the freedom-preserving relationship with the Other in terms of the leg up that children give each other to climb over a wall or an obstacle that could not otherwise be surmounted. One, through the simple weight of their free existence, supports the project of the other. But they each remain responsible only for their own action on their own journey. In a less static metaphor, which can also be seen as a (highly idealized) description of that dynamic, which had for years defined the life of Beauvoir and Sartre's "family," she expressed it like this: "Our freedoms support each other like the stones in an arch, but in an arch that no pillars support."[20]

OPEN FUTURE

By late August, Sartre and Beauvoir were once again on the way to Madame Morel's country house at La Pouëze. They planned to spend the rest of the summer writing there—Beauvoir, the beginning of her next novel, whose title, *The Blood of Others*, had been in her mind for some time; Sartre, a play for a small cast, which he planned to call *The Others*. More as a five-finger exercise, but above all in order to help Wanda, who like Olga was now an actress, to get her first part. (The play would later receive the title *Huis Clos*, or *No Exit*.)

The connecting train in Angers was late. While Beauvoir took a break in a café, Sartre came toward her from the station, "waving a newspaper." The time had come: "The first review of *She Came to Stay* had just come out, in *Comœdia*. . . . No article had ever pleased me so much. . . . Here was a review, written by a real critic, printed in a real paper, to assure me in black and white that I had written a real book—that I had become, overnight, a real writer. I could not contain my joy."[21]

Sartre had only good news. His screenplays had been accepted, and the money for them was assured: "Don't worry . . . we'll be comfortable next year."[22] Particularly since he had managed to find Beauvoir a well-paid job as an editor at Radiodiffusion Nationale, a state broadcaster, known colloquially as Radio Vichy.

When they got back to Paris in October, Beauvoir's novel was a hot topic of conversation even outside the Montparnasse scene. As expected, readers' imaginations were particularly stimulated by the ménage à trois at the center of the plot: "I did not jeopardize my pleasure by asking indiscreet questions, such as what absolute value there might be in my novel, or whether it would stand up to the passage of time. . . . For a moment it was sufficient that I had crossed the first threshold: *She Came to Stay* existed for other people, and I had entered public life."[23]

The book was even shortlisted for the Prix Goncourt. That was more than a first step, it was a breakthrough. And if the news coming through from the BBC was anything to go by, the Allied landing in Sicily meant that the liberation of France was also getting closer: "The important thing was that a day would come when the future was open again. We no longer had any doubts about this, and we even went so far as to predict that there would not be long to wait now."[24]

MESSAGE IN A BOTTLE

In New York that autumn of 1943, Hannah Arendt was also waiting with growing impatience for the infernal spectacle to be over. However, she had not in the meantime enjoyed similar breakthroughs. Quite the reverse. Aside from her disagreements with the city's Zionist groups, her contacts with the German exiled intelligentsia were becoming increasingly difficult. This applied primarily to Theodor Wiesengrund Adorno and Max Horkheimer and their Institute for Social Research. These antipathies dated back to Frankfurt in the early 1930s, when Günther Stern, Arendt's newly wedded husband, had unsuccessfully applied for a postdoctoral position in Adorno's immediate circle. The only thing that brought them together in this new world was concern over Walter Benjamin's legacy. As requested, Arendt had brought Benjamin's last writings to the Institute for archiving immediately after her arrival, but since then had heard nothing about their location or any use they might have been put to. That was now more than two years ago. In Jerusalem, Scholem, Benjamin's oldest and closest friend, was becoming increasingly aggravated. Why was nothing being done with the material? Why had nothing been published? Was no one answering questions?

"I'm sending you Benjamin's *Theses,* my only copy," Arendt wrote Scholem on November 4, 1943, in a letter whose New York directness would have done Ayn Rand proud. "Negotiating with Wiesengrund is worse than pointless. What they have undertaken to do with the estate, or have in mind to do with it, I haven't the foggiest idea. I spoke with Horkheimer when he was here in the summer, but nothing came of it. He maintains that the crate is in a safe (which is certainly a lie), and he hasn't even opened it. . . . I am entirely on my own here, without any support, and in dealing with this gang I am out of my element. . . . Added to this is that the Institute itself is about to go under. They still have money, but they are more and more of the opinion that they must use the money to spend their sunset years in comfort. The journal has stopped coming out: its reputation here is hardly stellar—for those who even know it exists, that is. Wiesengrund and Horkheimer are living it up in California. The Institute here is purely administrative, and what is being administered, besides money, no one knows. Through agents and intrigues they managed to relieve the American Jewish Committee of $10,000 for the purposes of a study on anti-Semitism."[25]

So that was Arendt's situation: without a network, a job, or a grant, she had to look on as Adorno and Horkheimer, of all people, won themselves a princely research grant for which she herself had been working with great concentration for years, even though "they complained to me that they had never been interested in Jews and their enemies, and now they have to waste their time with such crazy and 'marginal' issues. Wiesengrund and his cohorts meanwhile are writing the 'Message in the Bottle for the Future.' I'm assuming that for this they're getting some inspiration from the contents of the 'safe.'"[26]

Just a year later, Adorno and Horkheimer's "message in a bottle" would be published under the title *Dialectic of Enlightenment*; it would become one of the most influential philosophical works of the twentieth century. But as far as the history and above all the effects of anti-Semitism in Europe were concerned, these were also increasingly becoming the focus of public interest in the United States.

ON THE BRINK OF THE ABYSS

A year previously, in November 1942, the World Jewish Congress had delivered its first reports to journalists on the mass murder of Jews. As monstrous as the content of this information was, it did not begin to match the actual events of this phase. As we know today, between August 1942, when Wehrmacht troops advanced into Stalingrad, and October 1942, more than 1.4 million Jews were murdered by the SS. These included more than a million in the Operation Reinhard camps in Bełżec, Sobibór, and Treblinka: 14,000 people a day. The horror subsided in October only for logistical reasons. There was simply a temporary shortage of people to be murdered.[27]

But even in the context of the news at the time, the actions of the Nazis prompted disbelief, not least among experts and journalists. Above all because from outside, none of it seemed to make the slightest sense, either militarily or in any other way. Unless the Nazis, at the height of the war, were determined to demonstrate that this was something they were both capable of and willing to do.

It had also taken Arendt and Blücher months to accept that the reports might be true. From the spring of 1943, Arendt delivered lectures in which she expressed her conviction that "since the outbreak of the war and even before, a conspiracy of silence has covered the sufferings and the losses of the Jewish people."[28]

Nonetheless, she could not be persuaded to take part in publicly influential demonstrations of solidarity, like the "We Shall Never Die" concert organized by Ben Hecht and Kurt Weill in Madison Square Garden: her mistrust of any form of commitment backed by the Zionists was too deep.

For now there was nothing more meaningful to do than go on working away at her own message in a bottle. "I've been working a lot," she wrote to Scholem in November 1943. "If I ever write my book on anti-Semitism, it'll have to include plenty of very strange things. At present, I'm still writing and publishing parts of it in local journals."[29]

ELEMENTS AND ORIGINS

It was quite natural that the Judaist Scholem had gone his own way in his latest book, *Major Trends in Jewish Mysticism*, with regard to both his sources and his methods.[30] He had personally sent Arendt a copy the previous year. As she wrote in her notes on the book (which she enclosed with her November 1943 letter), his research broke in an almost visionary way from the pattern of interpretation that had for far too long defined and burdened modern Jewish historiography:

> Jewish historians of the last century tended to ignore all those facts of Jewish history that did not fit with the fundamental thesis of the history of the diaspora, according to which the Jews had no political history of their own, but were tirelessly innocent victims of a hostile and sometimes violent environment. . . . But Jewish

> mystical thought, which led in the Sabbatian movement, as we know, to political action, was such a serious obstacle to this interpretation that it could be overcome only by hasty defamation or by passing over it completely. Scholem's new presentation and appreciation of Jewish history not only fills a gap, but actually changes the whole picture of Jewish history.[31]

According to Scholem, the Sabbatianism mentioned in the quotation, a mystical salvation movement from the early eighteenth century based on Sabbatai Zevi's being the Messiah, marked the actual origin of the Jewish tragedy in Europe, when, with its repression as a distinct political movement, all hope was lost of finding an identity beyond assimilation or the role of victim. The failure of the Sabbatian movement thus meant the beginning of a profound identity crisis and an era of political agony that, fueled by the modern anti-Semitism and nationalism of the nineteenth century, reached an absolute nadir in the early 1940s. Ultimately, in terms of the National Socialist extermination campaign against the Jews, much more was at stake than mere despair about the internal definition of a people. It was about speechless horror in view of its total eradication by industrialized murder. The threatened loss of any hope of a future worthy of the name.

In the sense of Benjamin's angel of history, then, Scholem and Arendt initially turned their backs on the future in order to illuminate with their independent point of view on how the present-day mountains of rubble and corpses could have come about. Like Benjamin, they were convinced that what we call the past is not in any way more fixed than the future. And that in this darkest phase of the shock, everything depended on grasping the specific figurations that had led to this present and no other. Because, to quote one of Benjamin's "Theses on the Philosophy of History": "To articulate the past historically means . . . to seize hold of a memory as it flashes up at a moment of danger."[32] It was a matter of bringing together the elements and origins in which the present horror was suddenly crystallized.[33] That was a precise description of Arendt's current research project on the history of anti-Semitism. And, as she understood it, also Scholem's project as a visionary Judaist.

She concluded her notes in November 1943 with a quotation from his latest foundational work: "To speak of the mystical course which, in the great cataclysm now stirring the Jewish people more deeply perhaps than in the entire history of Exile, destiny may still have in store for us—and I for one believe that there is such a course—is the task of prophets, not of professors."[34]

To which Arendt immediately adds the proviso that it is not "the task of prophets to decide upon our ultimate political will."[35] Any more than it is the task of professors.

NO FATE

Arendt's own mission in this context was thus clearly outlined: she would write neither as a prophet nor as a professor. Neither betray the ideals of Kantian Enlightenment in the name of a dark dialectic nor escape into mystical whispers. Neither naively believe in "progress" nor abandon all hope of a better future forever. Neither naively relate history nor explain it with flat causality. But in the name of present-day thought—philosophizing in the cosmic sense[36]—repeatedly supply those disturbances that provided a glimpse of abysses, whether hidden or disguised. To be in between—to advance in between—carried by a warning with which she also concludes her notes on Scholem's book in 1943: "But what we ought not to forget is the fact that in the last instance it is up to man to decide upon his political fate."[37]

There was no better time to channel this memorializing work along new paths than at what was becoming increasingly clear was the origin of a new era in global politics. Even in the private sphere sparks of hope were appearing. Arendt's husband could still not really speak English, but by now he was teaching at a genuinely elite American university—his mission: to hold seminars with German-speaking officers of the U.S. Army on the organization and structure of the German and French armies.[38] That, too, was a form of enlightenment, and in fact an excellent one. In a letter to Scholem in November 1943, Arendt put it like this: "Monsieur has become a 'visiting professor' at Princeton. For the first time in many years, I'm not in the least worried about money."[39] Almost freedom.

FOOLISH FRUITS

"D*arlings*—the hot days are back, repeatedly interrupted by downpours. Not long now. They say September is often dry and sunny."[40] Simone Weil had been lying in a ward in Middlesex Hospital for four months now. In that time her condition had worsened constantly. She hardly had the strength to hold her cutlery. All her energy went into her letters. But rather than give Mime and Biri, on the other side of the Atlantic, an account of her situation, on August 4, 1943, Weil preferred to rhapsodize to her parents about London's summer street life, about parks and pints, girls and boys, first kisses and disappointing rendezvous, the ordinary joys of ordinary young people. Just as if she were part of this life. As if she ever had been.

She sensed it was her last letter to her parents, which is why she felt a profound need to correct an observation that she had communicated to them some months previously: the desserts that the English call "fruit fools" in fact consist not of fruit, but almost entirely of gelatin and chemicals. This made them quite the opposite of the fools in Shakespeare's plays, the only ones who tell the truth—while all the other characters express nothing but falsities. This provided Weil with a profound insight:

> In this world only those beings who feel extremely humbled, much more than by mere begging, who are not only of no social importance but also feel that they have been robbed of the first dignity of humankind, reason—they alone have the possibility of speaking the truth. Everyone else is lying.[41]

But since these fools have neither academic titles nor high offices, no one pays attention to their truths—they are neither heard nor understood.

> Darling M[ime], do you feel it, the kinship, the essential analogy between these fools and me—in spite of my degree and the hymns of praise to my "intelligence"? . . . In my case these eulogies have served one *purpose* alone, which is the avoidance of the question: is she telling the truth or not?[42]

INSOLUBLE

When Weil wrote these lines, she had been asking for some time to be transferred to a sanatorium. Against the advice of her doctors, she refused any further treatment.[43] She no longer wanted to fight. As mad as it might have seemed to everyone else, she no longer even wanted to want. After all, there were other forms of healing, of striving for freedom. Along the paths of the mind, the paths of philosophy. Because their actual method, as Weil begins her London notebook, consists of

> clearly conceiving all the insoluble problems in all their insolubility and then in simply contemplating them, fixedly and tirelessly, year after year, without any hope, patiently waiting.
>
> There is no entry into the transcendent until the human faculties—intelligence, will, human love—have come up against a limit, and the human being waits at this threshold, which he can make no move to cross, without turning away and without knowing what he wants, in fixed, unwavering attention.
>
> That is a state of extreme humiliation, and it is impossible for anyone who cannot accept humiliation.[44]

After years along the journey, Weil recognized that her earthly existence—the simple fact of being alive—was a problem of the kind she described. It was time for her to wait on the threshold, to abandon resistance. No foreign front, no other enemies. Just the most attentive, selfless perception. The way of mysticism. The way of salvation. Renouncing the most original, animalistic impulse of the will: the impulse to eat.

RELEASE

The ward doctor would remember her as "the most difficult patient he had ever seen."[45] From the day of her admission she categorically refused any special treatment. Not even the information that her tuberculosis was still infectious and therefore put other people in danger could convince her of the necessity of a single room. Both of her lungs were affected, but at first she appeared to have a good chance of recovery. She had only to allow herself absolute peace. And above all: eat enough.

But Weil refused to eat anything apart from tiny portions of porridge. Out of solidarity, she said, with the starving people in her homeland, the children especially. She repeatedly asked the nurses to send the milk they offered her directly to France. She spent the first weeks in the hospital writing and studying the Bhagavad Gita in the original Sanskrit.

By June, she was so weak that a French military chaplain was called. Weil didn't want to talk to him, let alone have him baptize her. Listening from his visitor's chair, the good man was unable to follow the whispered chain of associations about the gift of mercy and the path of the soul into light. Even to her former colleague Maurice Schumann, her trusted contact on de Gaulle's staff, Weil spoke only in prophetic suggestions, with no expectation of engaging in dialogue.

In her mind, the last ties had been cut. On July 26, 1943, she summoned all her strength once again to write a long letter to the executive staff of the Free France movement setting out the reasons for her deep disappointment. Rather than being sent, as she had expressly requested, on a mission in France, since her arrival in England she had for four long months been assigned tasks that were either presented to her in bafflingly vague terms or impossible for her to execute. Rather than letting her fight on the ground and die for her people, they had wanted to make use of her supposed intelligence. "Intellects that can be utilized abound on the market. Mine—I assure you that I am speaking in all sincerity and am well acquainted with what I am talking about—is not at all exceptional. . . . I myself cannot utilize my own intelligence; so how could I put it at [the disposal of others]?" For that reason she wanted it to be known for all time that "I do not wish to have any direct or indirect, or even very indirect, connection with the French Resistance. . . . This is no great loss for you. . . . I am finished, broken, beyond all possibility of mending, and that independent of Koch's bacilli. The latter have only taken advantage of my lack of resistance and, of course, are busily demolishing it a little further."[46]

Her letter to her parents was the last that she wrote by her own hand. In the margin of the fourth sheet she placed her farewell greeting: "A thousand kisses, darlings. Hope, but with moderation. Be happy. I hug you both again and again."

On August 17, 1943, Weil was moved to a sanatorium in Ashford, Kent.

GROUNDING

In spite of Weil's high temperature, the nurses found her in a good mood when she was admitted, and fully conscious. Her eyes were clear and lively. She looked out of the window at a view of trees and fields ("a beautiful room to die in"[47]). She even declared herself willing to eat. Ideally mashed potatoes, prepared in the French style. Would that be possible?

Dr. Broderick, the duty doctor, wanted to know who this new patient was and what she did for a living. Simone Weil answered with a smile, and in a single sentence, that "she was a philosopher and interested in humanity."[48]

CODA

In Hollywood, **AYN RAND** wrote the screenplay for *The Fountainhead,* which was filmed in 1949 with Gary Cooper in the leading role. Rand's fourth and last novel, *Atlas Shrugged,* was published in 1957 after more than ten years' work on the manuscript, and is, after *The Fountainhead,* considered her second major work.

Largely ignored by academia, in the 1960s Rand began to elaborate her philosophy, in the form of essays and textbooks, into a complete system of ontology, epistemology, ethics, political philosophy, and aesthetics. She gave her system the name "Objectivism"; she had originally planned to call it "Existentialism."

Rand's last book was published in 1982, the year of her death. It is titled *Philosophy: Who Needs It.* By this time she had been a cultural icon in the United States for decades, and one whose influence on political and social life, particularly in market-liberal circles of conservatism and libertarianism, can hardly be overestimated.

After her return to New York in 1951, Rand attracted a circle of loyal disciples. One of them was Alan Greenspan, chairman of the U.S. Federal Reserve from 1987 until 2006, appointed by President Ronald

Reagan. Greenspan had earlier been appointed chairman of the Council of Economic Advisers under President Gerald Ford, and Rand was present at Greenspan's swearing-in.

In retrospect, 1943—which saw the publication of not only *The Fountainhead* but also Isabel Paterson's *The God of the Machine* and Rose Wilder Lane's *The Discovery of Freedom*—can be seen as the birth year of the libertarian movement. The Libertarian Party in the United States was founded in 1971, and it continues to nominate its own presidential candidates.

With the financial crisis of 2008, Rand's influence was given a further boost, particularly in the form of the Tea Party movement, which absorbed considerable impulses from her novels into its programs and protests.

In the English-speaking world alone, Rand's books have sold (as of 2020) more than 29 million copies, with *The Fountainhead* accounting for about 10 million of those.

In 1945, **SIMONE DE BEAUVOIR** and Jean-Paul Sartre were part of the founding editorial board of the journal *Les temps modernes*, which also included Raymond Aron and Maurice Merleau-Ponty. In the same year the couple launched an "existentialist offensive" in the form of articles and lectures. In the wake of this, Parisian existentialism evolved into the most influential philosophical trend in the Western world, both politically and in terms of its approach to life.

In 1949, Beauvoir published *Le deuxième sexe* (*The Second Sex*), which is still seen as the founding document of modern feminism and a significant stimulus to the women's movement after 1968. In the book, far from essentialism and biologism, Beauvoir describes being a woman as a socially constructed "situation" based on specific physiological preconditions. She was thus, among other things, laying the foundation for the powerful later distinction between sex and gender. The book was an international success and eventually turned Sartre and Beauvoir into global iconic thinkers.

Beauvoir won the 1954 Prix Goncourt, France's most important literary prize, for her roman à clef about the left-wing intellectual postwar scene in Paris, *Les mandarins* (*The Mandarins*). Only slightly disguised, Albert Camus and Arthur Koestler play central roles in it alongside Sartre.

Beauvoir and Sartre increasingly came to see themselves as political activists in the 1960s and 1970s, above all with regard to questions of anticolonialism, socialist revolutionary movements, and the legal and social equality of women.

Active to the end as an author and as editor of *Les temps modernes*, Beauvoir died on April 14, 1986. She was buried at Montparnasse Cemetery, in the same grave as Jean-Paul Sartre, her lifelong companion in thought.

HANNAH ARENDT, who worked for various Jewish research and cultural institutions after the war, published *The Origins of Totalitarianism* in the United States in 1951—the same year she received her U.S. citizenship. The book, which was translated into many languages, is seen as one of the foundational documents of research on totalitarianism; it formed the basis of Arendt's worldwide fame.

At the end of 1949, Arendt returned to Germany for the first time. She met up with Karl Jaspers and Martin Heidegger. She remained friends with both throughout her life.

Arendt was active as a journalist, and from the late 1950s she was a professor at various American universities, including Princeton, the University of Chicago, and the New School for Social Research in New York.

In 1961, she was sent by *The New Yorker* to Jerusalem to cover the trial of Adolf Eichmann. Her book *Eichmann in Jerusalem: A Report on the Banality of Evil* was published in English in 1963, sparking a massive controversy. Arendt's description of Eichmann as a person whose primary shortcoming could be traced to his "inability to think" was seen as a whitewash. Her problematization of the behavior of the Jewish Councils during the deportations from Germany also caused a scandal, and led to further serious accusations concerning Arendt's relationship with both Zionism and Jewish intellectual life—and to a strain in her friendship with Gershom Scholem.

Other major works by Arendt include *The Human Condition* (1958) and a three-volume major philosophical work, *On the Life of the Mind: Thinking/Willing/Judging.* On December 4, 1975, while working on the third volume, *Judging,* Arendt died of a heart attack in her Manhattan apartment on Riverside Drive. She was buried beside Heinrich Blücher in the cemetery of Bard College.

Broadly ignored by academic philosophy over the decades, Arendt's thinking has gained an international influence since the 1950s that goes far beyond the spheres of political theory and historical research; it continues to gain in significance today.

SIMONE WEIL died on August 24, 1943, at the sanatorium in Ashford, England. The coroner's report identifies the cause of death as "cardiac failure . . . due to starvation and pulmonary tuberculosis," and adds, as a postscript: "The deceased did kill and slay herself by refusing to eat whilst the balance of her mind was disturbed."[1]

Only seven people attended Weil's funeral, including Maurice Schumann, who delivered a prayer at her graveside. A priest had also been booked, but he missed his train and didn't turn up.

The first extracts from Weil's *Cahiers* (*Notebooks*) were published in France in 1947, and *L'enracinement* (*The Need for Roots*) in 1949. In the early 1950s, Albert Camus took an interest in Weil's work and published many of her most important writings at Gallimard. In 1951, in a letter to Weil's mother, he wrote: "Simone Weil, I now understand, is the only great mind of our time.... For myself, I would be pleased if I could say I had played my own small part in disseminating her work and bringing it to people's attention—a body of work whose full impact we can as yet only guess."[2]

In 1958, Weil's grave in Ashford received a stone with the inscription "Her writings have established her as one of the foremost modern philosophers."

Weil's complete works are now available in an edition from Gallimard. For a long time her influence was restricted largely to the fields of Catholic theology, education, and political theory. Even today, Weil's thought is generally ignored by academic philosophy.

Her work is worth discovering.

ACKNOWLEDGMENTS

My thanks to Christiane Braun, Dr. Christoph Selzer, and Dr. Johannes Czaja, my editors, who saw this book through to publication with the greatest expert knowledge, specialized attention, and human forbearance.

My thanks to Tom Kraushaar and Michael Gaeb for crucial encouragement, confidence, and energy-giving "quarantinis," as well as Thomas Meyer for his goodwill and error-avoidance tips.

My thanks to the defining biographers of the four heroines of this book: Anne C. Heller (*Ayn Rand and the World She Made*), Simone Pétrement (*Simone Weil: A Life*), Kate Kirkpatrick (*Becoming Beauvoir: A Life*), and Elisabeth Young-Bruehl (*Hannah Arendt: For Love of the World*). Their works were constant companions throughout the writing process.

This book could not have come about in difficult times without a generous grant from the Brost Foundation; particular thanks to Sonja Villarreal, Dr. Boris Berger, and Professor Bodo Hombach.

I would like to thank Dr. Vera Schmit-Eilenberger for her always healing advice.

Above all, once again, to Pia, Venla, and Kaisa—the fires of my life.

Berlin, May 23, 2020

LIST OF WORKS

Many of these works are cited in the notes, indicated by abbreviated terms. See also the Selected Bibliography.

HANNAH ARENDT

Arendt/Anders = Arendt, H., and G. Anders (2018). *Schreib doch mal* hard facts *über dich: Briefe 1939 bis 1975.* Edited by K. Putz. Munich: Piper.

Arendt/Benjamin = Schöttker, D., and E. Wizisla, eds. (2017). *Arendt und Benjamin: Texte, Briefe, Dokumente.* Frankfurt am Main: Suhrkamp.

Arendt/Heidegger = *Hannah Arendt and Martin Heidegger: Letters 1925–1975.* Translated by A. Shields. New York: Harcourt, 2004. Translation of: *Hannah Arendt und Martin Heidegger: Briefe 1925–1975.* Edited by U. Ludz. Frankfurt: Vittorio Klostermann, 1998.

Arendt/Jaspers = Arendt, H., and K. Jaspers. *Hannah Arendt Karl Jaspers Correspondence 1926–1969.* Translated by R. Kimber and R. Kimber. New York: Harcourt Brace Jovanovich, 1993. Translation of: *Hannah Arendt/Karl Jaspers: Briefwechsel 1926–1969.* Edited by L. Köhler and H. Saner. Munich: Piper, 2001.

Arendt-Scholem = Knott, M. L., ed. (2010). *Hannah Arendt/Gershom Scholem: Der Briefwechsel 1939–1964.* Berlin: Suhrkamp.

Arendt/Scholem = Knott, M. L., ed. (2017). *The Correspondence of Hannah Arendt and Gershom Scholem.* Translated by A. David. Chicago: University of Chicago Press. Translation of Arendt-Scholem.

Aufbau = Knott, M. L., ed. (2004). *Vor Antisemitismus ist man nur noch auf dem Monde sicher: Beiträge für die deutsch-jüdische Emigrantenzeitung "Aufbau" 1941–1945.* Munich: Piper.

Augustine = Arendt, H. (1929/1996). *Der Liebesbegriff bei Augustin: Versuch einer philosophischen Interpretation.* Munich: Piper. English translation: *Love and Augustine.* Translated by J. Vecchiarelli Scott and J. Chelius Stark. Chicago: University of Chicago Press, 1996.

Böse = Arendt, H. (2006/2019). *Über das Böse: Eine Vorlesung zu Fragen der Ethik.* Edited by J. Kohn. Munich: Piper.

Briefe Freunde = Nordmann, I., ed. (2015). *Hannah Arendt: Wahrheit gibt es nur zu zweien: Briefe an Freunde.* Munich: Piper.

Denktagebuch = Ludz, U., and I. Nordmann, eds. (2016). *Hannah Arendt: Denktagebuch 1950–1973,* vol. 1. Munich: Piper.

Eichmann = Arendt, H. (1963). *Eichmann in Jerusalem: A Report on the Banality of Evil.* London: Faber & Faber.

EuU = Arendt, H. (1986). *Elemente und Ursprünge totaler Herrschaft: Antisemitismus, Imperialismus, totale Herrschaft.* Munich: Piper. Edited German translation of *The Origins of Totalitarianism.*

Finst. Zeiten = Arendt, H. (1968/2013). *Menschen in finsteren Zeiten.* Munich: Piper.

Freiheit = Arendt, H. (2018). *Die Freiheit, frei zu sein.* Munich: Piper.

JW = Arendt, H. (2007). *The Jewish Writings.* Edited by J. Kohn and R. Feldman. New York: Schocken.

KG = Arendt, H. *Kritische Gesamtausgabe.* Edited by B. Hahn. Göttingen: Universitätsverlag Göttingen (ongoing).

KG3 = Volume 3 of KG (2019). *Sechs Essays: Die verborgene Tradition.* Göttingen: Universitätsverlag Göttingen.

Origins = Arendt, H. (1948/1994). *The Origins of Totalitarianism.* San Diego: Harvest/ Harcourt.

Urteilen = Arendt, H., ed. (1982/2017). *Das Urteilen: Texte zu Kants politischer Philosophie.* Edited by R. Beiner. Munich: Piper.

Var = Arendt, H. (1997). *Rahel Varnhagen: The Life of a Jewish Woman.* Translated by R. Winston and C. Winston. Baltimore: Johns Hopkins University Press. Translation of: H. Arendt, *Rahel Varnhagen: Lebensgeschichte einer deutschen Jüdin aus der Romantik.* Munich: Piper, 1959/1981.

Vita = Arendt, H. (1960/2007). *Vita activa oder Vom tätigen Leben.* Munich: Piper.

WFW = Köhler, L., ed. *Within Four Walls: The Correspondence Between Hannah Arendt and Heinrich Blücher, 1936–1968.* Translated by P. Constantine. New York: Harcourt, 2000. Translation of: L. Köhler, ed., *Hannah Arendt/Heinrich Blücher: Briefe 1936–1968.* Munich: Piper, 1996.

Wir Juden = Knott, M. L., and U. Ludz, eds. (2019). *Hannah Arendt: Wir Juden: Schriften 1932 bis 1966.* Munich: Piper.

SIMONE DE BEAUVOIR

Beauvoir = Beauvoir, S. de. *Briefe an Sartre.* Vol. 1, *1930–1939.* Edited by S. Le Bon. Reinbek, Germany: Rowohlt, 2017.

Beauvoir/Sartre = Beauvoir, S. de (1991). *Letters to Sartre.* Translated and edited by Q. Hoare. London: Radius.

Blood = Beauvoir, S. de (1945/1948). *The Blood of Others.* Translated by Y. Moyse and R. Senhouse. London: Secker & Warburg.

Force = Beauvoir, S. de (1963/1965). *Force of Circumstance.* Translated by R. Howard. London: André Deutsch.

Mandarins = Beauvoir, S. de (1954/1969). *The Mandarins*. Translated by Leonard R. Friedman. Cleveland: World Books.
Memoirs = Beauvoir, S. de (1958/1963). *Memoirs of a Dutiful Daughter*. Translated by J. Kirkup. London: Penguin.
Men = Beauvoir, S. de (1946/2019). *All Men Are Mortal*. Translated by E. Cameron. London: Virago.
PoL = Beauvoir, S. de (1960/1962). *The Prime of Life*. Translated by P. Green. London: André Deutsch/Weidenfeld & Nicolson.
Pyrrhus = Beauvoir, S. de (1944/2004). "Pyrrhus and Cineas." In *Philosophical Writings*. Edited by M. A. Simons. Translated by M. Timmerman and M. B. Mader. Champaign: University of Illinois Press.
Sade = Beauvoir, S. de (1951–1952/1972). *Must We Burn Sade?* Translated by A. Michelson. London: New English Library.
SCtS = Beauvoir, S. de (1943/1990). *She Came to Stay*. Translated by R. Senhouse and Y. Moyse. New York: W. W. Norton.
Spirit = Beauvoir, S. de (1979/1982). *When Things of the Spirit Come First*. Translated by P. O'Brian. London: André Deutsch/Weidenfeld & Nicolson.
TSS = Beauvoir, S. de (1949/2011). *The Second Sex*. Translated by C. Borde and S. Malovany. London: Vintage.
WD = Beauvoir, S. de (1990/2008). *Wartime Diary 1939–1941*. Translated by A. Deing Cordero. Champaign: University of Illinois Press.

AYN RAND

Anthem = Rand, A. (1938/2010). *Anthem*. CreateSpace.
Atlas = Rand, A. (1957/2007). *Atlas Shrugged*. New York: Random House.
Fountainhead = Rand, A. (1943/1971). *The Fountainhead*. New York: New American Library.
Journals = Harriman, D., ed. (1997). *Journals of Ayn Rand*. New York: Dutton.
Letters = Berliner, M. S., ed. (1995). *Letters of Ayn Rand*. New York: Dutton.
New Intellectual = Rand, A. (1963). *For the New Intellectual*. New York: Signet.
Return = Rand, A. (1999). *The Return of the Primitive: The Anti-Industrial Revolution*. Edited by. P. Schwarz. New York: Meridian.
Romantic Manifesto = Rand, A. (1975). *The Romantic Manifesto: A Philosophy of Literature*. New York: New American Library.
Selection = Peikoff, L., ed. (1986). *The Early Rand: A Selection from Her Unpublished Fiction*. New York: Signet.
Three Plays = Rand, A. 2005. *Three Plays: Night of January 16th; Ideal; Think Twice*. New York: Signet.
Voice = Rand, A. (1990). *The Voice of Reason: Essays in Objectivist Thought*. New York: NAL.
WTL = Rand, A. (1936/2010). *We the Living*. London: Cassell.

SIMONE WEIL

APP = Weil, S. (1950/2013). *On the Abolition of All Political Parties*. London. Translated by S. Leys. New York: New York Review Books.

Corr 1942 = Weil, S., and J. Bousquet (2019). *Correspondance 1942: "Quel est donc ton tourment?"* Paris: Éditions Claire Paulhan.

FLN = Weil, S. (1970). *First and Last Notebooks*. Translated by R. Rees. London: Oxford University Press.

FW = Weil, S. (1987). *Formative Writings 1929–1941*. Edited and translated by D. T. McFarland and W. Van Ness. Amherst: University of Massachusetts Press.

Iliad = Weil, S. (2005). "The Iliad, or the Poem of Force." In S. Weil and R. Bespaloff, *War and the Iliad*. Translated by M. McCarthy. New York: NYRB Classics.

Notebooks = Weil, S. (1956). *The Notebooks of Simone Weil*. Translated by A. Wills. London: Routledge & Kegan Paul.

OC = Weil, S. (1988, ongoing). *Oeuvres complètes*, vols. I–VII. Paris: Gallimard.

OCII-2 = Weil, S. (1934–1937/1991). *Écrits historiques et politiques*. Paris: Gallimard.

OCII-3 = Weil, S. (1937–1940/1989). *Écrits historiques et politiques*. Paris: Gallimard.

OCIV-1 = Weil, S. (1940–1942/2008). *Écrits de Marseille*. Paris: Gallimard.

OCIV-2 = Weil, S. (1941–1942/2009). *Écrits de Marseille*. Paris: Gallimard.

OCV = Weil, S. (1943/2013). *Écrits de New York et de Londre*. Paris: Gallimard.

OCVII-1 = Weil, S. (2012). *Correspondance*. Paris: Gallimard.

OL = Weil, S. (1955/1958/1972). *Oppression and Liberty*. Translated by A. Wills and J. Petrie. London: Routledge & Kegan Paul.

Roots = Weil, S. (1949/1952). *The Need for Roots: Prelude to a Declaration of Duties towards Mankind*. Translated by A. Wills. London: Routledge & Kegan Paul.

SE = Weil, S. (1962). *Selected Essays 1934–43*. Translated by R. Rees. London: Oxford University Press.

SL = Weil, S. (1965). *Seventy Letters: Some Hitherto Untranslated Texts from Published and Unpublished Sources*. Translated by R. Rees. London: Oxford University Press.

Trotski = Weil, S. (2014). *Conversation avec Trotski*. Paris: L'Herne.

Venice = Weil, S. (1968/2019). *Venice Saved*. Translated by S. Panizza and P. Wilson. London: Bloomsbury.

Waiting = Weil, S. (1951). *Waiting for God*. Translated by E. Craufurd. London: Routledge & Kegan Paul.

NOTES

I. SPARKS: 1943

1. S. de Beauvoir, "Pyrrhus and Cineas," in *Philosophical Writings*, ed. M. A. Simons, trans. M. Timmerman and M. B. Mader (Champaign: University of Illinois Press, 2004), 90. All the quotations in this section are from Beauvoir's essay "Pyrrhus and Cineas" (Pyrrhus).
2. Pyrrhus, 91.
3. Pyrrhus, 91.
4. See S. de Beauvoir, *The Prime of Life*, trans. P. Green (London: André Deutsch/ Weidenfeld & Nicolson, 1962) (PoL).
5. *L'invitée*, published in 1943, and in English translation as *She Came to Stay*, trans. R. Senhouse and Y. Moyse (New York: W. W. Norton, 1990) (SCtS).
6. *Le sang des autres*, published in English as *The Blood of Others*, trans. Y. Moyse and R. Senhouse (London: Secker & Warburg, 1948) (Blood).
7. First performed in Paris in autumn 1945 under the title *Les bouches inutiles* (*The Useless Mouths*).
8. Pyrrhus, 98.
9. See K. Kirkpatrick, *Becoming Beauvoir: A Life* (London: Bloomsbury Academic, 2019), 182.
10. Pyrrhus, 108.
11. Pyrrhus, 113.
12. Pyrrhus, 115.
13. Pyrrhus, 91.
14. S. Weil, *First and Last Notebooks*, trans. R. Rees (London: Oxford University Press, 1970), 340 (FLN).
15. For the biographical details of this phase of her life, see S. Pétrement, *Simone Weil: A Life*, trans. R. Rosenthal (New York: Pantheon, 1976), 490–539.
16. Letter to Maurice Schumann, in S. Weil, *Seventy Letters: Some Hitherto Untrans-*

lated Texts from Published and Unpublished Sources, trans. R. Rees (London: Oxford University Press, 1965), 150–51 (SL).

17. Pétrement, 514.
18. S. Weil, *The Need for Roots: Prelude to a Declaration of Duties towards Mankind,* trans. A. Wills (London: Routledge & Kegan Paul, 1952) (Roots).
19. In S. Weil, *Selected Essays 1934–43,* trans. R. Rees (London: Oxford University Press, 1962), 211ff (SE).
20. SE, 217f.
21. Roots, 278.
22. Roots, 43.
23. FLN, 204.
24. A. Rand, *Letters of Ayn Rand,* ed. M. S. Berliner (New York: Dutton, 1995), 67 (Letters).
25. Letters, 69.
26. According to the Ayn Rand Institute, the total print run for this book now (in 2023) exceeds 10 million. For Rand's philosophical novels as a whole, the figure exceeds 30 million.
27. See A. C. Heller, *Ayn Rand and the World She Made* (New York: Nan A. Talese/ Doubleday, 2009), 117.
28. A. Rand, *The Fountainhead* (New York: New American Library, 1971), 965 (Fountainhead).
29. For biographical details concerning Rand's younger years, see Heller, 22–52.
30. For eyewitness accounts by inhabitants of the city, see A. Adamovich and D. Granin, *Leningrad under Siege: First-Hand Accounts of the Ordeal* (Barnsley, UK: Pen and Sword, 2007).
31. D. Harriman, ed., *Journals of Ayn Rand* (New York: Dutton, 1997), 281 (Journals).
32. Journals, 350.
33. H. Arendt, "We Refugees," in *The Jewish Writings,* ed. J. Kohn and R. Feldman (New York: Schocken, 2007), 271 (JW).
34. JW, 271.
35. JW, 273.
36. M. Heidegger, *Gesamtausgab: Ausgabe letzter Hand,* vol. 16, *Rede und andere Zeugnisse eines Lebensweges* (1910–1976) (Frankfurt am Main: Vittorio Klostermann, 2000).
37. E. Young-Bruehl, *Hannah Arendt: For Love of the World* (New Haven: Yale University Press, 1982), 261.
38. See Arendt's television interview with Günter Gaus, October 28, 1964: https://www.youtube.com/watch?v=J9SyTEUi6Kw&t=1820s. Transcript in German at: https://www.rbb-online.de/zurperson/interview_archiv/arendt_hannah.html.
39. JW, 271.
40. JW, 274.
41. See the epigraph of Arendt's later book *The Origins of Totalitarianism,* a quotation from Karl Jaspers: "Do not succumb to the past or the future. The important

thing is to be entirely in the present." H. Arendt, *The Origins of Totalitarianism* (San Diego: Harvest/Harcourt, 1994), ix (Origins).

II. EXILES: 1933–1934

1. Young-Bruehl, 106. The subsequent descriptions also come from Young-Bruehl.
2. Notgemeinschaft der Deutschen Wissenschaft: an organization set up by German scientists in 1920 to raise funds for science after the devastation of the First World War.
3. Young-Bruehl, 106.
4. As Thomas Meyer, who is currently working on a new biography, told me in conversation, Arendt—contrary to her own account—spent only a day in police custody.
5. Young-Bruehl, 93.
6. Young-Bruehl, 90.
7. Young-Bruehl, 84–85.
8. Young-Bruehl, 176.
9. H. Arendt and K. Jaspers, *Hannah Arendt Karl Jaspers Correspondence 1926–1969*, trans. R. Kimber and R. Kimber (New York: Harcourt Brace Jovanovich, 1993), 50 (Arendt/Jaspers).
10. K. Jaspers, *Max Weber: Deutsches Wesen im politischen Denken, im Forschen und Philosophieren* (Oldenburg, Germany: Stalling, 1932).
11. Arendt/Jaspers, 16.
12. Arendt/Jaspers, 19.
13. Arendt/Jaspers, 18–19.
14. Young-Bruehl, 107.
15. S. Weil, "The Situation in Germany," in *Formative Writings 1929–1941*, ed. and trans. D. T. McFarland and W. Van Ness (Amherst: University of Massachusetts Press, 1987), 97 (FW).
16. FW, 69.
17. Pétrement, 137.
18. Pétrement, 191.
19. S. Weil, *Correspondance* (Paris: Gallimard, 2012), 140, note 5 (OCVII-1).
20. OCVII-1, 150.
21. S. Weil, "Prospects: Are We Headed for the Proletarian Revolution?," in *Oppression and Liberty*, trans. A. Wills and J. Petrie (London: Routledge & Kegan Paul, 1958), 1 (OL).
22. It was reprinted several times in autumn 1933, and translated into both Spanish and Dutch.
23. OL, 7.
24. OL, 15.
25. OCVII-1, 154.
26. See the impressive study by A. Applebaum, *Red Famine: Stalin's War on Ukraine* (Toronto: Signal, 2017).
27. OL, 18.
28. Pétrement, 178.

29. The account of the meeting and quotations are from Pétrement, 188f.
30. Pétrement, 188.
31. Pétrement, 190. Leon Trotsky died on August 21, 1940, in Coyoacán, Mexico City, from injuries inflicted with an ice ax by the Soviet agent Ramón Mercader the day before. The murderer was awarded the Order of Lenin by Stalin in the same year.
32. Pétrement, 198.
33. OL, 36–115.
34. S. de Beauvoir, *The Prime of Life,* trans. P. Green (London: André Deutsch/Weidenfeld & Nicolson, 1962), 131 (PoL).
35. PoL, 162.
36. PoL, 126.
37. Sartre, who had failed the previous year, was awarded first place after lengthy discussion. Beauvoir, the youngest graduate in history, was placed second.
38. PoL, 126.
39. Kirkpatrick, 143.
40. S. de Beauvoir, *Memoirs of a Dutiful Daughter,* trans. J. Kirkup (Harmondsworth, UK: Penguin, 1963), 243 (Memoirs).
41. R. Descartes, *Meditations on First Philosophy, with Selections from the Objections and Replies,* trans. M. Moriarty (Oxford: Oxford University Press, 2008), 23.
42. PoL, 135.
43. In a later text from 1937, Sartre would poeticize this Husserlian relationship between world and consciousness: "[It] is purified, it is clear as a strong wind. There is nothing in it but a movement of fleeing itself, a sliding beyond itself. If, impossible though it may be, you could enter 'into' a consciousness, you would be seized by a whirlwind and thrown back outside, in the thick of the dust, near the tree, for consciousness has no 'inside.' Precisely this being beyond-itself, this absolute flight, this refusal to be a substance is what makes it be a consciousness. . . . When consciousness tries to recoup itself, to coincide with itself once and for all, closeted off all warm and cozy, it destroys itself. This necessity for consciousness to exist as consciousness of something other than itself is what Husserl calls 'intentionality.'" J.-P. Sartre, *The Transcendence of the Ego: An Existentialist Theory of Consciousness,* trans. F. Williams and R. Kirkpatrick (New York: Octagon, 1972), 6.
44. Quotations from PoL, 146ff.
45. PoL, 147.
46. PoL, 164.
47. PoL, 164.
48. For biographical details of this phase of Ayn Rand's life, see in particular Heller, 71ff.
49. Heller, 71.
50. Letters, 7.
51. Letters, 8.
52. Heller, 72.
53. Heller, 74.
54. Letters, 17f.
55. Letters, 18.

56. See A. Rand, *We the Living* (London: Cassell, 1936), 423.
57. Journals, 72.
58. Journals, 66.
59. J. Burns, *Goddess of the Market: Ayn Rand and the American Right* (New York and Oxford: Oxford University Press, 2009), 25.
60. Journals, 73.

III. EXPERIMENTS: 1934–1935

1. See Heller, 77.
2. A. Rand, *Three Plays: Night of January 16th; Ideal; Think Twice* (New York: Signet, 2005), 3f (Three Plays).
3. Three Plays, 3f.
4. J. Ortega y Gasset, *The Revolt of the Masses* (New York: W. W. Norton, 1994).
5. Journals, 71.
6. Episode quoted in Heller, 209.
7. Heller, 79.
8. PoL, 207.
9. See PoL, 207.
10. Later published as *La nausée*, and in English as *Nausea*, trans. L. Alexander (New York: New Directions, 1964).
11. PoL, 232.
12. PoL, 239f.
13. PoL, 240.
14. PoL, 254.
15. PoL, 171.
16. S. de Beauvoir, *Letters to Sartre*, ed. and trans. Q. Hoare (London: Radius, 1991), 50 (Beauvoir/Sartre).
17. Beauvoir/Sartre, 54.
18. Beauvoir/Sartre, 178.
19. Beauvoir/Sartre, 179.
20. S. de Beauvoir, *When Things of the Spirit Come First*, trans. P. O'Brian (London: André Deutsch/Weidenfeld & Nicolson, 1982), 8 (Spirit). Maritain's book has been published with the title *The Primacy of the Spirit*.
21. Quoted in D. Bair, *Simone de Beauvoir: A Biography* (London: Jonathan Cape, 1990), 190.
22. Bair, 194.
23. Bair, 193.
24. Bair, 205.
25. Spirit, 99.
26. Spirit, 111.
27. OL, 110f.
28. H. Bouchardeau, *Simone Weil: Biographie* (Paris: Gallimard, 1995), 132.
29. FW, 163.
30. See Pétrement, 227.
31. FW, 115.

32. OL, 42–43.
33. FW, 3.
34. OL, 46.
35. K. Marx and F. Engels, *The German Ideology* (London: International Publishers, 1970), 53.
36. OL, 46.
37. OL, 54.
38. OL, 102.
39. OL, 105.
40. OL, 113.
41. OL, 93.
42. OL, 79.
43. OL, 123.
44. OL, 163.
45. M. Nieradka-Steiner, *Exil unter Palmen: Deutsche Emigranten in Sanary-sur-Mer* (Stuttgart: Theiss, 2018), 67.
46. Nieradka-Steiner, 67.
47. Arendt interview with G. Gaus, October 28, 1964.
48. Arendt interview with G. Gaus, October 28, 1964.
49. Young-Bruehl, 110.
50. Young-Bruehl, 117.
51. Young-Bruehl, 117.
52. W. Benjamin, *The Correspondence of Walter Benjamin and Gershom Scholem, 1932–1940,* ed. G. Scholem, trans. G. Smith and A. Lefevere (New York: Schocken, 1989), 72.
53. Young-Bruehl, 119.
54. In L. Epstein, *The Dream of Zion: The First Zionist Congress* (Lanham, MD: Rowman & Littlefield, 2016).
55. Arendt interview with G. Gaus, October 28, 1964.
56. Origins, 73.
57. Enslaved people and especially people of African origin were expressly excluded in both documents, or simply omitted from consideration.
58. Origins, 291–92.
59. Origins, 381.
60. Arendt/Jaspers, 11.
61. Letter to Kurt Blumenfeld, July 17, 1946, in Hannah Arendt: *Wahrheit gibt es nur zu zweien: Briefe an Freunde,* ed. I. Nordmann (Munich: Piper, 2015), 63.
62. Young-Bruehl, 120.
63. Benjamin (1989), 168.
64. Young-Bruehl, 139.

IV. NEAREST AND DEAREST: 1936–1937

1. Letters, 23.
2. Letters, 23.
3. See Heller, 95.

4. Journals, 77.
5. Journals, 81.
6. Journals, 93.
7. Journals, 93.
8. Journals, 93f.
9. Journals, 95.
10. Journals, 95f.
11. Journals, 97.
12. Letters, 36.
13. L. Köhler., ed., *Within Four Walls: The Correspondence Between Hannah Arendt and Heinrich Blücher, 1936–1968*, trans. P. Constantine (New York: Harcourt, 2000), 21 (WFW).
14. Benjamin (1989), 183.
15. Benjamin (1989), 182.
16. I. Kershaw, *To Hell and Back: Europe 1914–1949* (London: Allen Lane, 2015), 287.
17. See G. Schreiber, *Der zweite Weltkrieg* (Munich: Beck, 2013), 12.
18. A. Applebaum, *Gulag: A History of the Soviet Camps* (London: Allen Lane, 2003), 73. For 1943 the figure is about four million.
19. See Kershaw, 11.
20. Kershaw, 408ff.
21. Kershaw, 413.
22. Young-Bruehl, 122.
23. See Young-Bruehl, 135.
24. H. Arendt, *Love and Augustine*, trans. J. Vecchiarelli Scott and J. Chelius Stark (Chicago: University of Chicago Press, 2018) (Augustine).
25. *Hannah Arendt and Martin Heidegger: Letters 1925–1975*, trans. A. Shields (New York: Harcourt, 2004), 237 (Arendt/Heidegger).
26. Augustine, 106.
27. Augustine, 111.
28. Augustine, 100.
29. WFW, 21.
30. WFW, 159.
31. PoL, 289.
32. PoL, 282.
33. Pol, 474.
34. Bair, 197.
35. For further reflections on this topic, see J. Webber, *Rethinking Existentialism* (Oxford: Oxford University Press, 2018), 57–73.
36. PoL, 261.
37. WFW, 31.
38. PoL, 260.
39. Bair, 200.
40. PoL, 288.
41. Sartre (1964), 170–71.
42. Sartre (1964), 227.
43. Sartre (1964), 209.

44. PoL, 285.
45. PoL, 290.
46. Pétrement, 299.
47. Pétrement, 283.
48. Pétrement, 274.
49. G. Bernanos, *The Great Cemeteries under the Moon*, trans. P. Morris (London: Cluny, 2016), 193.
50. SE, 172.
51. PoL, 290.
52. SE, 175.
53. SE, 156.
54. SE, 154.
55. SE, 156–57.
56. SE, 157.
57. SE, 165.
58. SE, 159–60.
59. OL, 65.
60. Pétrement, 295f.

V. EVENTS: 1938–1939

1. Pétrement, 339.
2. S. Weil, *Écrits historiques et politiques* (Paris: Gallimard, 1989), 93ff (OCII-3).
3. Pétrement, 338.
4. On political constraints in 1938, particularly in France, see M. Foessel, *Récidive: 1938* (Paris: Presses Universitaires de France, 2019).
5. Pétrement, 337.
6. Bouchardeau, 214.
7. J.-M. Perrin, *Mon dialogue avec Simone Weil* (Paris: Nouvelle Cité, 2009), 75.
8. Perrin, 74f.
9. Perrin, 75.
10. See Pétrement, 340.
11. FLN, 42.
12. S. Weil, *The Notebooks of Simone Weil*, trans. A. Wills (London: Routledge & Kegan Paul, 1956), 5 (Notebooks). Poem in *The Works of George Herbert*, ed. F. E. Hutchinson (Oxford: Clarendon Press, 1941), 188–89.
13. Pétrement, 340.
14. Pétrement, 340.
15. Pétrement, 341.
16. FLN, 47.
17. Pétrement, 337.
18. SE, 225. The last lines of the first verse of "The Internationale": "We'll change henceforth the old tradition, / and spurn the dust to win the prize," or, in another version, "The earth shall rise on new foundations, / We have been naught, we shall be all."
19. Heller, 98.

20. Applebaum (2017), 102.
21. Applebaum (2017), 99.
22. For the details of this period of Rand's life, see Heller, 102ff, and Burns, 49f.
23. Heller, 102.
24. See Heller, 102f.
25. A. Rand, *Anthem* (CreateSpace, 2010), 3 (Anthem).
26. Anthem, 2.
27. Anthem, 1.
28. Anthem, 32.
29. Anthem, 35.
30. Anthem, 40.
31. For the reference to Kallas and her work I am indebted to Dr. Pia Päiviö.
32. Letters, 4.
33. Burns, 50.
34. Heller, 105.
35. Journals, 95.
36. Heller, 117.
37. Burns, 51.
38. F. Nietzsche, *Ecce Homo: How to Become What You Are*, trans. D. Large (Oxford: Oxford University Press, 2007), 88–89.
39. Heller, 123.
40. Journals, 192.
41. Journals, 193.
42. Journals, 192.
43. Fountainhead, 5.
44. See J. Später, *Siegfried Kracauer: A Biography*, trans. D. Steuer (Cambridge, UK, and Medford, MA: Polity Press, 2020), 354f.
45. H. Arendt, *Rahel Varnhagen: The Life of a Jewish Woman*, trans. R. Winston and C. Winston (Baltimore: Johns Hopkins University Press, 1997), 244 (Var).
46. Var, 358.
47. Var, 245.
48. Var, 248.
49. Var, 249.
50. Var, 248.
51. Var, 240.
52. Var, 248.
53. Var, 249.
54. Var, 239.
55. Benjamin (1989), 217.
56. Origins, passim.
57. Var, xx.
58. WFW, 44.
59. Benjamin (1989), 240.
60. Benjamin (1989), 241.
61. To clarify, Scholem is referring to "Jewish settlement," and not the present-day sense of "Palestinian."

62. Benjamin (1989), 255–56.
63. Benjamin (1989), 257.
64. In fact, this would be the only copy in existence after the war: on Arendt's request, Scholem sent it (letter of October 17, 1941) to New York: it was published first in 1957 in English in London, in 1959 in German, and in 1974 in the United States.
65. PoL, 355.
66. Throughout her life, Beauvoir publicly denied having had sexual relationships with women.
67. See Kirkpatrick, 156ff.
68. Kirkpatrick, 158.
69. Kirkpatrick, 158.
70. Beauvoir/Sartre, 31f.
71. S. de Beauvoir, *Briefe an Sartre*, vol. 1, *1930–1939*, ed. S. Le Bon (Reinbek, Germany: Rowohlt, 2017), 95.
72. Kirkpatrick, 143.
73. PoL, 355.
74. PoL, 345.
75. PoL, 317.
76. See PoL, 318f.
77. PoL, 338.
78. PoL, 338.
79. PoL, 341.
80. Beauvoir's younger sister, Hélène, was on her way to becoming a painter at the time, as was her close friend Gégé.
81. PoL, 341.
82. SCtS, 151–52.
83. This configuration strongly resembles the later play *Huis Clos* (*No Exit*) by Sartre.
84. PoL, 339.
85. The radio play of H. G. Wells's *War of the Worlds* was broadcast in October 1938.
86. Beauvoir's book *Le deuxième sexe* (*The Second Sex*) would be published in French in 1949.
87. Beauvoir/Sartre, 31.
88. V. von Wroblewsky, ed., *Jean-Paul Sartre: Briefe an Simone de Beauvoir 1926–1939* (Hamburg: Rowohlt, 2008), 281f.

VI. VIOLENCE: 1939–1940

1. See Pétrement, 365.
2. This was published in English translation in 1947. See also the following note.
3. S. Weil, "The Iliad, or the Poem of Force," in S. Weil and R. Bespaloff, *War and the Iliad*, trans. M. McCarthy (New York: NYRB Classics, 2005), 3 (Iliad).
4. Iliad, 4.
5. Iliad, 8.

6. Pétrement, 354.
7. Iliad, 11.
8. Iliad, 14.
9. Iliad, 35.
10. Pétrement, 366.
11. On this episode, see A. Roberts, *The Storm of War: A New History of the Second World War* (London: Allen Lane, 2009), 77f.
12. Iliad, 14.
13. Iliad, 20.
14. M. Heidegger, *The Concept of Time*, trans. I. Farin (London: Continuum, 2011), 116.
15. Iliad, 22–23.
16. Iliad, 24.
17. Iliad, 26–27.
18. Iliad, 30.
19. Iliad, 30.
20. Iliad, 37.
21. Pétrement, 377.
22. Beauvoir/Sartre, 312.
23. J.-P. Sartre and S. de Beauvoir, *Lettres au Castor et à quelques autres*, vol. 1 (Paris: Gallimard, 1983), 277.
24. PoL, 442.
25. PoL, 443.
26. See Kirkpatrick, 175.
27. V. von Wroblewsky, ed., *Jean-Paul Sartre: Briefe an Simone de Beauvoir 1940–1963* (Hamburg: Rowohlt, 2004), 41f.
28. Beauvoir/Sartre, 258.
29. Beauvoir/Sartre, 260.
30. M. Heidegger, *Kant and the Problem of Metaphysics*, trans. R. Taft (Bloomington: Indiana University Press, 1997), 200.
31. PoL, 434.
32. PoL, 444.
33. Such scenes are historically established, but may be explained against the background of the often similar methods of Stalin's troops when they drove out the Wehrmacht. The hopes of the people were often soon badly shattered.
34. Von Wroblewsky (2004), 297.
35. S. de Beauvoir, *Wartime Diary 1939–1941*, trans. A. Deing Cordero (London: Penguin, 2009), 282 (WD).
36. PoL, 300.
37. PoL, 307.
38. PoL, 458.
39. PoL, 468.
40. PoL, 469.
41. Von Wroblewsky (2004), 209.
42. Beauvoir/Sartre, 314.
43. Beauvoir/Sartre, 328.
44. Beauvoir/Sartre, 328.

45. SCtS, 445.
46. Arendt/Scholem, 7.
47. Arendt/Scholem, 271.
48. Young-Bruehl, 156.
49. A. Koestler, *Scum of the Earth* (London: Jonathan Cape, 1941).
50. Koestler (1941), 190.
51. JW, 268.
52. H. Arendt, *Elemente und Ursprünge totaler Herrschaft: Antisemitismus, Imperialismus, totale Herrschaft* (Munich: Piper, 1986), 645.
53. Origins, 585.
54. Origins, 577.
55. Origins, 586.
56. JW, 265.
57. JW, 270.
58. Origins, 587.
59. Benjamin (1989), 638.
60. Arendt/Benjamin, 139.
61. Pétrement, 523.
62. *The Correspondence of Hannah Arendt and Gershom Scholem*, ed. M. L. Knott, trans. A. David (Chicago: University of Chicago Press, 2017), 8 (Arendt/Scholem).
63. W. Benjamin, "Theses on the Philosophy of History," in *Illuminations*, ed. H. Arendt, trans. H. Zohn (London: Fontana, 1973).
64. Benjamin (1973), 249.
65. Benjamin (1973), 264.
66. See H. Meyer-Moses, *Reise in die Vergangenheit* (Germany: Verlagregionalkultur, 2019), 10. Some 5,600 people were deported from Baden to Gurs. About a third of them died in Gurs or one of its subcamps.
67. Arendt/Scholem, 4.
68. Arendt/Scholem, 9.
69. See Young-Bruehl, 154.
70. Heller, 223.
71. Heller, 133.
72. Heller, 129.
73. Letters, 42.
74. See Heller, 116.
75. Journals, 209.
76. Journals, 215.
77. Journals, 209f.
78. Journals, 229.
79. Journals, 228.
80. Journals, 229.
81. Fountainhead, 802.
82. See Heller, 134.
83. See Burns, 43ff.
84. Journals, 345ff.
85. Journals, 345ff.

86. Journals, 345ff.
87. Journals, 350.
88. Journals, 351.
89. Journals, 355.

VII. FREEDOM: 1941–1942

1. PoL, 484f.
2. PoL, 479f.
3. PoL, 482.
4. Schreiber, 58.
5. Schreiber, 42.
6. Schreiber, 56.
7. PoL, 406.
8. Bair, 254.
9. PoL, 502.
10. WD, 319.
11. WD, 319f.
12. J.-P. Sartre, *Being and Nothingness*, trans. H. E. Barnes (London: Methuen, 1969), 159.
13. Sartre (1969), 810.
14. J.-P. Sartre, *Existentialism Is a Humanism*, trans. C. Macomber (New Haven: Yale University Press, 2007), 17–73.
15. Here we may agree unconditionally with the judgment of Kirkpatrick, 189: "So it has been mistakenly assumed that Sartre developed the ethics of existentialism, one of the most popular movements in twentieth-century philosophy, when in fact Beauvoir did."
16. PoL, 393.
17. PoL, 397.
18. See Kirkpatrick, 178.
19. PoL, 505.
20. PoL, 504.
21. J.-P. Sartre, *Situations, III* (Paris: Gallimard, 1949), 11.
22. WD, 321.
23. WD, 323.
24. Pétrement, 425.
25. Pétrement, 434f.
26. Pétrement, 435.
27. See S. Weil, *Écrits de Marseille 1940–1942* (Paris: Gallimard, 2008) (OCIV-l).
28. The notebooks from this period have been published in English as *The Notebooks of Simone Weil*, trans. A. Wills (London: Routledge, 1956).
29. The term "existentialism" was first used by the (Catholic) philosopher Gabriel Marcel (1889–1973) to characterize Sartre's philosophy. There is a terminological similarity with the term "Existenzphilosophie" (philosophy of existence) used by the German philosopher Karl Jaspers to characterize his own approach (also in the tradition of Kierkegaard), an approach also close to

Marcel's thought. Here it is not quite clear whom Weil is referring to—but her critical point is directed against Jaspers (and Heidegger) and against Sartre and Beauvoir.

30. Notebooks, 203.
31. Notebooks, 206.
32. Notebooks, 279.
33. Notebooks, 278.
34. Notebooks, 336.
35. Notebooks, 361.
36. Notebooks, 258.
37. Notebooks, 291.
38. Notebooks, 298.
39. Notebooks, 466.
40. Notebooks, 349.
41. Notebooks, 466.
42. Notebooks, 466.
43. Notebooks, 466.
44. Notebooks, 618.
45. Notebooks, 447.
46. Notebooks, 596.
47. Notebooks, 552.
48. Notebooks, 505.
49. Notebooks, 292.
50. Notebooks, 297.
51. Notebooks, 255.
52. Notebooks, 289.
53. Notebooks, 298.
54. Notebooks, 205.
55. Notebooks, 358.
56. Notebooks, 364.
57. Notebooks, 267.
58. See B. Spinoza, *Ethics*, ed. and trans. E. Curley (London: Penguin, 1996).
59. See L. Wittgenstein, *Tractatus Logico-Philosophicus*, trans. C. K. Ogden (London: Kegan Paul, Trench, Tubner, 1922).
60. Notebooks, 610.
61. Notebooks, 309.
62. See L. Wittgenstein, *Philosophical Investigations*, trans. G. E. M. Anscombe (Oxford: Blackwell, 1953).
63. Pétrement, 458.
64. Notebooks, 156.
65. J.-M. Perrin and G. Thibon, *Simone Weil As We Knew Her*, trans. E. Craufurd (London: Routledge, 1953), 172.
66. Pétrement, 466.
67. Arendt/Scholem, 12–13.
68. Arendt/Scholem, 13.

69. In *Vor Antisemitismus ist man nur noch auf dem Monde sicher: Beiträge für die deutsch-jüdische Emigrantenzeitung "Aufbau"1941–1945,* ed. M. L. Knott (Munich: Piper, 2004) (Aufbau).
70. Aufbau, 28. Article from November 14, 1941.
71. H. Arendt, "A Way toward the Reconciliation of Peoples," in *The Jewish Writings*, 263 (JW).
72. Aufbau, 28. Article from November 14, 1941.
73. Schreiber, 64ff.
74. JW, 346.
75. JW, 352.
76. JW, 344.
77. Aufbau, 122.
78. Aufbau, 120.
79. E.g., Aufbau, 82: "Little today is as important for our politics as keeping the liberation struggles of the oppressed peoples clean of the fascist plague. This war will only be won if all peoples are freed in its course, and that means all 'races' are transformed into peoples."
80. Arendt/Scholem, 18.
81. Young-Bruehl, 210.
82. Young-Bruehl, 172.
83. Letters, 68.
84. See Burns, 80.
85. See Heller, 143ff.
86. See Burns, 80.
87. Letters, 63f.
88. Journals, 69.
89. Journals, 221.
90. Journals, 221.
91. Fountainhead, 954.
92. Fountainhead, 980.
93. Fountainhead, 958.
94. Fountainhead, 961.
95. Fountainhead, 961.
96. Fountainhead, 961.
97. Fountainhead, 965.
98. Fountainhead, 967.
99. Fountainhead, 968–69.

VIII. FIRE: 1943

1. Heller, 165.
2. Heller, 55.
3. During these months Rand became a regular consumer of benzedrine, an amphetamine that was frequently prescribed in the United States.
4. Heller, 165.

5. Letters, 87f.
6. Letters, 88.
7. Finally published in 1957 as *Atlas Shrugged*.
8. Letters, 174.
9. Burns, 96.
10. Heller, 160.
11. Heller, 160.
12. Heller, 161.
13. Journals, 234.
14. Beauvoir/Sartre, 377.
15. Beauvoir/Sartre, 377f.
16. S. de Beauvoir, "Pyrrhus and Cineas," in *Philosophical Writings*, ed. M. A Simons, trans. M. Timmerman and M. B. Mader (Champaign: University of Illinois Press, 2004), 77–150 (Pyrrhus).
17. Pyrrhus, 137.
18. Pyrrhus, 129.
19. Pyrrhus, 135.
20. Pyrrhus, 140.
21. PoL, 440.
22. Von Wroblewsky (2004), 329.
23. PoL, 441.
24. PoL, 435.
25. Arendt/Scholem, 16f.
26. Arendt/Scholem, 17.
27. See L. Stone, "Quantifying the Holocaust: Hyperintense Kill Rates during the Nazi Genocide," *Science Advances* 5, no. 1 (January 2, 2019).
28. See Young-Bruehl, 182.
29. Arendt/Scholem, 17f. The planned book became the second part of Arendt's *The Origins of Totalitarianism*.
30. G. Scholem, *Major Trends in Jewish Mysticism* (New York: Schocken, 1946.).
31. Quoted in Arendt-Scholem, 469.
32. Benjamin (1963), 247.
33. Arendt/Benjamin, 40.
34. Scholem (1946), 350.
35. Scholem (1946), 350.
36. See I. Kant, *Anthropology from a Pragmatic Point of View*, trans. A. P. Louden (Cambridge, UK: Cambridge University Press, 2006).
37. Arendt/Scholem, 280.
38. See Young-Bruehl, 184.
39. Arendt/Scholem, 18.
40. E. Gabellieri and F. L'Yvonnet, eds., *Simone Weil* (Paris: L'Herne, 2014), 195.
41. Gabellieri and L'Yvonnet, 195.
42. Gabellieri and L'Yvonnet, 196.
43. Biographical details for this part of Weil's life are taken from Pétrement.
44. FLN, 335.
45. Pétrement, 526.

46. Pétrement, 530–31.
47. Pétrement, 535.
48. Pétrement, 537.

CODA

1. Pétrement, 537.
2. Reported in the French newspaper *L'express*, February 11, 1961.

SELECTED BIBLIOGRAPHY

Adamovich, A., and D. Granin (2017). *Leningrad under Siege: First-Hand Accounts of the Ordeal*. Translated by C. Burrell and V. Kisselnikov. Barnsley, UK: Pen and Sword.

Adorno, T. W., and W. Benjamin (1999). *The Complete Correspondence 1928–1940*. Edited by H. Lonitz. Translated by N. Walker. Cambridge, UK: Polity Press.

Alain. (1939). *Suite à Mars*. 2 vols., *Convulsions de la force*; *Échec de la force*. Paris: Gallimard.

Applebaum, A. (2003). *Gulag: A History of the Soviet Camps*. London: Allen Lane.

—— (2017). *Red Famine: Stalin's War on Ukraine*. Toronto: Signal.

Bair, D. (1990). *Simone de Beauvoir: A Biography*. London: Jonathan Cape.

Bakewell, S. (2016). *At the Existentialist Café: Freedom, Being and Apricot Cocktails*. London: Chatto & Windus.

Benjamin, W. (1972–1989). *Gesammelte Schriften*. Vol. 1. Frankfurt am Main: Suhrkamp.

—— (1973). *Illuminations*. Edited by H. Arendt. Translated by H. Zohn. London: Fontana.

—— (1989). *The Correspondence of Walter Benjamin and Gershom Scholem, 1932–1940*. Edited by G. Scholem. Translated by G. Smith and A. Lefevere. New York: Schocken.

—— (2019). *The Correspondence of Walter Benjamin, 1910–1940*. Edited by G. Scholem and T. W. Adorno. Translated by M. R. Jacobson and E. M. Jacobson. Chicago: University of Chicago Press.

Bernanos, G. (1938/2018). *The Great Cemeteries under the Moon*. Translated by P. Morris. Providence, RI: Cluny.

Blume, D., M. Boll, and R. Gross, eds. (2020). *Hannah Arendt und das 20. Jahrhundert*. Munich: Piper.

Boehm, O. (2021). *Haifa Republic: A Democratic Future for Israel*. New York: New York Review Books.

Boschwitz, U. A. (1939/2021). *The Passenger*. Translated by P. Boehm. London: Pushkin Press.

Bouchardeau, H. (1995). *Simone Weil: Biographie*. Paris: Gallimard.

Bovenschen, S. (1979). *Die imaginierte Weiblichkeit: Exemplarische Untersuchungen zu kulturgeschichtlichen und literarischen Präsentationsformen des Weiblichen*. Frankfurt am Main: Suhrkamp.

Branden, B. (1986). *The Passion of Ayn Rand*. New York: Doubleday.

Branden, N. (1989). *Judgment Day: My Years with Ayn Rand*. Boston: Houghton Mifflin.

Burns, J. (2009). *Goddess of the Market: Ayn Rand and the American Right*. New York and Oxford: Oxford University Press.

Cavell, S. (1982). *The Claim of Reason: Wittgenstein, Skepticism, Morality, and Tragedy*. Oxford: Oxford University Press.

—— (2005). *Philosophy the Day after Tomorrow*. Cambridge, MA: Harvard University Press.

Cohen-Solal, A. (1985/1987). *Sartre: A Life*. London: Heinemann.

Collado Seidel, C. (2016). *Der spanische Bürgerkrieg: Geschichte eines europäischen Konflikts*. Munich: Beck.

Descartes, R. (1641/2008). *Meditations on First Philosophy, with Selections from the* Objections *and* Replies. Translated by M. Moriarty. Oxford: Oxford University Press.

Eiland, H., and M. W. Jennings (2014). *Walter Benjamin: A Critical Life*. Cambridge, MA: Harvard University Press.

Eilenberger, W. (2020). *Time of the Magicians: Wittgenstein, Benjamin, Cassirer, Heidegger, and the Decade That Reinvented Philosophy*. Translated by S. Whiteside. New York: Penguin Press.

Epstein, L. (2016). *The Dream of Zion: The First Zionist Congress*. Lanham, MD: Rowman & Littlefield.

Fest, J. (1973/1974). *Hitler*. Translated by R. and C. Winston. London and New York: Harcourt Brace Jovanovich.

Foessel, M. (2019). *Récidive: 1938*. Paris: Presses Universitaires de France.

Gabellieri, E., and F. L'Yvonnet, eds. (2014). *Simone Weil*. Paris: L'Herne.

Gladstein, M. R., and C. M. Sciabarra, eds. (1999). *Feminist Interpretations of Ayn Rand*. University Park: Pennsylvania State University Press.

Hampe, M. (2014/2018). *What Philosophy Is For*. Translated by M. Winkler. Chicago: University of Chicago Press.

Hegel, G. W. F. (2018). *Phenomenology of Spirit*. Translated by M. Inwood. Oxford: Oxford University Press.

Heidegger, M. (1924/2011). *The Concept of Time*. Translated by I. Farin. London: Continuum.

—— (1927/1962). *Being and Time*. Translated by J. Macquarrie and E. Robinson. Oxford: Blackwell.

—— (1929/1962). *Kant and the Problem of Metaphysics*. Translated by R. Taft. Bloomington: Indiana University Press.

—— (2000). *Gesamtausgabe: Ausgabe letzter Hand*. Vol. 16, *Reden und andere Zeugnisse eines Lebensweges* (1910–1976). Frankfurt am Main: Vittorio Klostermann.

Heller, A. C. (2009). *Ayn Rand and the World She Made*. New York: Nan A. Talese/ Doubleday.

Herbert, G. (1941). *The Works of George Herbert*. Edited by F. E. Hutchinson. Oxford: Clarendon Press.

Hobsbawm, E. (1994). *The Age of Extremes: A History of the World, 1914–1991*. New York: Pantheon.

Homer (1990). *The Iliad*. Translated by R. Fagles. New York: Penguin.

Jaspers, K. (1932). *Max Weber: Deutsches Wesen im politischen Denken, im Forschen und Philosophieren*. Oldenburg, Germany: Stalling.

Kant, I. (2006). *Anthropology from a Pragmatic Point of View*. Translated by A. P. Louden. Cambridge, UK: Cambridge University Press.

Kershaw, I. (2015). *To Hell and Back: Europe 1914–1949*. London: Allen Lane.

Kirkpatrick, K. (2019). *Becoming Beauvoir: A Life*. London: Bloomsbury Academic.

Koestler, A. (1937). *Spanish Testament*. London: Left Book Club Edition/Victor Gollancz.

—— (1941). *Scum of the Earth*. London: Jonathan Cape.

Labatut, B. (2020). *When We Cease to Understand the World*. Translated by A. N. West. London: Pushkin.

Lepore, J. (2019). *These Truths: A History of the United States*. New York: W. W. Norton.

Louette, J.-F. (2019). *Sartre et Beauvoir, roman et philosophie*. Geneva: La Baconnière.

Marx, K., and F. Engels (1946/1958). *Marx-Engels-Werke*. Vol. 3. Berlin: Dietz.

Meyer-Moses, H. (2019). *Reise in die Vergangenheit: Eine Überlebende des Lagers Gurs erinnert sich an die Verfolgung während der NS-Diktatur*. Ubstadt-Weiher, Germany: Verlag Regionalkultur.

Nieradka-Steiner, M. (2018). *Exil unter Palmen: Deutsche Emigranten in Sanary-sur-Mer*. Stuttgart: Theiss.

Nietzsche, F. (1888/2007). *Ecce Homo: How to Become What You Are*. Translated by D. Large. Oxford: Oxford University Press.

—— (2013). *Philosophische Werke in sechs Bänden*. Edited by C.-A. Scheier. Hamburg: Felix Meiner.

Nye, A. (1994). *Philosophia: The Thought of Rosa Luxemburg, Simone Weil, and Hannah Arendt*. London: Routledge.

Ortega y Gasset, J. (1930/1994). *The Revolt of the Masses*. New York: W. W. Norton.

Peikoff, L. (1991). *Objectivism: The Philosophy of Ayn Rand*. New York: E. P. Dutton.

Pelz, M. (2007). *Simone de Beauvoir*. Frankfurt am Main: Suhrkamp.

Pétrement, S. (1976). *Simone Weil: A Life*. Translated by R. Rosenthal. New York: Pantheon.

Perrin, J.-M. (2009). *Mon dialogue avec Simone Weil*. Paris: Nouvelle Cité.

Perrin, J.-M., and G. Thibon (1953). *Simone Weil As We Knew Her*. Translated by E. Craufurd. London: Routledge.

Poirier, A. (2018). *Left Bank: Art, Passion and the Rebirth of Paris, 1940–50*. London: Bloomsbury.

Prinz, A. (1998). *Hannah Arendt oder Die Liebe zur Welt*. Frankfurt am Main: Beltz & Gelberg.

Reckwitz, A. (2017). *Die Gesellschaft der Singularitäten*. Berlin: Suhrkamp.

Rees, R., and H. T. Moore (1978). *Simone Weil: A Sketch for a Portrait*. Carbondale: Southern Illinois University Press.

Rhodes, R. (2015). *Hell and Good Company: The Spanish Civil War and the World It Made.* New York and London: Simon & Schuster.

Roberts, A. (2009). *The Storm of War: A New History of the Second World War.* London: Penguin/Allen Lane.

Rowley, H. (2005). *Tete-à-Tête: Simone de Beauvoir and Jean-Paul Sartre.* New York: HarperCollins.

Sartre, J.-P. (1936/1972). *The Transcendence of the Ego: An Existentialist Theory of Consciousness.* Translated by F. Williams and R. Kirkpatrick. New York: Octagon.

—— (1938/1964). *Nausea.* Translated by L. Alexander. New York: New Directions.

—— (1943/1957). *Being and Nothingness.* Translated by H. E. Barnes. London: Methuen.

—— (1946/2007). *Existentialism Is a Humanism.* Translated by C. Macomber. New Haven: Yale University Press.

Scholem, G. (1946). *Major Trends in Jewish Mysticism.* New York: Schocken.

Schreiber, G. (2013). *Der zweite Weltkrieg.* Munich: Beck.

Sciabarra, C. M. (2013). *Ayn Rand: The Russian Radical.* University Park: Pennsylvania State University Press.

Seghers, A. (2021). *Transit.* Translated by M. B. Dembo. London: Virago.

Seymour-Jones, C. (2009). *A Dangerous Liaison: Simone de Beauvoir and Jean-Paul Sartre.* London: Arrow.

Shklar, J. N. (2020). *Über Hannah Arendt.* Edited and translated by H. Bajohr. Berlin: Matthes & Seitz.

Smith, T. (2006). *Ayn Rand's Normative Ethics: The Virtuous Egoist.* Cambridge, UK: Cambridge University Press.

Später, J. (2020). *Siegfried Kracauer: A Biography.* Translated by D. Steuer. Cambridge, UK, and Medford, MA: Polity Press.

Spinoza, B. (1677/1996). *Ethics.* Edited and translated by E. Curley. London: Penguin.

Stone, L. "Quantifying the Holocaust: Hyperintense Kill Rates during the Nazi Genocide." *Science Advances* 5, no. 1 (January 2, 2019).

Suhr, M. (2015). *Jean-Paul Sartre zur Einführung.* Hamburg: Junius Verlag.

von Redecker, E. (2013). *Gravitation zum Guten: Hannah Arendts Moralphilosophie.* Göttingen: Lukas Verlag.

von Wroblewsky, V., ed. (2004). *Jean-Paul Sartre: Briefe an Simone de Beauvoir 1940–1963.* Hamburg: Rowohlt.

—— (2008). *Jean-Paul Sartre: Briefe an Simone de Beauvoir 1926–1939.* Hamburg: Rowohlt.

Webber, J. (2018). *Rethinking Existentialism.* Oxford: Oxford University Press.

Weil, S. (2009). *Chez les Weil: André et Simone.* Paris: Buchet Chastel.

Weinstock, N. (1975). *Das Ende Israels? Nahostkonflikt und Geschichte des Zionismus.* Berlin: Wagenbach.

Wildt, M., and C. Kreutzmüller, eds. (2013). *Berlin 1933–1945.* Munich: Siedler Verlag.

Wimmer, R. (1990). *Vier jüdische Philosophinnen: Rosa Luxemburg, Simone Weil, Edith Stein, Hannah Arendt.* Tübingen: Attempto Verlag.

—— (2009). *Simone Weil: Person und Werk*. Freiburg im Breisgau: Herder Verlag.

Winch, P. (1989). *Simone Weil: "The Just Balance."* Cambridge, UK: Cambridge University Press.

Wittgenstein, L. (1922). *Tractatus Logico-Philosophicus*. Translated by C. K. Ogden. London: Kegan Paul, Trench, Trubner.

—— (1953). *Philosophical Investigations*. Translated by G. E. M. Anscombe. Oxford: Blackwell.

Young-Bruehl, E. (1982). *Hannah Arendt: For Love of the World*. New Haven: Yale University Press.

Zamyatin, Y. (1924/1952/1993). *We*. Translated by C. Brown. London: Penguin.

ILLUSTRATION CREDITS

Hannah Arendt: akg-images

Ayn Rand: © picture alliance/Everett Collection

Simone Weil: picture alliance © Whiteimages/Leemage

Simone de Beauvoir: akg-images/Denise Bellon

Excerpts from "The Iliad, or the Poem of Force," in Simone Weil and Rachel Bespaloff, *War and the Iliad*, trans. Mary McCarthy (New York: NYRB Classics, 2005), courtesy of Sylvie Weil and the Simone Weil estate.

Excerpt from *Oppression and Liberty* by Simone Weil, translated by Arthur Wills and John Petrie, translation copyright © 1958 by Routledge & Kegan Paul (London: Routledge & Kegan Paul, 1958). Reproduced by permission of Taylor and Francis Group, LLC, a division of Informa plc.

Excerpt from *Formative Writings, 1929–1941* by Simone Weil, edited and translated by Dorothy Tuck McFarland and Wilhelmina Van Ness, translations, introductions, and all new matter copyright © 1987 by The University of Massachusetts Press (Amherst: University of Massachusetts Press, 1987). Reproduced by permission of Taylor and Francis Group, LLC, a division of Informa plc.

Excerpts from *Selected Essays 1934–43* by Simone Weil, chosen and translated by R. Rees (London: Oxford University Press, 1962), courtesy of Sylvie Weil and the Simone Weil estate.

Excerpts from *Seventy Letters* by Simone Weil, trans. R. Rees (London: Oxford University Press, 1965), courtesy of Sylvie Weil and the Simone Weil estate.

Excerpts from *Hannah Arendt: For Love of the World* by Elisabeth Young-Bruehl (1982), copyright © 1982 by Elisabeth Young-Bruehl. Used by permission of Yale University Press and Georges Borchardt, Inc., on behalf of the author's estate.

INDEX

INDEX